AIA Design for Aging Knowledge Community

Design for Aging
Review 14

AIA Design for Aging Knowledge Community

Design for Aging
Review 14

images
Publishing

Dedicated to

Robert 'Rob' Nathan Mayer, Ph.D.

It is the tradition of *Design for Aging Review* to distinguish exemplary projects, individuals, or organizations in the book's biennial publication with the 10-Year or Lifetime Achievement awards. This acknowledgement is made by the emeriti members of the Design for Aging Advisory Group. With the too-soon passing, in late 2015, of Rob Mayer, the emeriti members are foregoing those awards in *DFAR14*. Instead, this volume is dedicated to the memory and good work of Rob, accomplished through the Hulda B. & Maurice L. Rothschild Foundation in the pursuit of enhancing the lives of the elderly. As a top leader in the industry, Rob was an implementer, thought leader, eldercare reformer, mentor, challenger, and friend. The section later in this book is a look back at a sampling of the many studies, papers, guidelines, task forces initiated and impacted by an exceptional champion for today's seniors.

Published in Australia in 2018 by
The Images Publishing Group Pty Ltd
ABN 89 059 734 431

Offices
Australia
6 Bastow Place
Mulgrave, Victoria 3170
Australia
Tel: +61 3 9561 5544

United States
6 West 18th Street 4B
New York, NY 10011
United States
Tel: +1 212 645 1111

books@imagespublishing.com
www.imagespublishing.com

A catalogue record for this
book is available from the
National Library of Australia

Title: Design for Aging Review 14: AIA Design for Aging Knowledge
          Community // The American Institute of Architects (AIA)
ISBN: 9781864708028

Photography credits for individual projects and works are listed throughout the book, with the
following exceptions:
Courtesy of individual jurors 12–13
Sarah Mechling 14–15 *(original image has been edited)*
Gensler / Ryan Gobuty 172–73 *(original image has been edited)*
Courtesy of Georgia Tech 233
Debra Weese-Mayer 235
Benjamin Benschneider Photography 236–37 *(original image has been edited)*

This title was commissioned in IMAGES' Melbourne office and produced as follows: *Editorial
coordination* Rebecca Gross, *Layout design and coordination* Rod Gilbert, *Production* Nicole
Boehringer, *Senior editorial* Gina Tsarouhas, *Senior graphic design* Ryan Marshall

Printed on 140gsm GoldEast matte art paper by
Everbest Printing Investment Limited, in Hong Kong/China

IMAGES has included on its website a page for special notices in relation to this and its other
publications. Please visit www.imagespublishing.com

Contents

9   Foreword

10   Overall Jury Statement

12   The Jury

Projects and Awards
Small Projects

16   North Ridge at Tacoma Lutheran Ⓜ
Shoesmith Cox Architects

26   Cuthbertson Village Town Center Renovation
CJMW Architecture

30   The Burnham Family Memory Care Residence at Avery Heights
Amenta Emma Architects

Building Projects

34   Rose Villa Pocket Neighborhoods & Main Street Ⓜ
RLPS Architects and MGA Architects

44   The Cottage at Cypress Cove Ⓜ
SFCS Architects

54   The Summit at Rockwood South Hill Ⓜ
Perkins Eastman

64   Abiitan Mill City Ⓢ
BKV Group

72   Caleb Hitchcock Memory Care Neighborhood at Duncaster Retirement Community Ⓢ
Amenta Emma Architects

80   Elm Place Ⓢ
Duncan Wisniewski Architecture

88   Fountainview at Gonda Westside Ⓢ
Gensler

96   Linden Park Apartments Ⓢ
Wiencek + Associates Architects + Planners

104   Babcock Health Care Center
CJMW Architecture

108   Edenwald Café
RLPS Architects

112   Goodwin House Alexandria
Perkins Eastman

116   Hillcrest Country Estates
AG Architecture

120   Legacy Place Cottages
RLPS Architects

124   The Plaza at Waikiki
Wattenbarger Architects

128   The Woodlands at John Knox Village
RDG Planning & Design

Planning / Concept Design Projects

132   Brightview Bethesda Ⓜ
Hord Coplan Macht

142   The Seasons at Alexandria Ⓜ
c.c. hodgson architectural group

152   EmpathiCare Village
c.c. hodgson architectural group

156   Frasier Meadows Retirement Community Independent Living Additions and Renovations
Hord Coplan Macht

160   Shenyang Senior Living
Perkins Eastman

164   The Trousdale Assisted Living and Memory Care
SmithGroupJJR

168   Well-Spring Resident Activity Center + Expansion
CJMW Architecture

Design for Aging Knowledge Community

174   DFAR14 Insights and Innovations

204   Student Design Awards

224   Rob Mayer: A Look Back

Appendix

238   Project Data

255   Index of Architects

Ⓜ   Merit recipient

Ⓢ   Special Recognition recipient

Foreword

Our Lifecycle is Our Guide for Design

America's population continues to grow with each successive generation, and each generation is living longer than the one before it—including my own, the famous (or infamous) baby boomers. According to the U.S. Centers for Disease Control (CDC), the number of Americans over the age of 65 will double during the next 25 years to a whopping 72 million people. By 2030, the CDC notes, older adults will account for one fifth of the U.S. population.

More effective health care and better overall health have contributed to a longer lifespan for us boomers. Good news: Those advances will contribute to even longer lifespans for Gen Xers and millennials, as well as all those who come after. It has never been more important than now to get aging in place, senior living, or "design for aging" right.

In the pages that follow, you'll read about projects recognized by a blue-ribbon jury in an important biennial design competition sponsored by the American Institute of Architects Design for Aging (DFA) Knowledge Community. Regardless of how the jurors premiated these projects, one dominant theme emerged: the degree to which the architects could create a strong connection between interior spaces and the natural world.

It's not a new idea, but architects in every sector of the built environment have found interesting and innovative ways to keep us connected to nature, even if we inevitably spend 90 percent of our lives indoors—in our homes, cars, at school, and work.

One day, that number might decrease, since the well-documented (and intuitive) health benefits of "getting out" are fundamental to holistic design. The lifecycle of a work of architecture, as it maps to our own lifecycle, is also fundamental to holistic design—and we all deserve an architecture that can sustain us throughout our lives.

This edition of *Design for Aging Review*, in a series that began more than a quarter-century ago as a vital expression of DFA, reminds us that good design is a lifelong right. Congratulations to DFA for shepherding another excellent volume into the hands of architects—young and not-so-young—who ensure that right in the work they do.

Carl Elefante, FAIA
2018 AIA President

Overall Jury Statement

We are living and designing in an ever-faster-moving world with new technology and new information on how the environment, both natural and built, affects our bodies and our brains. How do we as individuals involved in this unique and complex sector stay in front of and use this information to create a better built environment? That is what we hoped to see in the submissions to the 14th edition of *Design for Aging Review*. We believe the projects selected respond to this evolving world.

The trends that emerged in the preceding *Design for Aging Review*—household and neighborhood design, community connections, and affordable housing models—are now the well-established design and operational base line for communities. So where do we go from here? Clients, designers, and residents are looking for more thoughtful and timeless design; communities that engage and give back to the neighborhood; and more integrated, sustainable, and healthy environments for residents, families, staff, and owners.

The jury looked for designs that realized the owner's objectives, established at the beginning of the project and executed throughout the process with a clear vision of the stated goals to be achieved. This ranged from a parti of a hillside village, a single focal point, working within the restrictive boundaries of an urban site, to creating an affordable yet sustainable model using technology and green design principles, which now include biophilia and WELL Building principles.

Top right: Caleb Hitchcock Memory Care Neighborhood at Duncaster
Retirement Community
   Photography: Robert Benson Photography
Bottom right: Brightview Bethesda
   Rendering: courtesy of Hord Coplan Macht
Opposite: Abiitan City Mill
   Photography: Troy Thies Photography

The jury was composed of a dedicated group of volunteers representing the design industry, both architecture and interior design, as well as owner / operators of large aged care communities or systems. Each was a valued member who brought a range of perspectives to the review of the projects. Through the process of individual evaluations and initial group discussions, the jury was able to clearly identify the merits of the submissions. Having a well-rounded jury led to insightful discussions about the projects with jury members bringing their unique perspectives and convincing others of ideas and approaches they had not seen or thought about before.

Three themes emerged from the submissions for *Design for Aging Review 14*. Some of these are similar to the last cycle of the biennial competition, which indicates not so much an emerging trend but an indicator of where this sector is moving. These trends are affordable senior housing, community integration, the emphasis on nature and technology.

Affordable senior housing

Four key points made the affordable housing projects stand out not just for the designs, but for how they positively affected the local communities and ensured they would remain affordable in the future. This was the use of higher quality materials and construction methods for better energy savings; technology that enables residents to monitor how they are helping to achieve the goal of affordability for them and future residents; the emerging and creative methods of public / private partnerships to develop and finance projects; and the transformation of existing affordable housing to rejuvenate a neighborhood.

Community integration

The increasing integration of affordable housing into the urban fabric of local communities reinforces this theme as now being a major shift in the market sector. This is reflected in the projects that are positioned as part of the overall urban renewal of a city; communities that are helping transform industrial areas into mixed-use housing, thereby revitalizing or creating a neighborhood; and designs that respond to the local character of a district and the desire of communities to be part of and support the social fabric.

Nature and technology

In addition to the conscious use of energy, there are more projects following biophilia, WELL Building, and LEED principles to achieve healthier, energy efficient, and better designed buildings for the long-term health of residents and staff. These principles are being achieved with a focus on nature and technology, for example a winding path that opens up to views and sunlight around every curve; the introduction of natural light into resident bathrooms; communal spaces and resident rooms that look out to a single tree as a shared focal point; and clever solutions based on the study of natural and artificial light to better maintain the natural circadian rhythm of residents.

Design for Aging Review has long been established as the standard bearer for innovative and thoughtful designs for our ever-growing elderly population. This jury challenges our industry to keep pushing the envelope for new ideas and better use of technology and materials for the environment you are designing in. Always keep in mind that our collective clients are the ultimate end users: the residents of the communities we design.

On behalf of the DFAR14 Jury,

David L. Banta, AIA
Wiencek + Associates Architects + Planners
Washington, D.C.

The Jury

David Banta, AIA

Wiencek + Associates
Architects + Planners
Washington, D.C.

David Banta is a licensed architect in the state of Maryland and works at Wiencek + Associates Architects + Planners in Washington, D.C. where he is involved in all aspects of the firm's senior living projects. He has worked across the senior living sector since 1999 and has been at the forefront of industry discussions through his affiliations with the AIA Design for Aging Knowledge Community where he is also a member of the Advisory Group, and the American Seniors Housing Association. David has developed an astute understanding of the evolving global trends amongst seniors. He has applied innovative principles to a range of communities, including independent living, assisted living, skilled nursing, and memory care facilities. He has successfully managed the planning and design of retirement communities, residential projects, urban infill, transit-oriented, and mixed-use developments with major developers in cities throughout the United States and China. The needs associated with the aging process are universal, and David has been invited to give educational lectures nationally and internationally.

Paul Donaldson, AIA, LEED AP

PRDG Senior Living
Architecture
Dallas, Texas

Paul Donaldson is a licensed architect in the state of Texas, where he is the Managing Principal of PRDG. Paul has an extremely diverse background, with more than 25 years in architectural design, planning, and construction of senior living and health care facilities. Paul has combined his knowledge of construction technology, code research, and Continuing Care Retirement Community (CCRC) planning with real-world project experience. Paul has devoted his career to improving the quality of care in senior living environments through creative, functional architectural solutions. Through this work, Paul's residential designs parallel advancements in the personal care industry, offering inviting services and environments for the elderly. Paul's work includes a series of resort-style high-rise CCRC projects that changed the paradigm for urban senior living communities. His work represents more than a billion dollars of senior housing construction in 20 states. Today he manages a firm of 25 people completing work for senior living clients such as Life Care Services, Greystone Communities, Elmcroft Senior Living, and Formation Development Group.

Karla M. Jackson, MS, RID

StudioSIX5
Austin, Texas

Karla M. Jackson is a registered interior designer in the state of Texas and is Design Director and Principal at StudioSIX5 in Austin. Karla holds bachelor's and master's degrees in interior and environmental design and has been practicing for 28 years, the last 13 at StudioSIX5 focusing exclusively on the design of senior living communities across the country. While attending graduate school at Texas Tech University, Karla taught studio design classes and concentrated her studies on gerontology and the effects of the built environment on individuals living with Alzheimer's and other forms of dementia. In 1991, *Southwest Journal of Aging* published her master's thesis on the design of adult day care centers to accommodate seniors with dementia. Karla has been interviewed for articles in *Senior Housing News*, *McKnight's Long-Term Care News*, and *Multi-Housing News*, and was a featured speaker at the 2017 and 2018 Environments for Aging Conferences. She is passionate about elevating senior housing design by creating unique, engaging environments and optimizing quality of life for residents and their families.

Dayle Krahn, BBA, EDAC

Baptist Housing Ministries Society
Vancouver, B.C., Canada

Dayle Krahn has been Vice President of Property Maintenance and Development at Baptist Housing Ministries Society for 12 years. With extensive experience in construction and land development, Dayle is the lead project manager on all Baptist Housing development opportunities. He has been involved in researching and studying design for senior environments and is involved in all aspects of new developments from conception to move in. He works very closely with architects, consultants, and contractors to build a physical environment that enhances residents' independence and team members' ability to deliver care. Dayle oversaw the design and construction of Baptist Housing's new award-winning 260-bed residential care building, The Heights at Mt. View. He continues to look for latest trends and innovative designs that will improve resident experience.

David F. Lacy

Southminster, Inc.
Charlotte, North Carolina

David Lacy is President and Chief Executive Officer at Southminster, Inc. He spent the first 11 years of his career working in the area of city planning. Since 1982, David has focused on management of Continuing Care Retirement Communities as Associate Director for Finance and Planning at Carol Woods Retirement Community in Chapel Hill, North Carolina, and Executive Director at Trinity Terrace in Fort Worth, Texas, before becoming President and CEO of Southminster in 1999. He also held various positions on the Board of the Armed Forces Retirement Homes in Washington, D.C., finally serving as Chairman of the Board and COO. David currently serves as Chairman of the Board of the LeadingAge North Carolina Foundation. Previous affiliations include member of the House of Delegates of LeadingAge and member of its Continuing Care Community Advisory Committee; member of the Continuing Care Advisory Committee of the NC Department of Insurance; member of the Financial Advisory Panel of CARF/CCAC; and an evaluator and team leader for numerous site visits. David's professional awards include the LeadingAge North Carolina Career Excellence for Lifetime Achievement in 2018; LeadingAge North Carolina Distinguished Service Award in 2003; and the U.S. Department of Defense Medal for Distinguished Public Service in 2002. David earned a Bachelor of Arts degree from Bucknell University and a Masters in Regional Planning from the University of North Carolina in Chapel Hill. He is a licensed Nursing Home Administrator in North Carolina.

Projects and Awards

SMALL PROJECTS // BUILDING PROJECTS // PLANNING / CONCEPT DESIGN PROJECTS

Shoesmith Cox Architects

North Ridge at Tacoma Lutheran
Tacoma, Washington // Tacoma Lutheran Retirement Community

Facility type (year of completion): Assisted living—dementia / memory support (2016)
Target market: Middle / upper middle
Site location: Suburban; greenfield

Gross square footage of the new construction involved in the project: 10,234 (additions: 9704)
Gross square footage of the renovation / modernization involved in the project: 530
Provider type: Faith-based non-profit

Below: Sketch view of North Ridge entry from within courtyard
Opposite: Aerial sketch showing connection to existing independent living / assisted living building

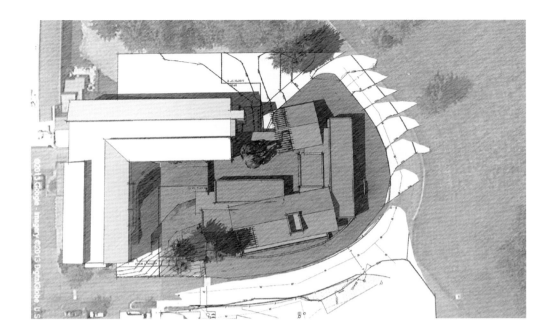

Overall Project Description

Tacoma Lutheran, a life care community, recognized that they were not able to sufficiently provide support for residents in the early to middle stages of dementia within the existing environment. To better serve these residents, Tacoma Lutheran envisioned creating an environment where seniors could "explore, engage in stimulating activities, and live in a beautiful supportive, homelike atmosphere." The result is North Ridge, a 14-resident memory care small house addition to Tacoma Lutheran's existing assisted living building. The site and building plans emerged directly from relationships discovered through diagramming and discussion with the client. North Ridge reflects a high level of thoughtfulness and detailing in a relatively small project. It focuses on enhancing the quality of life of each resident by providing memory care within the comfort, privacy, and familiar setting of "home."

Project Goals

What were the major goals?

- To create an appropriately scaled home for residents. North Ridge is a home for 14 assisted living residents, designed exclusively with single bedrooms and single baths. These bedrooms are subdivided into two groups along two short residential hallways to allow the common spaces more direct connection to the outdoors and to maximize natural light. The layout of North Ridge is intuitive—spaces are found as they would be in any home. The kitchen, dining room, and living room open to each other and to the short residential hallways. Residents may visit the living room for socializing with friends and family. A den is located adjacent to the living room to allow for quieter activity or visits with family. The dining room accommodates residents, staff, and family at meal times. A lower seating

area is built into the kitchen island so that residents can participate in meal preparation or baking activity—familiar and meaningful activities of family life. Gable roofs over the common living spaces and over the service "garage" help to break the overall building into smaller residential-scaled masses. These more prominent roofs not only hierarchize the building mass to emphasize common areas and entries from the exterior, the vaulted ceilings celebrate these spaces on the interior. Common living and dining spaces are oriented to views of gardens beyond. Each resident room is generously sized to accommodate residents' choice of furnishings, books, and artwork, and to be a place where each resident can enjoy privacy. Care was taken to locate service and support areas to be convenient yet discrete from and secondary to the main living spaces.

- To promote green / sustainable design. All rainwater is channeled to a rain garden located on site just north of the building, and the planter located at the perimeter of the resident patio is a stormwater planter. Landscaping primarily consists of native plant varieties. Large windows allow daylight to reach deep into small house resident rooms and common areas. Each room is served by a high-efficiency mini split-system heat pump with individual thermostat allowing residents to control the temperature in their room. Low VOC paints and finishes are used throughout the building.

- To create a warm and rich visual environment. Exposed trusses and mechanical systems add character, scale, and visual interest to the interior environment. Similar trusses exist within independent living community spaces at Tacoma Lutheran so are a familiar feature for residents moving from other parts of

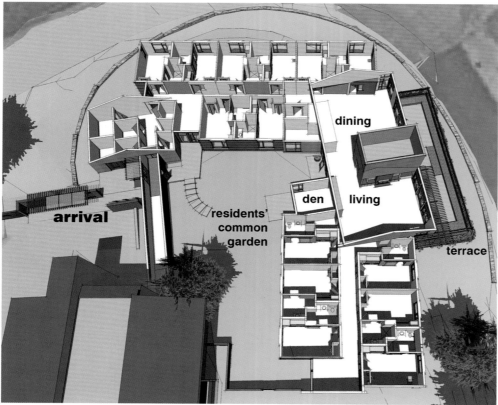

arrival

residents'
common
garden

den living

dining

terrace

Study model

the community. Stained cedar trellises and headers over resident-room windows add warmth and scale to the building exterior. The interior color palette utilizes warm tones and contrast where appropriate to demarcate changes in surface and make the environment more readable to the residents. The live-edge mantle over the fireplace adds visual and textural interest to the living room.

Innovations: What innovations or unique features were incorporated into the design of the project?

Lighting in hallways outside resident rooms is dimmable so that light levels can be reduced by staff at night, cueing residents to the shift

from day to night. This is less disruptive to the sleep of residents who choose to leave their hallway doors open. Residential-looking medicine cabinets are located at the entry to each resident room to allow individualized medicine storage and distribution. These cabinets were designed in partnership with staff and provide both a fold-out work space for charting and a double-locked compartment for storing narcotics. Resident rooms are designed with direct visual access to the bathroom to help cue self-toileting. The oversized "chimney" above the kitchen hides kitchen exhaust, HVAC units, condensers, and roof access from the adjacent three-story independent living apartment building.

In addition to rain gardens, the terrace wall of the patio is designed as a stormwater planter that captures roof rainwater from the chain downspouts.

Challenges: What were the greatest design challenges?

The soils and slopes challenged the project budget and influenced the design solution. The project site is a bluff created 30 years prior during the excavation of Tacoma Lutheran's existing assisted and independent living buildings. Because of the organic composition of this fill, the bearing capacity of the soil was poor. Suitable bearing material was located deep enough that although costly, the building foundation needed to be supported on pin piles to eliminate the potential for differential settlement to the existing assisted living building. This drove up the foundation cost of the project, requiring the design team to be creative in how this additional cost could be absorbed within the budget for the project without sacrificing the perceived quality or detailing of the project. While the bluff location afforded the potential for pleasant off-site views from resident common spaces, the relatively steep slopes of the bluff dictated that the building entry and visitor parking be located to the west to allow an accessible entry without the added cost of extensive ramping.

The zoning requirement that North Ridge be an addition created a paradox for the design team: how to attach the project to the existing building in a way that it would technically classify as an addition but feel very much like the separate, standalone small house building envisioned by the client. Thus, North Ridge is attached to the existing building only by a simple corridor. This corridor is an accessible exit and connecting path for visitors and service from the existing campus buildings, and creates the western and final

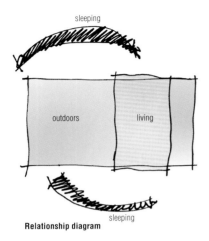

Relationship diagram

sleeping

outdoors | living

sleeping

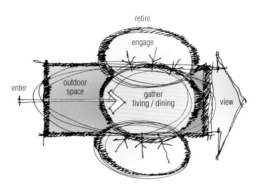

Relationship / arrival diagram

retire

engage

enter

outdoor space

gather living / dining

view

Relationship / spatial hierarchy diagram

retire | gather eat live | retire

enclosing wall of North Ridge's courtyard, visually and physically separating the courtyard from visitor parking and service areas. The corridor becomes the entry gate for visitors to North Ridge as they travel through this "fence" to the courtyard and on to North Ridge's front door.

North Ridge was one of the first projects to be approved in Washington state with an open residential kitchen in a residential-occupancy assisted living licensed building. To gain approval, the design team proposed equivalency measures similar to those recently allowed by CMS in nursing home settings. This included the use of an induction cooktop, providing keyed timers on all cooking appliances, strategically locating sprinkler heads and smoke detectors, and the use of a high CFM residential rangehood.

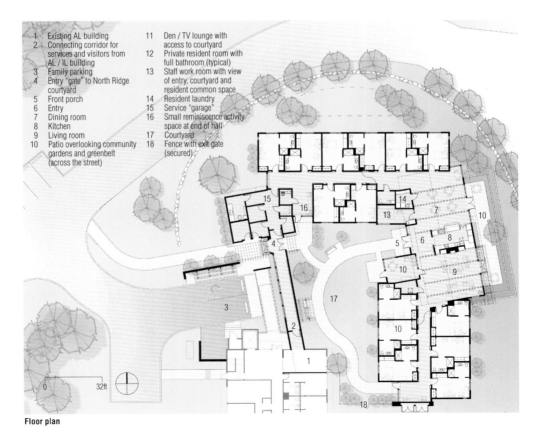

1 Existing AL building
2 Connecting corridor for services and visitors from AL / IL building
3 Family parking
4 Entry "gate" to North Ridge courtyard
5 Front porch
6 Entry
7 Dining room
8 Kitchen
9 Living room
10 Patio overlooking community gardens and greenbelt (across the street)
11 Den / TV lounge with access to courtyard
12 Private resident room with full bathroom (typical)
13 Staff work room with view of entry, courtyard and resident common space
14 Resident laundry
15 Service "garage"
16 Small reminiscence activity space at end of hall
17 Courtyard
18 Fence with exit gate (secured)

Floor plan

0   32ft

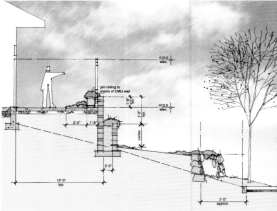

Section at patio and stormwater planter

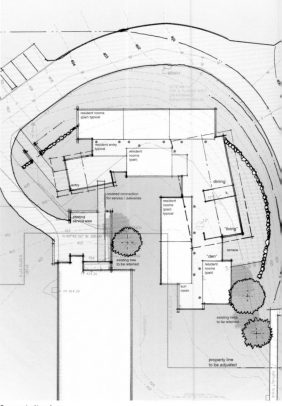

Concept site plan

Above: Initial view of North Ridge from entry drive looking toward patio with living room beyond
Opposite top left: Patio and trellis
Opposite top right: View south to patio, common spaces, and resident room, with existing assisted living beyond
Opposite bottom left: Courtyard path
Opposite bottom right: Study model illustrating how all paths lead to successful outcomes for residents

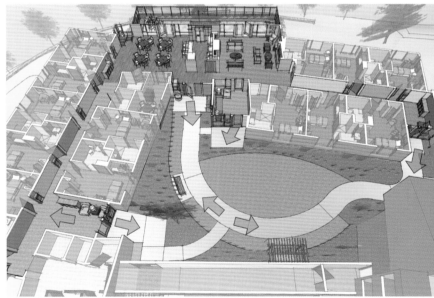

As a single-story building, the roof of North Ridge is visible from units in the adjacent three-story independent living building. Considerable care was taken by the design team to conceal kitchen exhaust, rooftop mechanical equipment / condensers, and roof access to the greatest extent possible. To accommodate this, a "chimney" is located over the kitchen to minimize the visual impact of these items. In addition, the roof vents and plumbing stacks are ganged together and located to minimize visual impact on adjacent independent apartments.

Collaboration: How did stakeholders, occupants, the design team, and / or others collaborate during the planning and / or design process?

One of the most unique features of the project is one that isn't seen. Fire alarm horns cause anxiety and agitation for memory care residents who don't understand what they mean, and for staff who are trying to ensure their safety. Fire horns support self-evacuation and that is the last thing that is desired with memory care residents. Using the principles of private mode signaling allowed in hospitals (where only staff is alerted in case of an emergency), the design team and client worked with the wireless nurse call provider and electrical engineer to propose a fire alarm system that would eliminate horn / strobes and report to staff pagers. Via their staff pager, nurses are alerted to a specific fire or CO event uniquely from a nurse call. The proposed system was modified and approved through a series of meetings with state and local building and fire officials. The final approved system eliminates all fire alarm horns from the building in favor of signaling staff via pager. Strobes remain in the resident common spaces as a compromise with fire officials who were concerned that family members and visitors still need a means of notification, other than by staff, in an emergency.

Above: Living and dining patio with landscaped edge
Opposite: Detail of trellis and chain downspout at patio

Green / Sustainable Features: What green / sustainable features had the greatest impact on the project's design?

The key sustainable features are site design considerations, energy efficiency, and maximized daylighting.

Primary motivations: What were the primary motivations for including green / sustainable design features in the project?

The primary motivations were to support the mission / values of the design team, lower operational costs, and improve the building for occupants.

Challenges: What challenges did the project face when trying to incorporate green / sustainable design features?

While many of the green features were new to the client, the design team explained a number of them during early project discussions and found that the notion of sustainable design aligned well with the client's values. Many systems were selected based on lower operating cost in spite of slightly higher first cost.

Technology: How is innovative / assistive / special technology used by the project to deliver care or services?

While common in hospital settings, the elimination of fire alarm horns in the building in favor of private mode signaling is unique in an assisted living licensed memory care building. Elimination of upsetting horns removes technology as a harmful intrusion in the lives of the residents while allowing staff to best protect them in case of an emergency. In line with Tacoma Lutheran's goal to allow full access to the courtyard, none of the doors to the courtyard include locks.

Doors to the courtyard at the ends of the hallway are instead equipped with sensors that can be programmed to page staff if a resident identified as needing assistance in the courtyard passes through it. This maintains the residents' ability to freely access the courtyard, while alerting staff in a manner unobtrusive to the resident.

Jury Comments

The new assisted living memory care residence at North Ridge at Tacoma Lutheran is a wonderful execution of how this type of housing should be built. The scale and spacing of the interior of this project creates a warm and inviting atmosphere. The large windows allow for ample natural daylight as well as views of the exterior landscape. The connection to the outdoors appears to work very well with secure patios and courtyard, which give residents free and independent access to the exterior areas.

The jury liked the simple design of this small house. The 14-bed assisted living memory care cottage is laid out well with appropriately scaled exterior, living, and private spaces. Considerable thought went into the design. An example of this is the nested bathrooms between the bedrooms. This allows for the resident to view the toilet from the bed, thus acting as a visual cue. The jury also liked the modified fire alarm system, which uses the nurse call system to notify staff of an emergency and eliminate strobes and horns, as well as the short distance down the hallways to get from the private to public areas, and the simple interior design. North Ridge is a positive contribution to the quality of care for older adults with memory care needs.

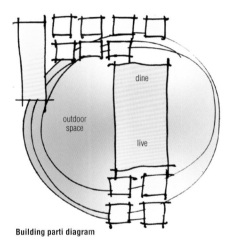

Building parti diagram

Top left: Resident room with oversized windows, view to bath, and individual medicine cabinet inside entry door

Bottom left: Den with direct access to courtyard

Above right: Living room with "windows" to open kitchen and dining

Opposite: Dining room with open kitchen and patio access

Photography: Benjamin Benschneider Photography (exterior); Jesse Young (interior)

Cuthbertson Village Town Center Renovation
Charlotte, North Carolina // Aldersgate Retirement Community

Facility type (year of completion): Assisted living—dementia / memory support (2016)
Target market: Middle / upper middle
Site location: Suburban

Gross square footage of the new construction involved in the project: 4726
Purpose of the renovation / modernization: Upgrade the environment
Provider type: Faith-based non-profit

Below: The area has been opened up with the central atrium space defined by a colonnade, around which activity spaces are located
Opposite left: The entry to each household is distinct in color, furnishings, and artwork
Opposite right: The theater now has better and more comfortable seating, improved sight lines, and actual doors to isolate sound (both in and out)

Overall Project Description

Cuthbertson Village Town Center is the commons area of Aldersgate's assisted living memory support unit, built in 2003. Originally consisting of three 15-bed households, the addition of a new household and another 16 people to the Village prompted a re-evaluation of the condition of the Town Center. Although relatively new, the Town Center appeared old and out of date. The Center consisted of periphery spaces surrounding a skylit central area. Originally organized as a Village Square, periphery spaces had false storefronts and a mixed retro aesthetic. Store frontages in the Village Square appeared artificial and for the most part, the spaces—a five and dime, soda fountain, and potting shed—no longer fit resident needs or interests and were little used. Large planters, a stage, a water feature, and railings littered the center of the area, and the Town Center had little usable space as a result. Hard surfaces and inefficient acoustic materials made it difficult for

residents to hear. Lighting was a problem, either very harsh and direct, or almost non-existent in certain corners. The lack of comfortable seating was also an issue as many chairs had no cushions and some had no arms. Staff had difficulty organizing group activities, partly because of these problems and partly because very little space in the area was actually usable for groups.

Aldersgate, at the time, was in the midst of a series of projects that would ultimately transform the campus—building a new health care center, new types of independent living apartments, and modernizing the independent living commons areas—and the Town Center did not reflect this forward-looking vision. The Town Center renovation project was completed as a standalone scope of work, although certain decisions were integrated with decisions made for the new memory care household that was added around the same time.

The courtyard, which previously felt large and overwhelming, is now light and airy with detailing that gives it a relatable scale and context. It provides a comfortable environment for residents to gather, visit, or simply sit, with plenty of seating and acoustics and lighting deficiencies addressed.

Since completion, the space has been used for concerts, fitness classes, and other events. The cafe tables have proven to be a great place for birthday parties. Background music is often playing, adding to the general relaxing atmosphere. In addition, seemingly small improvements, such as unique identifiers for each household—a different color door or a special light fixture—help residents find their way back to their rooms with less assistance. These changes are also designed to make the entry feel more like the front door to a person's home.

aesthetic is carried throughout the space, and details, such as pilasters, faux balconies, trellis, and pergola effects, add relief to flat walls.

- Entries to households from the Town Center all looked similar, with no distinguishing features to help residents tell them apart. Now, each household entry is uniquely identified by color, art, and furnishings to assist residents with wayfinding.

- Existing acoustics and lighting were a major issue. With primarily hard surfaces and little to soften reverberation, it was very difficult for residents to hear in the Town Center. Acoustic panels were added to dampen noise, but installed to resemble second-story windows around a balcony. In this way the panels are both functional and decorative. New lighting includes decorative lantern fixtures and LED cove lighting, which offer soft but ample light.

Innovations: What innovations or unique features were incorporated into the design of the project?

This project is an example of how a space can be completely transformed with a few very specific ideas. It presents an example of a well-thought-out design geared towards supporting residents and their interactions with staff, visitors, and each other. The design creates a visually stimulating space without becoming overly literal in its references, and demonstrates how small changes and details can make a big difference in this type and size of space. Creating the faux balconies and windows, for example, provided a way to incorporate absorptive acoustic panels visually and logically into the design.

In addition, because the space is small and difficult to understand in renderings, the design team created an interactive 3D model to assist Aldersgate with portraying the space to residents and their families. Wood from trees felled for another new building on campus have been repurposed as decorative wood behind the water feature inside the Town Center.

Project Goals

What were the major goals?

- To design a space that supported operational goals and residents' needs, but didn't say "this is senior living." The intent was to create a sophisticated residential space that speaks more to a large home rather than attempting to look like a small town. This included creating flexible space for gatherings, such as picnics and fitness classes; establishing a new aesthetic; and creating new uses for periphery areas to support residents and operations.

Changes included creating a larger and more functional salon, a larger movie theater, a large gathering space for worship, and a new satellite kitchen that resolves difficulties with food delivery from the main kitchen.

- Taking inspiration from the gracious courtyard gardens of Charleston, Savannah, and New Orleans, the space was refocused on the skylight area, creating an "outdoor" garden with comfortable and supportive seating, surrounded by a colonnade giving definition to circulation paths. The southern-city-courtyard

Challenges: What were the greatest design challenges?

The Town Center had bad acoustics due to its primarily hard surfaces, including stained concrete floor, brick wall tile, and skylight. Sound bounced and residents found it difficult to hear. The existing acoustical ceiling tile was low grade and not very helpful. New vinyl flooring with a sound absorptive backing reduces footfall and cart-traffic noise. The flooring resembles slate tile, but has no joints to create noise or a trip hazard. Absorptive acoustical panels near the skylight also help dampen noise and reflective echoes, while adding visually to the space. The team also selected a higher grade acoustical ceiling tile in the coffered ceilings, and the community room has acoustical wall and ceiling panels and a hearing loop. The Town Center had little area residents and staff could actually use. It was cluttered and full of unmovable objects (water feature, planter boxes, brick columns, metal railings, large wooden stage). Residents could navigate around these objects, however there was little actual usable space for group activities. The only place residents could sit to enjoy the atrium was in front of the soda fountain, an area populated with uncomfortable metal furniture. (Many of the chairs had no arms.) In addition, the surrounding corridor / walkway was impinged on by the architectural features of the faux storefronts. Removing all objects created a flat open courtyard easily used for gatherings or activities. Plenty of comfortable seating allows residents to enjoy the space and the sunshine, and streamlined peripheral walls create a more open area. Aldersgate wanted a large worship / event space separate from the courtyard. Services / events were being held in the theatre, which couldn't accommodate enough residents. With no room to expand outside of the existing space, the design team incorporated part of the corridor / walkway into what had been the five

and dime, creating a large space separate from the center atrium and giving definition and a focal point to the courtyard. The loss of this corridor / walkway doesn't adversely affect circulation, as the majority of staff, residents, and visitors enter from the independent living building doors and navigation to the furthest household is equally distant with / without that part of the corridor. Although the four-sided corridor was originally designed to provide a continuous walking path, few residents used it as such. Since the center is open, residents can now walk within the courtyard instead of having to circle it.

Collaboration: How did stakeholders, occupants, the design team, and / or others collaborate during the planning and / or design process?

The design team met with administration as well as all levels of staff throughout the planning and design phases of this project. Aldersgate staff had ideas about what new functions should be part of the perimeter, based on their experience with the residents. In addition, the team worked with a resident committee, which reviewed the design at each phase and provided feedback and input. This depth of experience and access was invaluable to the project.

Green / Sustainable Features: What green / sustainable features had the greatest impact on the project's design?

The key sustainable features are maximized daylighting and conscientious choice of materials. The design firm specified sustainable materials as a no-added-cost alternative and the client was very happy with the strategy.

Primary motivations: What were the primary motivations for including green / sustainable design features in the project?

The primary motivations were to support the mission / values of the design team and make a contribution to the greater community.

Jury Comments

The jury was impressed with the transformation of the Town Center at Cuthbertson Village. The original town center appeared old and outdated with a number of planters and features that divided the space into unusable small spaces, and with furniture that was not resident-friendly. The transformed space has been opened up to create spaces that are welcoming and user-friendly. This is a marked improvement. By removing the artificial storefront spaces that clutter the hallways in the town hall, the design team were able to enlarge the chapel and movie theater to accommodate the growing community.

The jury appreciated the use of acoustical panels and sound-absorbing flooring, which blend in nicely with the design, to reduce the reverberations that were an issue in the original hard-surfaced space. The use of lighter colored walls, added light, and resident-appropriate furniture makes the space look more inviting. The jury felt the wayfinding through artwork and differentiating colors for each house is an improvement as well.

Opposite: The newly expanded worship / community center can be set up so residents can participate in or enjoy a variety of programs and activities
Above: Corridor areas are decluttered; ceiling treatments delineate the space and provide scale
Photography: RH Wilson Photography

The Burnham Family Memory Care Residence at Avery Heights

Hartford, Connecticut // Avery Heights Senior Living Community

Facility type (year of completion): Assisted living—dementia / memory support (2017)
Target market: Middle / upper middle
Site location: Suburban

Gross square footage of the renovation / modernization involved in the project: 10,000
Purpose of the renovation / modernization: Repositioning
Provider type: Faith-based non-profit

Below: Great room
Opposite: Memory garden zone one

Project Goals

What were the major goals?

- To maximize daylight and views. Strategically positioned common space with two exterior exposures offers views to the garden and beyond with new larger windows. The memory garden fence is detailed with open lattice to afford western winter views to the valley beyond.

- To maximize ceiling height. Careful coordination of mechanical ductwork with existing 1990s structure permitted thoughtful soffit creation to allow for maximum ceiling height. Discreet uplighting enhances the lofty feel.

- To create a discreet resident entry / exit with visitor appeal. Having a clear view to an exit or entrance can cause anxiety for dementia residents, but it is also important for visitors to have a good first impression and enter into the nicest part of the space. The design team created an alcove with a bookcase at the main entrance for visitors, while shifting and narrowing the entrance to the common space to obscure the entry / exit from residents' view.

- To have independent yet secure outdoor access. Outdoor spaces exist in two zones to create a sense of freedom for residents. Zone one allows independent access directly from and visible from the common space. It is used for social gathering, outdoor dining, and activities. Zone two has a gate for assisted access from zone one and is a more natural, private experience with a meandering walking path while still being secure.

- To create an environment for daytime stimulation and restful nighttime experience. Calming and soothing interior finishes and color choices, and artificial and natural lighting control—for bright, cool daytime light, and warm, soft nighttime light—are key in helping residents regulate circadian rhythms. Red umbrellas in outdoor gathering space are visible from the interior public space to stimulate the senses and draw views outward.

Overall Project Description

Avery Heights is a 45-acre Life Plan Community, but its 26-year-old facilities had no space or services for an increasing population of residents suffering from dementia. The renovation of a 10,000-square-foot independent living apartment wing now provides a secure memory care environment for a "population previously closed off to opportunity and allowing them to be in an active, engaging living space." The new facility accommodates 20 apartments in a small house concept, with active areas and quiet zones, a large outdoor living space, and a secure garden with walking path. Security features, such as window locks, are disguised in unobtrusive ways so as not to distract residents. Non-glare lighting and dimmer switches, along with special physical features contribute to resident well-being, including supporting circadian rhythms so that they are active during the day and sleep in the evening. A quiet room,

set off from the main community living area by shoji screens, provides a haven for individuals who become anxious or agitated. Here, they experience aromatherapy, meditation, and calming music. It also provides a place for families to visit privately, or a place for residents to engage in exercise. The community area, with a cozy fireplace, provides space for games, puzzles, conversation, and dining. The program director and nurse share a room that provides privacy to residents needing attention. While visitors come and go through a main entry area, staff can come and go discretely through the country kitchen, thus not disrupting and distracting residents. This small detail is something the staff value highly. Each space in the memory care environment is utilized throughout the day. Soothing colors and graphic imagery evoke smiles and compliments from residents and their families.

- To encourage socialization and respect privacy. Designers created a multi-zoned common area with spaces for group socialization and quiet reflection. For example, varied dining table sizes (two tops, four tops, and community table for family-style dining); fireplace group seating area; two-person seating area near the television and library; relaxing semi-private Snoezelen-type room, or relaxation area, with patterned translucent sliding glass shoji screens.

Innovations: What innovations or unique features were incorporated into the design of the project?

Patterned translucent sliding glass shoji screens separate public and semi-public spaces. The pussy willow, which is one of the first signs of spring, was chosen for the screen pattern as symbolic of an optimistic, positive view of life, and the oversized graphic makes it easily recognizable. Red umbrellas visually connect indoors to outdoors and stimulates the senses. Multi-zoned open living / dining public space allows choices of more social or private experience. Country kitchen induction cooktop ensures safety. Beamed ceiling detail creates openness. Area rugs are actually carpet cut to resemble area rugs in size, but framed to be flush with hardwood flooring to prevent falls. LED night-lights provide a low-light path from bed to bathroom, not only increasing safety but helping residents avoid bright lights so as not to disturb circadian rhythms.

Top: Red umbrellas draw views outside
Bottom left: Semi-private Snoezelen room
Bottom right: Subtle carpet and ceiling transitions and varied lighting break the apparent length of the long corridor to private apartments
Opposite: Memory garden zone two
  Photography: Robert Benson Photography

Challenges: What were the greatest design challenges?

The greatest design challenge was having to work within the existing building constraints of the 1990s facility. The low existing floor-to-ceiling height required careful coordination of mechanical ductwork and thoughtful soffit creation to allow for maximum ceiling height, and concealed uplighting in the wooden beams enhance the lofty feel. The long existing space made for long corridors. Subtle carpet and ceiling transitions, and varied lighting break the apparent length of the corridor. The egress door was offset at the end of the corridor and replaced with an accent wall and large artwork to add interest and visually bring the wall closer.

Collaboration: How did stakeholders, occupants, the design team, and / or others collaborate during the planning and / or design process?

It took a creative collaboration of the varied ideas and talents of architect, interior designer, graphic designer, landscape architect, and visionary owner to create a space that engages dementia residents in indoor / outdoor activity while honoring their dignity and providing them with opportunities not otherwise available in existing circumstances of assisted living or nursing care facilities. The design leverages practical solutions to make the community safe, while addressing the challenging needs of staff who seek to maximize the daily activity and evening restfulness of their charges with flexible spaces that are utilized fully.

Green / Sustainable Features: What green / sustainable features had the greatest impact on the project's design?

The key sustainable features are energy efficiency, maximized daylighting, and conscientious choice of materials.

Primary motivations: What were the primary motivations for including green / sustainable design features in the project?

The primary motivations were to support the mission / values of the client / provider, to stay competitive against other similar / local facilities, and to lower operational costs.

Challenges: What challenges did the project face when trying to incorporate green / sustainable design features?

Seniors who require dementia care need two to three times greater lighting levels than younger residents. This creates a challenge in meeting energy-code watts per square feet. Designers utilized all LEDs that allow dimming to overcome this challenge.

Technology: How is innovative / assistive / special technology used by the project to deliver care or services?

The Snoezelen-type room is equipped with a smart TV primarily used for resident meditation. Users can enjoy aromatherapy, hand massages, and soft music as calming influences. The technology is also used as a diversionary response, for example, if one resident needs to be isolated from others and can be entertained with a movie.

Jury Comments

This project is a creative renovation of existing independent living apartment space to serve those with memory care needs. The design team clearly worked well together to integrate creative solutions needed to overcome the limitations of the existing building. The neighborhood incorporates many current practices for small house design. The jury was particularly impressed with the attention given to lighting, entry and exit points, and resident public spaces. The lighting solution uses existing beams to allow substantial indirect LED lighting that can give cool light during daytime and warmer light after dark. The entry to the neighborhood is creatively designed to be attractive to visitors, but is less obvious from inside the neighborhood. The exit point at the other end of the neighborhood is offset so as not to be obvious to residents, but an interior design feature at that end of the hall creates interest. The indoor common spaces are warm and subtle with simple but very effective detailing. The generous exterior spaces are separated into an "outdoor room" and a larger garden area. Both allow for more expansive views from the property. This is a great example of a successful collaborative design process with a well-executed renovation outcome.

RLPS Architects and MGA Architects

Rose Villa Pocket Neighborhoods & Main Street

Portland, Oregon // Rose Villa

Facility type (year of completion): Independent Living (2016)
Target market: Middle / upper middle
Site location: Suburban

Gross square footage of the new construction involved in the project: 139,580
Provider type: Non-sectarian non-profit

Below: Garden amenities include arbors, boulder seating walls, rose gardens, fire pits, and pet drinking fountains
Opposite: Pocket neighborhoods transition up to the new Town Center

Overall Project Description

This garden community, originally opened in 1960, faced several challenges contributing to declining occupancy. Known for its lush landscaping and relaxed lifestyle, the campus consisted of linear one-story garden apartments that no longer met consumer expectations. Navigating the steep 22-acre hillside site was challenging for existing residents and daunting for those considering the community. The first phase of gradual replacement or exterior renovation of all 263 units (some of which had been converted to non-resident uses) introduced pocket neighborhoods organized around gardens stepping down the hillside. Each pocket neighborhood is comprised of seven cottage homes overlooking an intimate courtyard. The result creates smaller, pedestrian-friendly neighborhoods within the larger community, which capitalize on garden connections and outdoor views. The "over-under" cottages in each pocket neighborhood maximize site utilization while providing compact floor plans that are sized to

be affordable, yet maintain open living spaces with views in multiple directions. The pocket neighborhoods transition up to a new Main Street and Town Center with resident amenities at street level and loft apartments on floors above. The loft apartments provide a residential option for consumers who prefer "downtown" living with interior connection to common spaces. Situated at the highest point of the site overlooking Willamette River, Main Street provides a unique and appealing first impression of the campus, as well as reinforcing a sense of place within the larger community. To provide a true downtown ambience, the street-level amenities, including a bistro grill, garden center, art studio, wellness, and performing arts center, are directly accessible from both the street and internal corridors. A wine bar is envisioned for the rooftop garden overlooking Main Street with views to the river. The completion of the first-phase updates revived Rose Villa's appealing, accessible garden setting, as the community was originally conceived.

Project Goals

What were the major goals?

- To improve occupancy and create a vibrant town center that allows Rose Villa residents to engage with the surrounding Portland community. The pocket neighborhoods doubled the amount of density and tripled the usable open space by stacking cottages while providing at-grade porches for each cottage. The other half of the solution was more traditional loft apartments in the two- and three-story Main Street buildings. While the pocket neighborhoods have outdoor connections to the courtyard gardens, all of the apartments have balconies that favor the views down to the river. Each and every balcony can be accessed from two rooms in the residences. The new housing combined with the Main Street amenities, has resulted in a sustainable and pedestrian-oriented campus that is connected to surrounding

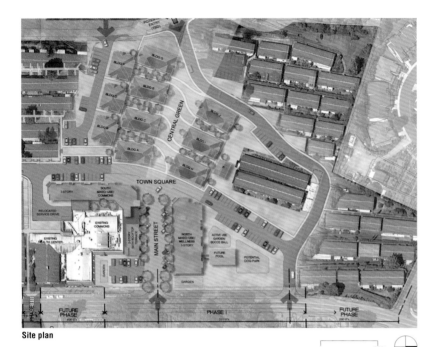

Site plan

0   80ft

residential neighborhoods, schools, and other senior living communities. Amenities such as a performing arts center, newsroom, cafe, garden nursery, full-service salon, wellness center, pool, and spa have all been designed to look and operate as individually branded businesses. Most of these services are open to the public and these amenities, encompassed in a strategic master plan, give residents the ability to live an active lifestyle and provide a social connection to the surrounding community.

- To provide "third-place" spaces where people can casually gather and interact on a regular basis. This led to the creation of the new Main Street and Town Center with loft-style housing above common areas. The inclusion of a lazy river and waterslide in the saline chlorinated lap pool and spaces such as the

resident-operated garden center reflect the unique qualities of Rose Villa. To provide a true downtown ambience, many of the street-level resident amenities are open to the surrounding community. Each pocket neighborhood consists of seven cottage homes organized around an intimate garden setting that promotes a close-knit sense of community. Neighbors are naturally acquainted by the simple fact of shared space and small-scale living. The cottages are sized to be affordable, yet maintain open floor plans that maximize daylight and views in multiple directions. The active rooms of the homes, including the main living areas and front porches, face the common courtyards rather than turning their back to neighbors. Layering of public to private space, using landscape strategies, along with careful placement of windows,

facilitates privacy for each dwelling. Multiple clusters of pocket neighborhoods form a larger aggregate community, all contributing to the character and life of Rose Villa and are connected via walking / cart paths leading up to the Main Street town center and housing. For residents where the travel distances from the pocket neighborhoods is undesirable, the loft apartments located directly above the new common areas along Main Street provide a true sense of downtown living.

Innovations: What innovations or unique features were incorporated into the design of the project?

Introducing a pocket neighborhood concept in combination with an "over-under" cottage design was instrumental in achieving Rose Villa's programming and marketing goals within the constraints of a built-out site with steep grade-level variations. The stacked design, in which the lower-level cottage overlooks a courtyard in one pocket neighborhood while the upper-level cottage facing the opposite direction takes advantage of the grade to form another neighborhood with its own courtyard, provides a gradual and pedestrian-friendly transition up the hillside. Despite the significant grade changes, the pocket neighborhoods are organized to create a low slope, accessible path from the bottom of the hill up to the Main Street and Town Center at the highest elevation. The pathways were designed not only to be pedestrian and pet-friendly but also wide enough to allow for golf-cart service to the front door of any residence. Each garden is themed and provided with various amenities such as arbors, boulder seating walls, rose gardens, fire pits, and even pet drinking fountains. A multi-use pavilion structure bounding one of the gardens is available for social gatherings and events.

Challenges: What were the greatest design challenges?

The greatest design challenges were addressing declining occupancy, severe lack of curb appeal, and undersized social spaces with little available property for new construction. The solution required careful development using a multi-phased approach to reinvent the campus with ultimately all 70-plus existing buildings being replaced or extensively remodeled. To initiate the first phase of demolition and construction, 100 of the existing 260 villa units were taken out of inventory, some held open for redevelopment and others converted to alternate uses. Those units, combined with additional unoccupied units, allowed for resident relocations to implement the first phase of improvements envisioned by the master plan. By introducing two new housing options, Rose Villa has greater marketing depth to accommodate varying levels of independence and meet the needs of a more diverse population.

To achieve financial viability the planning and design team developed a housing model that addressed the steep slopes while maintaining the necessary density. An "over-under" cottage plan was developed where each cottage has both a front and back door with an abundance of natural light in this garden-living setting. The buildings act as retaining walls to address the steeply sloping site, but maintain level gardens throughout. Ultimately, increasing not only occupancy but also the total number of housing units through higher density models without overbuilding the site provided the necessary revenue for the new Main Street spaces that further contribute to long-term community relevance and viability.

Previously, the entrance to the Rose Villa campus from the surrounding neighborhood was not immediately apparent and a distinctive campus core or activity hub was lacking. To create a

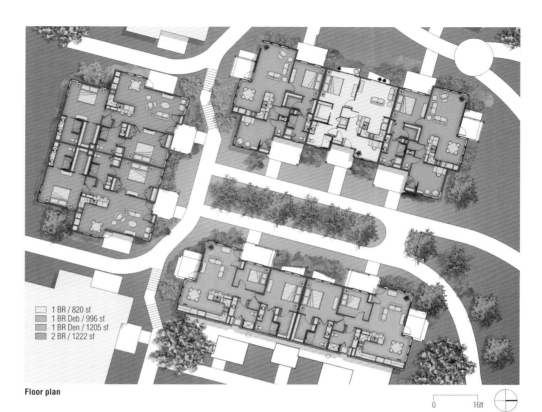

Floor plan

1 BR / 820 sf
1 BR Deb / 996 sf
1 BR Den / 1205 sf
2 BR / 1222 sf

0   16ft

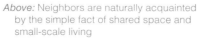

Above: Neighbors are naturally acquainted by the simple fact of shared space and small-scale living

Top right and right: Before: The low-slope accessible pathway is wide enough for golf-cart service to the front door of any residence

Top left and right: Small-scale communities in a large-scale world
Above: A saline chlorination system was utilized for the pool
Right: Bistro garage doors can be opened to Main Street

sense of arrival at the community, the new Town Center is located directly off the main public road and provides a curbless Main Street / Plaza that can be closed off to vehicles to provide a safe, accessible, pedestrian environment. This allows Rose Villa to host community events such as farmers markets and art fairs. The Town Square sits at the precipice of the site looking down through the linear gardens and pocket neighborhoods to Willamette River.

Collaboration: How did stakeholders, occupants, the design team, and / or others collaborate during the planning and / or design process?

In addition to traditional marketing studies, the design team conducted five separate focus groups comprising senior management, staff members, independent living residents, adult children of residents, and family members. Each group responded to a series of open-ended questions regarding existing facilities and programs, as well as potential areas of improvement utilizing the owner and design team's shared interest in the pocket neighborhood concept as a guide. A review of publications including Ross Chapin's *Pocket Neighborhoods: Creating Small Scale Community in a Large Scale World*, and Ray Oldenburg's *The Great Good Place*, along with the tabulated focus group results, helped the development team prioritize and refine programming goals. The team of owner, development consultant, civil engineer, local design architect, and architect of record further collaborated throughout a four-month master planning process. This included a two-day on-site design charrette. This collaborative, interactive process provided an efficient and cost-effective forum for debate, clearly defined relevant design and development issues, structured alternative solutions, and concluded with a graphic presentation of preliminary project designs.

Following subsequent refinement culminating in the final master plan, the team continued to advance the design concepts though a series of collaborative review sessions both on site and utilizing web conferencing technology for real-time reviews from multiple locations.

Green / Sustainable Features: What green / sustainable features had the greatest impact on the project's design?

The key sustainable features are energy efficiency, maximized daylighting, and recycling construction waste and / or diversion from landfills.

Primary motivations: What were the primary motivations for including green / sustainable design features in the project?

The primary motivations were to support the mission / values of the client / provider, stay competitive against other similar / local facilities, and lower operational costs.

Jury Comments

Rose Villa Pocket Neighborhoods is an exceptional reimagining of a linear single-story garden apartment complex in a great location but in need of an update to meet current market expectations. The concept of pocket neighborhoods joined by pathways and gardens, situated along the sloping hillside, reinforces the residential character of the community and makes creative use of a challenging topography.

The jury felt this concept was a thoughtful response to the needs of the community and demands of a difficult site. The "over-under" cottage configuration provides accessible entries and plans for all residents. The beautifully landscaped gardens connect the cottages and encourage neighborhood engagement and sense of community. The sloping paths may challenge some residents but there are numerous opportunities to pause and rest along the way.

The loft apartments in the Town Center at the top of the hill provide an urban alternative to cottage living, which supports the current focus on providing multiple options to residents to personalize their lifestyles. The comprehensive wellness center provides residents the opportunity to socialize while focusing on their health and well-being. Retail amenities opening to Main Street are well executed and inviting destinations for residents and families, as well as the public, which reduces the isolation felt in more suburban communities and enhances the connectivity with the outside world.

The jury agreed that this property embodied all the current directions in senior living toward choice of living space, focus on wellness and socialization, and connection with the outdoors and with the greater community.

Above: To address 40 feet of grade change, pocket neighborhood clusters step up the hillside to the new Town Center through an interconnected series of accessible walkways
Opposite: Pocket neighborhoods provide the basis for a sense of belonging and meaning

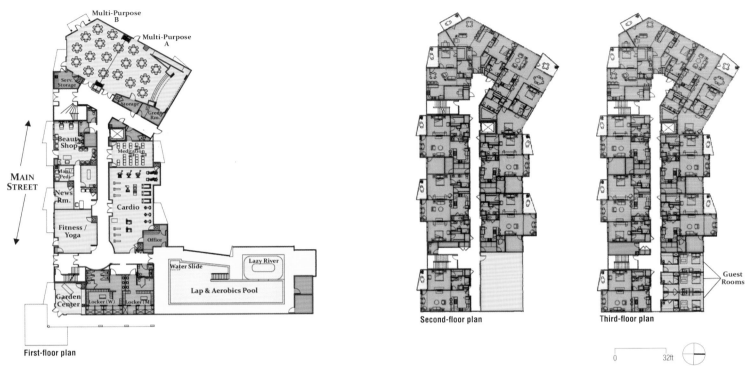

Multi-Purpose B

Multi-Purpose A

Serv. Storage

Storage

Green Rm.

Beauty Shop

Meditation

Mani/ Pedi

MAIN STREET

News Rm.

Cardio

Fitness / Yoga

Office

Water Slide

Lazy River

Lap & Aerobics Pool

Garden Center

Locker (W)

Locker (M)

First-floor plan

Second-floor plan

Third-floor plan

Guest Rooms

0   32ft

Left: Town Center
Top: Pedicure stations in spa
Bottom: Residence

Photography: Nathan Cox Photography; Steve Wanke Photography

SFCS Architects

The Cottage at Cypress Cove

Fort Myers, Florida // Cypress Cove

Facility type (year of completion): Assisted living—dementia / memory support (2016)
Target market: Upper
Site location: Suburban

Gross square footage of the new construction involved in the project: 39,533
Provider type: Non-sectarian non-profit

Opposite: Exterior

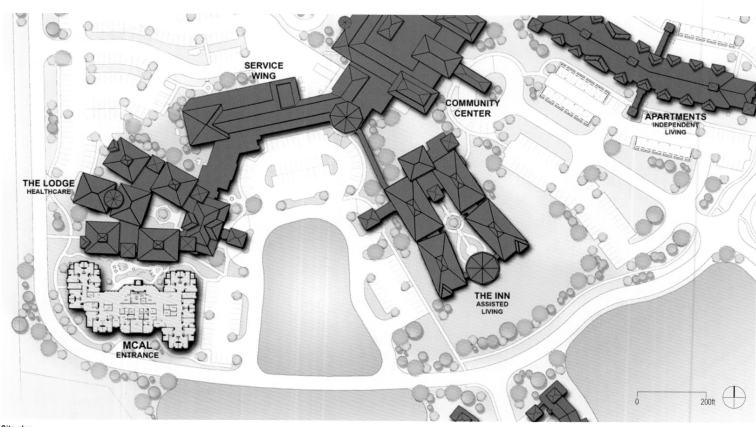

Site plan

Overall Project Description

The Cottage at Cypress Cove is a new assisted living memory care residence that specifically caters to residents with Alzheimer's disease and other dementia-related conditions. It is a visionary, state-of-the-art environment, program, and operation utilizing comprehensive best practices and research. The 39,533-square-foot two-story Cottage establishes a neighborhood of 44 private residential apartments with four separate smaller households that accommodate 11 residents. Each household is approximately 8000 square feet with 3800 square feet of shared core spaces per floor. The Cottage at Cypress Cove was purposefully created so that every aspect of its design best serves the residents. The U-shaped household layout is designed to minimize corridor lengths and provide visual cueing from the bedrooms to the common spaces. This helps residents to find their way and eliminates confusion. Each household is designed with a different distinct aesthetic authentic to the Southwest Florida area.

The exterior of the building matches the aesthetic style of the existing campus and is designed around a specialty sensory and activity courtyard, which is accessible from all households and provides a safe and enriching outdoor extension. The project was developed based on factors that include: a collaborative "project guiding principles" document; various site constraints; program requirements; owner, resident, and family feedback; site visits to other innovative programs and environments; best practices in household design; outdoor spaces; and code requirements. The project team is an integrated and highly diverse group of design professionals including two internationally recognized leaders in the field of environments for elderly with dementia. This project is part of a holistic improvement to the existing health care programs and adds a specialized level of care not previously provided on the campus. The design promotes healthy living through a well-rounded holistic approach addressing the physical, social, spiritual, and emotional needs of elders suffering from dementia-related diseases.

Project Goals

What were the major goals?

- To develop a visionary, state-of-the-art environment, program, and operation utilizing comprehensive best practices and research. The project team envisioned a therapeutic environment and program that actually treats the symptoms of the disease while creating a familiar, comfortable home. Drawing on significant prior and developing research on many memory care design elements, including small house design, artificial lighting, natural light, access to the outdoors, privacy, wayfinding / visual cueing, color and spatial theories, the overarching goal was to create the best memory care small house in the country in which residents live longer, healthier, happier lives. The initial research on the impacts of the circadian lighting systems actually show greater positive results than any pharmacological intervention currently available.

- To create a holistically designed, operated, and programmed memory care environment that offers residents better comprehensive outcomes then elsewhere. The Cottage at Cypress Cove specifically caters to residents with Alzheimer's disease and other dementia-related conditions. The layout considers the memory care resident by minimizing corridor length and by providing visual cueing to the residential commons space. Heat gain and harsh sunlight / glare is minimized by limiting glazing along the south face of the building, while the design allows for a maximum amount of light to enter the building from the north through the dining and living spaces. This allows for abundant visual connections to the outdoor courtyard, which is accessible by all residents.

The incorporation of a tunable circadian lighting system throughout the community commons has a satellite real-time / place solar connection. This technology simulates natural sunrise and sunset patterns and has been proven to help maintain circadian rhythms and mitigate sleep disorders for memory care residents. The system is inconspicuously located in the cove lighting located in all common areas. This provides residents exposure to the illumination process 24 hours a day as light therapy. Additionally, the highly visible connection to the resident bathroom has an exterior window for additional natural light, all within a very tight and efficient footprint. To maintain and reduce stimulating the resident's circadian system during the night, bathrooms also include sufficient warm amber night lights to support healthy sleep. Often in people with dementia-related disorders, the internal circadian rhythms and sleep-wake cycle become significantly disrupted, which have significant impacts on residents and caregivers. Research indicates that the exposure to a supplemental lighting system can help residents maintain synchronization with the solar day. The Cottage is the first purpose-built dementia environment in the world to utilize this technology to help with light-related symptoms of dementia. Appropriate lighting also helps with providing visual information for maintenance of postural stability, helping to limit and manage falls, which increase due to age-related changes that occur in the vestibular and somatosensory systems. A specific example of this is amber night lighting in order to minimize both sleep disruptions and potential falls.

Innovations: What innovations or unique features were incorporated into the design of the project?

The team specifically focused on elements that foster aging with integrity, promote resident comfort, create a peaceful sense of safety and security, promote independence, and nurture mental, physical, and emotional health of each resident. Floor plans carefully position dining rooms, corridors, gathering areas, and restrooms, plus other spaces, for optimal flow, practicality, and convenience. Private resident rooms have all elements, such as hardware, lighting, furniture, and visual cues, designed to best serve residents. Activities and programs include physical exercise programs, art therapy, computer interface activities, Montessori activities, and other sensory stimulation activities such as baking or music performances. Interior and exterior environments bring daylight and elements of the natural world into the built environment. Embedded discrete staff spaces allow for unobtrusive observation of household commons. Layouts minimize the intrusion of institutional services, which can disrupt resident life. The design of unique resident room layout maximizes natural light, floor space, flexibility, and storage, while minimizing resident confusion. By locating the resident bathroom on the exterior wall, natural light is introduced to both the bedroom and bathroom spaces. This move also maximizes flexible, open-plan floor space within the apartments and provides significant storage options. The design team specifically focused on the promotion of independence, as well as the mental, physical, and emotional health and welfare of each resident, through purposeful design techniques. The centrally located living room provides areas for socialization and activities. Each household is designed with a different distinct aesthetic authentic to the Southwest Florida area to cater to varying resident tastes. Families love the ability to spend time with their loved ones in the comfortable and private parlors within each household.

Residents are encouraged to explore the outdoors within the tropical memory garden, which has been designed to be a space that is pleasant, reflective, restorative, and an engaging experience. Relaxing elements include a rain chain waterfall, rain gardens, dancing water jets, and fountains. Ornate rain chains provide a unique visual connection to the outdoor courtyard and promote conversation without distracting, disruptive noises heard during a rainstorm. Residents can watch and listen to the soft water sound of a waterfall while inside the household or from the adjacent covered porch areas. The design team and project initially included a small extensive green roof area over the back porch overlooking the courtyard garden. This green roof area was to provide direct outdoor access for the upper level households. Due to concerns about maintenance and water issues the extensive green roof was converted to a roof with large potted plants. The owner and design team elected at that time to add a third elevator to the project, allowing the upper-level residents with direct outdoor access to the courtyard garden on grade, thus achieving the original goal of direct outdoor garden access for every resident in the building.

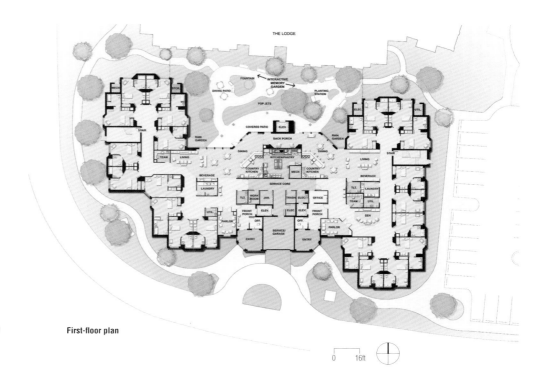

First-floor plan

0   16ft

Opposite: Household entry
Right: Dining and rooftop garden

Resident room layout

0   8ft

Challenges: What were the greatest design challenges?

The greatest design challenge was building placement and siting, while allowing for direct outdoor access for all residents, plus unobtrusive stealth services and deliveries for the building. Building design and site arrangement needed to work technically while supporting the project guiding principles of "it's their home," "small house concept," "person-centered," and "purposeful living and integrated programming." One of the first and most significant challenges was finding a way to design and place the almost 40,000-square-foot program on a very small and tight, three-sided existing corner lot, which backs up to the existing nursing home. To accomplish all of the necessary, and in some cases conflicting parameters, the building was designed around a center service core, accessed through the street-facing residential

garage. This center core allows all stealth services to serve each household in a discrete manner, which truly limits the infiltration of noise, clutter, and institutional artifacts. To allow all residents direct access and visual connection to the outdoors, the team incorporated a second-floor viewing roof garden and a secondary elevator, allowing the two upper households to directly access the memory garden.

A second challenge was to maximize both natural day lighting and resident visual cueing while minimizing corridors throughout the households and incorporating operational and staff efficiencies throughout the design. By developing a unique resident room layout, corridor lengths are minimized and resident rooms provide direct visual cueing from and to the household commons spaces. Staff spaces are discretely integrated throughout

the household and these subtle shifts in environmental design promise to increase staff efficiencies and create a more satisfying working environment. In turn, this yields time for deeper relationships with the residents and family members.

Another challenge was to incorporate and design the best elements of a supportive memory care environment into each private resident room and bathroom to support autonomy, independence, and maintenance of resident capability while endeavoring to limit the confusion and frustration. Due to the small site, the overall design of The Cottage had to be very efficient, starting with the layout of the private resident rooms and

Opposite top left: Open kitchen
Opposite top right: Living room
Opposite bottom left and right: Living and dining
Above left: Resident room entry

bathrooms. The design of unique resident room layouts maximize natural light, floor space, flexibility, and storage while minimizing resident confusion. The open-plan design incorporates a sitting area, sleeping area, large closet, plus additional storage. The highly visible connection to the resident bathroom has an exterior window for additional natural light, all within a very tight and efficient footprint. Many dementia-specific supportive details are incorporated, including various open and closed storage options, a barn door to the bathroom, and direct view to the toilet. The use of integrated amber night-lighting in the bathrooms was incorporated as well.

Collaboration: How did stakeholders, occupants, the design team, and / or others collaborate during the planning and / or design process?

The entire project team participated in a very collaborative approach from the outset. Initial planning sessions included the multi-disciplinary project and owner team. The visioning process included visits and tours to six memory care communities to study best practices in programming, operations, staffing, training, and environment, researching the "best of the best."

These tours, the information discovered, plus the project guiding principles created a foundation for the team to work from. The guiding principles were developed with input from all stakeholders including leadership, staff, residents, family members, and the multi-disciplinary design team. The title headings of the principles are: it's their home; small house concept; it's about our people; it's person-centered; purposeful living and integrated programming; and financial stewardship. Periodic updates were provided to stakeholders during project development, with input and feedback solicited. Prospective residents and family members toured The Cottage when nearing completion and provided preliminary feedback.

Outreach: What off-site outreach services are offered to the greater community?

Alzheimer's Association: The Cottage was the official sponsor of all Purple Mug events leading up to the Alzheimer's Association Walk to End Alzheimer's last year, as well as the kick-off events leading up to the walk this year. The Cottage had hundreds of attendees at these events last year and approximately 80 percent

of all attendees were health care professionals. The Cottage raised more than $7000 from the sale of Purple Mugs and raffle tickets—the most successful Purple Mug events in the state of Florida. The Cottage participated in the Longest Day at Bell Tower Shops in June, promoting its memory care services along with the upcoming kick-off events. The Cottage is also the official sponsor of the Alzheimer's Association Grand Opening event for its new offices.

Alvin A. Dubin Alzheimer's Resource Center: The Cottage is the primary sponsor of the Caregiver's Day-off event held each December at Westminster Church. This event typically has 60 to 80 attendees who are part-time or full-time family caregivers. In addition, The Cottage participates in and sponsors the annual Brushstrokes From The Soul, A Light to Remember, and Handbag Fundraiser events. The Cottage presented to the Early Diagnosis Support Group at the Dubin Center and received positive feedback regarding the presentation, which is being offered to the Alzheimer's Association based on the response. Health and wellness fairs typically occur in-season and are primarily attended by seasonal residents. These events provide an excellent opportunity to educate the community about the services and amenities available at The Cottage and network with other communities, organizations, and agencies. Lee Health Case Manager Meet and Greet is an invitation-only annual vendor fair for health care providers, including facilities, home-health agencies, and non-profit organizations, sponsored by Lee Health.

The Cottage has participated in monthly meetings with key health care professionals in Lee County to coordinate and plan the annual Southwest Florida Coalition for Optimal Behavioral Health and Aging conference. It has also participated in monthly meetings for Lee County Injury Prevention Coalition to review safety and injury prevention initiatives. Cypress Cove won an award from this Coalition for its scooter program. The Cottage also participates in other off-site annual or biennial events and fundraisers for: Lee County Medical Society, Senior Friendship Center Adult Day Care, Dr. Piper Center for Social Services, Senior Blue Book Senior Symposium, Sanibel Island, Caribbean American Medical Educational Organization, ARNP, Florida Geriatrics Society, and Professional Guardians.

Green / Sustainable Features: What green / sustainable features had the greatest impact on the project's design?

The key sustainable features are energy efficiency and water efficiency.

Opposite top left: Resident bathroom
Opposite top right: Resident bedroom
Top: Living room
Bottom: Private parlor

Primary motivations: What were the primary motivations for including green / sustainable design features in the project?

The primary motivations were to support the mission / values of the client / provider, lower operational costs, and improve the building for occupants.

Technology: How is innovative / assistive / special technology used by the project to deliver care or services?

The community common areas are fully equipped with advanced circadian lighting technology that simulates natural sunrise and sunset patterns and has been proven to help maintain circadian rhythms and mitigate sleep disorders for memory care residents. The highly visible connection to the resident bathroom has an exterior window for additional natural light, all within a very tight and efficient footprint. To maintain and reduce stimulating the resident's circadian system during the night, bathrooms also include sufficient warm amber night-lights to support healthy sleep.

Top: Salon and day spa
Bottom: Parlor
Opposite left: Resident courtyard
Opposite right: Tropical memory garden

Photography: Alise O'Brien Photography; Thomas Watkins

Jury Comments

The jury felt that The Cottage at Cypress Cove is a very successful execution of the household model. The plan centers on shortened resident corridors opening onto common spaces shared by two households. The visual and physical access to living areas encourages engagement and provides ample space for wandering and exploring the environment.

The thoughtful use of both natural and artificial lighting provides open and airy living and dining spaces, all with views into the gardens. The sundowning effect, often experienced by residents with dementia, is mitigated through use of lighting technology designed to mimic the body's circadian rhythm, promoting more natural sleep-wake cycles. The design team cites research indicating that light therapy has also been attributed with reduced anxiety and depression, which will hopefully be measured in this community as a case study.

Maximizing the daylight in the apartments is also a feature that the jury appreciated. The outboard bathroom with a large clerestory window enhances the appeal of the whole space and makes it feel larger. Important direct visual access to the bathroom from the bed is achieved with an angled entry and decorative barn door. The amber night-light is cleverly concealed in a running trim detail, providing a warm indirect glow with no visible light source, so as not to disturb sleep patterns for residents.

The jury also loved the ample storage space provided in the resident apartment. It is simple but functional and well designed.

The common spaces are well detailed, tasteful, and homelike in their aesthetic, which combined with the indirect lighting provides a calm, relaxed atmosphere. The outdoor gardens are accessible to the residents, via an elevator for second-floor units, and provide safe, flexible walking paths, and a variety of seating and activity areas.

The jury agreed that much thought was clearly given to this small house design, and the result is a state-of-the-art environment and a positive contribution to the pursuit of high-quality dementia care.

Perkins Eastman

The Summit at Rockwood South Hill
Spokane, Washington // Rockwood Retirement Communities

Facility type (year of completion): Independent Living (2016)
Target market: Middle / upper middle
Site location: Suburban; greyfield

Gross square footage of the new construction involved in the project: 216,568
Gross square footage of the renovation / modernization involved in the project: 16,640
Purpose of the renovation / modernization: Upgrade the environment
Provider type: Faith-based non-profit

Below: The Summit tower
Opposite: The entry lobby is the confluence of the Riverwalk circulation from the day-lit social activities hall and corridor leading to dining activities

Overall Project Description

Rockwood Retirement Communities wanted an innovative home for its older adult residents to deeply connect them to the natural world from within an environment that offers improved amenities and living spaces. Using biophilic design to illuminate and support the seven dimensions of wellness, The Summit (and The Ridge) now offers the opportunity for a healthy, productive lifestyle in a LEED-Silver Certified building. The site offered views of distant mountains and nearby pine forests from its location atop a butte, and the existing community had two living options: Forest Estate homes and The Ridge tower, a high-rise building with undersized apartments, sparse amenities, and poor energy performance. The design team initiated a two-strategy approach for repositioning. First, build a new tower, The Summit, with 65 larger independent living apartments ranging from 900 to

2200 square feet. Second, add an expanded first-floor community space focused on wellness, while tying the existing Ridge with the new Summit and orienting it toward the estate homes to create a cohesive, connected community. A major feature of the addition is The Riverwalk connecting The Ridge to The Summit. This curvilinear circulation path of discovery winds through an array of new amenity spaces. The material palette reflects natural colors and textures drawn from Rockwood's surroundings. Ample windows and clerestory openings repeatedly frame views of the woods and sky following biophilic principles. The Riverwalk's four new dining venues offer choice in their varied design, operating hours, and menus. Other amenities include a grand ballroom, art studio, cinema, library, lounge, and a wellness center with an aerobics studio, state-of-the-art fitness equipment, beauty salon, and spa.

Project Goals

What were the major goals?

- The Ridge—an eight-story 1960s glass-box building—consisted of small apartments, outdated and limited amenity spaces, inadequate parking, and skyrocketing energy bills. The occupancy rate was declining. There was a waiting list for larger apartments and homes, and not an adequate supply. The Summit—a new 11-story high-rise luxury tower with amenity space and underground parking—provided 65 new, larger apartments and allowed for the reinvention of The Ridge with additional common spaces, using entry fees from new tower apartments.

- Knit the existing Ridge and new Summit towers with the Forest Estate homes to provide a greater social connection among the residents and reinforce the essence of a whole community. To encourage an easy connection to residents in the community's active adult portion, the community's main entry was relocated to face estate homes on the building's west side. On the main level, the community added a host of enticing educational and vocational activities with a grand ballroom for concerts and events, art studio, movie theatre, library, and casual lounge spaces that overlook the main entry drive. The community also added a wellness center that addresses the resident's physical needs with aerobics, weights, yoga, and personal coaching. The salon includes spa functions as well. These activities are a drawcard for all and have created new friendships in the community.

- Incorporate whole-person wellness as a core value throughout the community. Rockwood was clear that wellness relates to everything it offers, including food services, activity

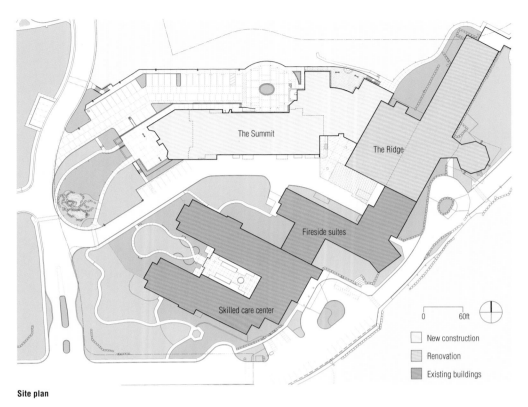

Site plan

The Summit

The Ridge

Fireside suites

Skilled care center

0   60ft

☐ New construction

▨ Renovation

■ Existing buildings

programs, community connections, and creative endeavors. Venues have been expanded for those activities. The wellness center now includes personal training, strength building, yoga studios, massage and aromatherapy areas, and a future pool addition. Dining is no longer in one large room, and is divided up to create casual, theatrical, and formal dining options. A new auditorium provides space for concerts, lectures, and community celebrations. Casual areas to socialize, with views to the outside, were added, as well as spaces for art, movies, library, and spiritual programs. Outdoor terraces spill out from the south and west sides of the building from the activity spaces.

Innovations: What innovations or unique features were incorporated into the design of the project?

Rockwood is a community that focuses on the wellness of its residents in all its programs. To create architecture in support of this goal, the design incorporates biophilic design principles that recognize an inherent human affinity to affiliate with natural systems and processes. Natural light floods the main spaces helping with melatonin production and encouraging natural circadian rhythm. The Riverwalk is the main serpentine corridor connecting first-floor common spaces and entices residents to satisfy an innate curiosity to explore. Spaces are designed to fulfill a person's emotional need for "prospect and refuge," for example the library with views to the main entry from a room with a more secluded feeling.

Boundaries between indoors and outdoors are blurred to create a connection with nature, and natural elements are embraced with places to enjoy the warmth of a fire, watch forest and wetland wildlife, sense the dynamic nature of the sky, and track the sun's movement throughout the course of the day. Interior design elements rely on the use of natural materials such as stone and wood, within touch of the residents, and the artwork and fabric shapes evoke natural scenes based on fractal patterns found in the natural environment.

Challenges: What were the greatest design challenges?

The first design challenge was to eliminate the sense that there would be separate groups of residents on campus. The design proceeded with an intention to not create a hierarchy on campus. Attention needed to be paid equally to the renovation of the building as well as the new construction of the building and the existing residents needed to be considered and respected throughout the design process. This extended to considering the location of the new elevator, the proximity of parking to the existing residents' apartment homes, minimizing view blockages of the existing tower, and recognizing that continued dialogue was important between staff and residents throughout all phases of the project.

The second design challenge was that the current buildings looked worn and Rockwood needed to be perceived as the community of choice to the market while the rest of the project was being developed. An interior design makeover of the key existing community spaces considered furniture that might be used in the overall project, making sure it kept within budget, and creating a new, more vibrant image when potential residents visited.

The recession hit as the marketing commenced at the end of the design development phase of the project, which made it a challenge to market. The project was therefore reconsidered and downsized with fewer units on a smaller footprint, and fewer amenity spaces in an effort to reduce costs. The design utilized the same concepts of site organization, circulation, and major program layout and apartment home design, along with the exterior skin concept, but tightened up the building. This made it easier to reach the target sales goals and reduced the project development costs, making it successful to build while construction costs were still relatively low and pricing competitive.

Collaboration: How did stakeholders, occupants, the design team, and / or others collaborate during the planning and / or design process?

A study to assess the before and after effects of the building on the wellness of the residents included circulating a questionnaire to current and future residents prior to opening the new building. Another resident survey will be taken after approximately nine months of living in the community to determine the effectiveness of biophilic design in relation to occupant wellness.

Green / Sustainable Features: What green / sustainable features had the greatest impact on the project's design?

The key sustainable features are energy efficiency and maximized daylighting. A "Green Team" of residents and staff who were keenly interested in sustainable design worked together to advise the architects of design suggestions and also initiate more immediate ideas that could be implemented while the building design was underway. For example, residents and staff researched photovoltaic and solar water technology, implemented a recycling program, and changed the detergents used in the washing to eliminate phosphate.

Second-floor to seventh-floor plan

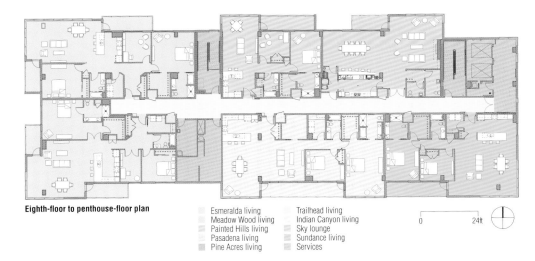

Eighth-floor to penthouse-floor plan

Esmeralda living
Meadow Wood living
Painted Hills living
Pasadena living
Pine Acres living
Trailhead living
Indian Canyon living
Sky lounge
Sundance living
Services

0   24ft

Primary motivations: What were the primary motivations for including green / sustainable design features in the project?

The primary motivations were to lower operational costs, improve the building for occupants, and create a more sustainable community.

Challenges: What challenges did the project face when trying to incorporate green / sustainable design features?

There was a desire to make more modifications to The Ridge's existing envelope and building systems to increase resident comfort and improve energy efficiency. The pro forma did not stretch to allow for covering the cost of those changes. However, a lifecycle cost analysis on The Summit tower allowed for integration of better systems and envelope efficiencies on the new building.

Left: The library with fireplace encourages casual socializing with views to forest beyond

Top: A new auditorium with reception space provides a place to bring residents of the entire community together

Bottom: There has been a notable increase in the level of activity in the dining program

Jury Comments

The Summit at Rockwood South Hill is a strong independent living element that complements and enhances an existing campus. The jury particularly liked the curvilinear corridor through the amenity spaces. This element of the design opened up different views around each bend and linked the amenity spaces in a seamless and relaxed flow. There are both intimate and expansive spaces along the way. Views to the outside are available all along this primary corridor and from within amenity spaces. There was extensive use of natural light. The interior design and decor are sophisticated, clean, warm, and modern. Multiple state-of-the-art dining options were added with this plan and are located close to where existing buildings are connected. The open and flexible design of the event space includes overflow space on an outside terrace. The fitness facilities are also located to take advantage of outside views.

The apartments in the building incorporate features to take advantage of natural light. Each residence has access to the outside with a patio. The overall up-to-date style is appropriate for this high-rise independent living building.

Right: Embers Grille, located adjacent to the bar, serves food all day and offers display cooking that engages residents

Left: The library uses the biophilic principles of prospect and refuge

Above: Open-plan apartments support a casual lifestyle and offer views onto the landscape beyond

Photography: Benjamin Benschneider Photography

BKV Group

Abiitan Mill City
Shoreview, Minnesota // Ecumen

Facility type (year of completion): Assisted living—dementia / memory support (2018)
Target market: Middle / upper middle / upper
Site location: Urban; greyfield

Gross square footage of the new construction involved in the project: 145,000 (housing), 67,000 (parking)
Provider type: Faith-based non-profit

Below: Abiitan Mill City and the larger master plan site design was inspired by the historic area and developed through a focus on urban connectivity
Opposite: View from the north

Overall Project Description

Abiitan Mill City is a nod to the past and a vision for the future. Respectfully borrowing from the Ojibwe word for "live in," Abiitan and the larger master plan site design were inspired by the area history and developed with a future focus on urban connectivity. The site is located a few hundred yards from St. Anthony Falls, a historic site for Native Americans and the birth place of Minneapolis. As the area developed, the site was filled with rail lines connecting to the city's many flour mills and main rail station. Within this framework, the design team created a plaza space that bridges two buildings around the historic rail-spur location. A shared street concept called a *woonerf* was designed to create connectivity between the buildings, the downtown core, and the Mississippi River Parkway. The *woonerf* is a Dutch-inspired urban concept that places pedestrians and bicycles ahead of cars.

Abiitan has 86 independent living units and 48 memory care units across five stories. It is the first major senior-focused development built in downtown Minneapolis in the last 20 years. Seniors will have the opportunity to age gracefully in an urban environment with easy access to the city's many attractions and amenities, plus multiple modes of public transit, which can reduce or eliminate the need to drive. Current Minneapolis residents will be able to remain within their own community, even as they age and their needs change. The urban nature of the project promotes an active lifestyle, with a high level of access to bike trails, walking paths, the river parkway, city parks, restaurants, theaters, and other downtown amenities. The overall design of the streetscape of Abiitan utilizes its position in the city to create new connectivity and promote resident health through walkability and rich pedestrian experiences. The primary building entry and common spaces are organized around the *woonerf*. Abiitan further promotes connectivity by activating the remaining streetscapes with the fitness room, courtyards, and walk-up units.

The building design was influenced in a number of ways primarily by the historic district in and focus groups. Historical building patterns of the St. Anthony Falls Historic District feature smaller footprints that guided the massing and exterior material selection locations. Focus groups with the local senior community directly engaged possible residents for their input. The feedback was invaluable and integral to the overall design of the development. They wanted to see a metropolitan style of building (contemporary and refined yet comfortable and inviting), modern interior spaces, fresh and current food selections, and large windows allowing for lots of natural light. The building features a solid masonry base with expansive glass openings at the public spaces. The upper resident levels reflect an industrial aesthetic through the use of form and the placement of openings. These levels also incorporate brick, metal panels, and glass as their primary materials.

Project Goals

What were the major goals?

- To create a building for local seniors to age gracefully within their community, which was accomplished by the overall design of the facility.

- To create a destination building for those drawn to walkable senior living, which was also achieved through the overall design of the facility.

- To promote health through an active lifestyle with access and walkability to the city's amenities.

- To create a strong sense of place and activity hub within the building. Focusing on the common spaces primarily on level one brings the main building activity together to enhance the residents' connectivity to one another.

- To provide fresh and contemporary food options across a multitude of dining experiences, including an open kitchen, bar, cafe, and private dining room.

Innovations: What innovations or unique features were incorporated into the design of the project?

The memory care environment was designed with particular consideration. The spaces, finishes, and furniture are an integral feature of the circle of care offered by the provider, leveraging the Awakenings care approach. The design of the memory care spaces incorporate concepts that reduce distractions associated with Alzheimer's including glare-free lighting, private rooms, activity stations (indoor and outdoor), and discrete directional cues. This design presents the opportunity to create a private-public *woonerf*, a Dutch-inspired shared street where bikes, cars, and pedestrians co-exist and car speeds are reduced. The space will be curbless, and vehicular travel lanes will be defined via bollards and changes in paving-surface type and color. *Woonerfs* are designed for very slow speeds (10 miles per hour), similar to those typically found in European cities. They allow pedestrians and cyclists to become the focus of the space, while the car is treated as the visitor.

The design of the project was committed to demonstrating a number of best management practices for stormwater management and low-impact development. Some of the concepts and techniques include rainwater harvesting, vegetated walls, pervious paving, pixilated parking, green roofs, and underground retention system, which was of particular note. The stormwater from both properties is directed to a communal underground retention system below the *woonerf*. This system includes a large perforated pipe gallery that is embedded in a porous rock section. Stormwater is allowed to infiltrate into the soils below the system. An impervious liner is installed vertically surrounding the perimeter of the system to limit lateral spreading of the infiltrating stormwater. The system also has a raised outlet that connects to the City of Minneapolis storm sewer in South 2nd Street. The outlet regulates the allowable rate that is discharged to the city sewer.

Challenges: What were the greatest design challenges?

The greatest design challenge was responding to a changing market. Being the first major downtown senior-focused development in 20 years, the market study had to project the possible future residents. The study focused on primarily one-bedroom units. However, as the construction drawings were completed and early construction began, it became clear through preleasing that the building needed to change. The development team of the owner / operator, architect, and contractor worked closely together to combine several stacks of living units. Through the combination, the independent unit count was modified from 103 to 86.

Another challenge was incorporating memory care and independent housing in a single building within an urban environment. Urban connectivity to the building guided the design to focus the resident amenity spaces and walk-up units at the street edges. This required the memory care residence and outdoor gardens to be placed on the second level of the building, which created many complexities for the design, particularly with the stacking of units and inherent complexities to the structural and mechanical systems. Additionally, locating this use on the second level required additional building code collaboration with the City of Minneapolis for occupancy and exiting.

The heritage preservation guidelines in the Historic Mills District Master Plan created conflict with the St. Anthony Falls District guidelines and urban-infill thinking. The traditional models follow a principle of hard street edges and setbacks in conformance with existing buildings. The Historic Mills District Master Plan recommended green space and setbacks along Third and Fifth Avenues. This would violate these

Opposite: Woonerf and building entry

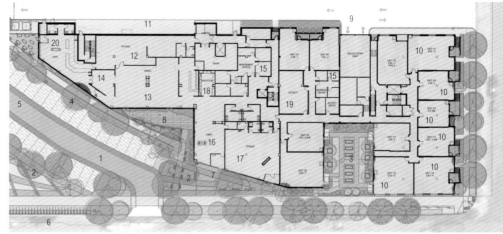

First-floor plan

1	*Woonerf*
2	Public plaza
3	Private courtyards with elevated planters
4	Permeable paver tree planting zone
5	Connection to river parkway
6	Bike racks
7	Residential lobby entry
8	Commercial / retail entry
9	Underground parking entry
10	Walk-up resident entry
11	Service court
12	Kitchen
13	Public restaurant
14	Private dining
15	Office
16	Entry lounge
17	Neighborhood fitness center
18	Mailroom
19	Activity
20	Cafe

0   60ft

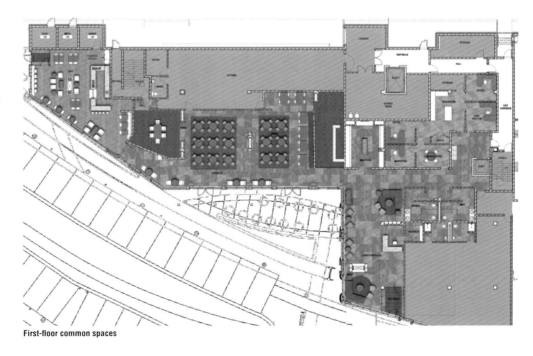

First-floor common spaces

familiar urban forms and create a monolithic public space scheme that is unrepeated on the opposing corners and street edges. The *woonerf* is therefore in place of creating a more pronounced and interactive public space in the middle of the development.

After the mills and train tracks were removed and the city developed around this site, it became cluttered with parking easements for all of the neighboring buildings. The site is also challenged by the moderate bedrock depth below grade and ground water at the top of the bedrock. The design challenge was to accommodate the parking needs of building as well as 100 additional spaces for the neighboring buildings. The project provides two levels of below grade parking.

City regulations required that the site add no new stormwater to the existing sewers and repair some drainage issues at the edges of the site. This required a particularly complex underground stormwater management system in which stormwater from both properties is directed to a communal underground retention system below the *woonerf*. Stormwater will infiltrate into the soils through a large perforated pipe gallery embedded in a porous rock section. An impervious liner surrounding the perimeter of the system limits lateral spreading of the infiltrating stormwater, and a raised outlet connects to the City of Minneapolis storm sewer in South 2nd Street.

Collaboration: How did stakeholders, occupants, the design team, and / or others collaborate during the planning and / or design process?

A great deal of collaboration was required as the site is owned by three different entities with varying interests. The grand vision of the senior campus and *woonerf* based on the historic rail lines was key to working together to create a high-quality project for all of the parties involved. Additionally, a great deal more collaboration was

necessary in order to receive financing and gain city historic, parkland, and zoning approvals. Many different entities came together to help clean up the site, create the *woonerf*, fund the affordable housing, and fund the non-profit housing. Special care was also given to the collaboration with multiple neighborhood groups. These are the people that will interact with the building daily and will be the future residents. There were many meetings to ensure this was a project that everyone could be proud of.

Outreach: What off-site outreach services are offered to the greater community?

The community reaches out to the public, particularly seniors, offering them access to internal services to the building. The restaurant, bar, cafe, and fitness center are open to the public.

Green / Sustainable Features: What green / sustainable features had the greatest impact on the project's design?

The key sustainable features are site selection, site design considerations, and maximized daylighting.

Primary motivations: What were the primary motivations for including green / sustainable design features in the project?

The primary motivations were to lower operational costs, improve the building for occupants, and to create a more sustainable community.

Challenges: What challenges did the project face when trying to incorporate green / sustainable design features?

Pulling together the overall development to remove the greyfield site was the largest challenge. With a number of property owners and parking easements on the site, it took several months and many public and private meetings to untangle the site for the creation of a future development.

Technology: How is innovative / assistive / special technology used by the project to deliver care or services?

Independent living residence within Abiitan is offered with additive services as needed with the goal of aging in place. This ranges from small services to nursing care. It is further reinforced by the provider's network offering a continuum of care—they want to keep residents in their homes as long as possible. The high-quality design of the living environment is an integral feature of the circle of care provided by Ecumen, leveraging the Awakenings care approach. Some of the subtle features that reduce distractions associated with Alzheimer's include glare-free lighting, private rooms, activity stations (indoor and outdoor), and discrete directional cues. The other elements to the care approach include leadership, enriching programming, continuing education for care providers, Honor Portrait life stories for a personalized understanding of each resident, and medication reduction strategies. This proven approach has led to a reduced need for psychotropic medication in many patients.

Jury Comments

Abiitan Mill City is a dense urban infill project that has a strong connection to the greater community through a wonderful street-level pedestrian walking path. This feature respects the city's master plan and visual connection to the *woonerf*, a Dutch-inspired concept of public and private spaces. This walkable community promotes an engaged healthy lifestyle, so important to today's seniors.

The historic architecture reflects the industrial context with a material palette of glass and brick. The designers also integrated vegetated walls, green roofs, and pervious paving to soften the edges of the building as it meets the street level. While the character of the building is more industrial than traditional retirement communities, the mixed-use setting is perfectly scaled, and the park-like amenities make it very approachable.

The common spaces that are placed along the main street are inviting and open to the public. The dining venue, club rooms, and fitness areas are visible from the street, but secure within the community. The notion of an intergenerational community is clearly supported with walking paths, biking paths, and accessible mass transit. The project includes apartments to serve a low-income population without compromising the quality of the spaces and character of the building something that is vital in senior housing.

Top left: Sky deck
Top right: Outdoor dining
Bottom: Building entry

Top: Living room
Bottom: Welcoming lobby seating
Right: Smith and Porter Restaurant + Bar

Photography: Troy Thies; Mike Krych; Julie Murray

Amenta Emma Architects

Caleb Hitchcock Memory Care Neighborhood at Duncaster Retirement Community

Bloomfield, Connecticut // Duncaster Retirement Community

Facility type (year of completion): Assisted living—dementia / memory support (2015)
Target market: Upper
Site location: Suburban; greenfield

Gross square footage of the new construction involved in the project: 8918
Purpose of the renovation / modernization: Upgrade the environment
Provider type: Faith-based non-profit

Below: South facade
Opposite: Charter Oak

Overall Project Description

By 2050, the number of senior Americans with Alzheimer's disease or some other kind of dementia is estimated to reach 13.8 million, triple the number today. Organizations that provide senior living accommodations are struggling with increased demand for memory care services, both from their existing populations and new families seeking such care for their loved one. How we design these facilities has a significant impact on helping people navigate dementia. To meet this need, Duncaster Retirement Community engaged an architect and interior designer to design an addition to its assisted living memory care neighborhood known as Dogwood in the Caleb Hitchcock building. The addition adds 12 resident rooms and incorporates small house project concepts, which offer a model for long-term care designed to look and feel like a real home. Connection to nature was a driving force

in the design concept. This was emphasized by "bringing the outside in" through an abundance of natural light in every space, corner windows that provide two-sided views in resident rooms, and a focused view of a majestic 100-year-old oak tree that is affectionately known on campus as the Charter Oak, which became an organizing element in the design.

Project Goals

What were the major goals?

- To provide better care by way of the environment for the whole person—not just medical but social as well—through the collaboration of architects and owners.

- To design for cognitive clarity to help compensate for cognitive losses that accompany dementia. Perceptual clarity was achieved by dramatically reducing the

amount of detail in the environment, thus reducing the stimuli. Spaces were defined by introducing simple architectural features such as columns and beams, beadboard ceilings, and contrasting white-paneled entry alcoves that make reference to elements typical in New England homes, thus making the environment more understandable and familiar. Residents are showing signs of improved memory and less directional confusion and are able to better negotiate their surroundings.

- To offer a sense of privacy, yet provide inviting glances of activities, through proper location of activity spaces with subtle separation between resident rooms and common areas. The floor plan was developed based upon the small house concept in which resident rooms are arranged around a central organizing space containing a country kitchen, dining room, and living room designed and detailed to reflect the character of a familiar home. Residents are more social and participating in more activities, helping to create a camaraderie between care partners and residents.

- To create lighting closer to the natural spectrum for visual clarity and a calming effect by maximizing daylighting and views to the outdoors, installing exceptionally even and higher artificial lighting levels, and selecting highly efficient lighting with a color temperature of 3000-plus kelvins. Owners are seeing a drop in resident sleep disorders as the bright and natural light is helping maintain residents' circadian rhythm.

Innovations: What innovations or unique features were incorporated into the design of the project?

Simple features and details, such as the beadboard ceiling, column, and beam dividers, define the space and reference elements typical of New England homes. Older adults may experience additional cognitive losses that accompany dementia, which can have a dramatic effect on safety and the ability to perform basic daily functions. A careful and thoughtful approach to design can help compensate. While this design principle guides all senior living spaces, it is exponentially more critical in the design of memory care facilities. Examples include: subtle color transitions in flooring to prevent confusion and a sense of "visual cliffing" in those with memory and visual impairment; deliberate use of contrasting colors between walls and floors with a white base to help residents distinguish boundaries; the maximization of daylighting and views to the outdoors; careful selection of artificial lighting in terms of color rendition, higher than average luminance, and programmable controls to reduce light levels in the evening, which helps regulate residents' normal circadian rhythms, reduces sundowning, and fulfills a desire for an outdoor connection. A majestic 100-year-old oak tree to the south, known by the residents as the Charter Oak, was used as an organizing element for the form and placement of the building, and was the inspiration in the connection-to-nature theme of the interior design. The designers centered the building on the tree, stepped the footprint to bring southern light and glimpses of the tree to each resident room, and opened up the end of the building to a glassed activity room where it can be viewed in all its glory. When inside the activity room (dubbed "the conservatory" by the owner), the tree is truly the star as it is often the subject of paintings or drawings created by residents of art therapy classes. The connection-to-nature theme is further emphasized in the selection of a warm and natural palette of materials, colors, textures, patterns, and fixtures.

It is also reinforced with the organic pattern of the earthy green and tan carpet (akin to leaves on the ground), wood tones used for millwork, warm grass-cloth textured wallcovering, soft organic-shaped shades on pendant light fixtures in the dining area, and natural patterns in the furniture fabrics.

Challenges: What were the greatest design challenges?

The greatest challenge was the site, distinguished by elevated earthen barriers along the east and west, and pinched available buildable land getting narrower from north to south. However, the pinch created an opportunity to strengthen the design concept, providing natural light and a connection with nature. The building was centered on the oak tree and stepped in plan to allow for corner windows in each room to bring southern light and glimpses of the tree. The end of the building is opened up to a glassed activity room, or conservatory, where the tree can be viewed in all its magnificence.

Collaboration: How did stakeholders, occupants, the design team, and / or others collaborate during the planning and / or design process?

The overarching criterion, as a result of collaboration between the owner and architects, was to design for cognitive clarity, simplicity, and wayfinding ease in order to create a homelike environment that would promote health, wellness, and safety for residents with dementia. While the architects provided research on current best practices from around the country, staff at the facility contributed expertise on the realities of caring for this special population and discussed how they wanted to care for them.

Opposite: Country kitchen and dining

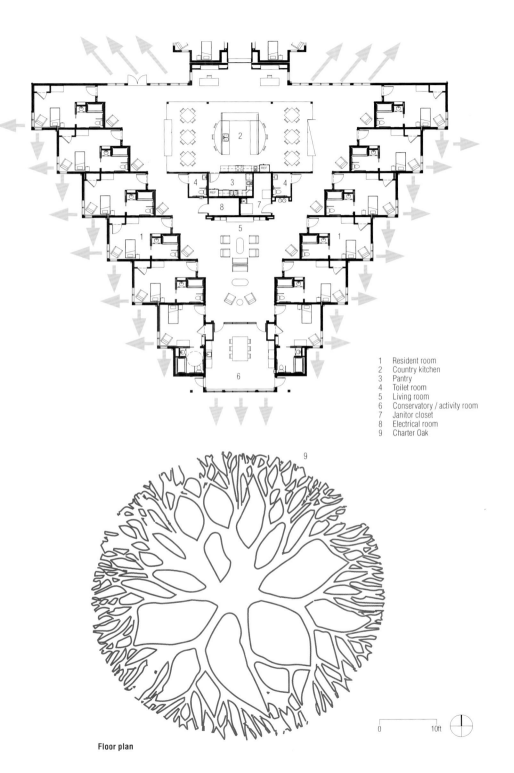

1   Resident room
2   Country kitchen
3   Pantry
4   Toilet room
5   Living room
6   Conservatory / activity room
7   Janitor closet
8   Electrical room
9   Charter Oak

0   10ft

Floor plan

Green / Sustainable Features: What green / sustainable features had the greatest impact on the project's design?

The key sustainable features are energy efficiency and a conscientious choice of materials. The Dogwood Memory Care Neighborhood is a clear example of biophilic design. It focuses on the Charter Oak, a strong use of natural materials and their inherent patterns, and 360-degree nature views. There is an abundance of natural light, artificial lighting, and lighting control to balance circadian rhythms, and an overall connection to nature.

Primary motivations: What were the primary motivations for including green / sustainable design features in the project?

The primary motivations were to support the mission / values of the client / provider, stay competitive against other similar / local facilities, and lower operational costs.

Challenges: What challenges did the project face when trying to incorporate green / sustainable design features?

Seniors and dementia-care residents require two to three times greater lighting levels than younger residents. This creates a challenge in meeting energy-code watts per square feet. The design utilized all LEDs that allow dimming to overcome this challenge.

Technology: How is innovative / assistive / special technology used by the project to deliver care or services?

With an It's Never 2 Late® system available around the clock, entertainment or diversional activity is always an option to address boredom or anxiety. The system is built on a picture-based, touch-screen interface that allows users to simply "touch" their way to find engaging, educational, spiritual, and personalized content that is appropriate to their level of ability. With a NuStep exercise apparatus in a safe area, residents are encouraged to maintain their physical strength to prevent falls and maintain mobility.

Jury Comments

The 12-resident memory care small house at Caleb Hitchcock Memory Care Neighborhood reflects a thoughtful solution to current memory care research. The design team / developer used a combination of technology and connection to nature in this innovative triangularly designed house. The focus is a 100-year-old oak tree visible through large windows in the conservatory, making an impactful connection with nature. With many large windows, nature and light stream into many of the spaces.

The house focuses on a connection to nature. Residents are encouraged to use the secure courtyard whenever they want. By using a triangular shape, the design has corner windows in each bedroom creating multiple views to the outside. The artificial lighting was designed to be a close match to the natural light spectrum and the staff has noticed a reduction in sleep disorders. The wayfinding for residents is made easy as each bedroom opens up to the more public spaces in the house. Overall, Caleb Hitchcock Memory Care Neighborhood is a positive solution to current memory care research.

Above: Country kitchen with walker storage
Opposite left to right: Kitchen pendant; dining pendant; "Arboretum" carpet pattern; stone fireplace; chair fabric; stained quarter-sawn oak millwork

    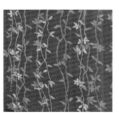 

Opposite: Resident rooms are expressed as "tiny houses"

Left: Conservatory

Top: All resident rooms have unobstructed views of the campus grounds, providing each room with an abundance of natural light

Bottom: Resident painting the Charter Oak

Photography: Robert Benson Photography

Duncan Wisniewski Architecture

Elm Place

Milton, Vermont // Cathedral Square Corporation

Facility type (year of completion): Independent Living (2017)
Target market: Low income / subsidized
Site location: Suburban; greenfield

Gross square footage of the new construction involved in
the project: 28,607
Provider type: Non-sectarian non-profit

Below: Located within the town's growth center,
the project aims to be a catalyst for shifting the
suburban character of the area to something
more walkable and urban

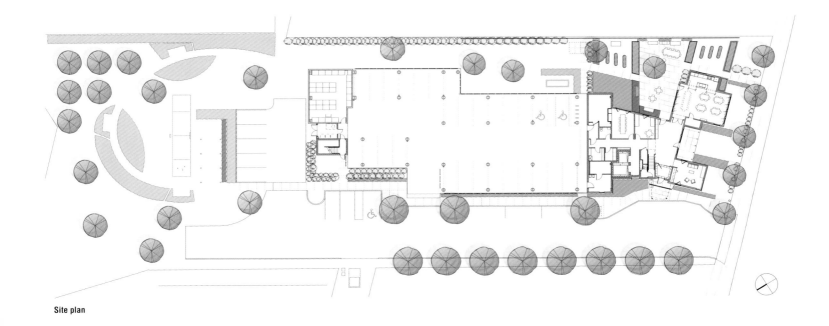

Site plan

Overall Project Description

Vermont has one of the oldest populations in the country, and demographics suggest it will continue to grow older, with projections estimating 25 percent of residents will be over 65 years of age by 2030. While some can afford to age in their own home with a la carte services, or move to a retirement community, many cannot. Elm Place provides 30 affordable homes with support and services to older adults with modest incomes. Beyond affordability, the project creates a healthy and energy efficient environment that promotes healing and allows residents to age gracefully within their community. Without affordable housing communities such as Elm Place, lower-income Vermonters would be forced to make difficult decisions that might compromise their health or financial stability. Investing in affordable, healthy, and efficient homes for seniors bolsters our communities and increases access to preventative care. Good architecture combined with a moral mission can help bring down health care costs

through reduced emergency room visits, better disease management, and promotion of exercise. Located within the town's growth center, Elm Place aims to be a catalyst for shifting the suburban character of the area to be more walkable and urban. Although the context is relatively suburban, residents have ready access to multiple off-site services, and they can walk to the town library, a small medical practice, multiple churches, and a senior center, pharmacy, and grocery store.

Project Goals

What were the major goals?

- To reduce energy use, increase resident comfort and safety, and create community, while still carefully stewarding public resources that went into producing the project. At the opening, Governor of Vermont, Phil Scott, pointed to the project as "the wave of the future" and applauded the project for meeting low energy goals with careful design and robust insulation. All of the Cathedral Square's

communities are permanently affordable, which is an overarching public policy goal for all publicly financed affordable housing in Vermont. Building to the Passive House standard reduces energy costs significantly (65 percent less than the same building built to code minimums). These key features enabled lower energy use through increased shell insulation, robust air sealing, low u-factor windows, and balanced ventilation with heat recovery. Increasing the amount of insulation was relatively straightforward, though the design team required multiple iterations to settle on the most economical approach. The project ended up with R40 at the foundation, R60 at the garage ceiling, R38 exterior walls, and an R70 roof. Similarly, specified windows are uPVC R7.8 tilt / turn windows. Both increased insulation and better windows have led to better comfort inside the apartments. The ventilation system provides tempered fresh air to all areas and is

Innovations: What innovations or unique features were incorporated into the design of the project?

Elm Place is remarkable for the breadth of progressive features that support residents and staff. Balanced ventilation provides fresh air while exhausting stale air, creating healthy indoor air quality for seniors, some of whom have multiple chronic conditions and compromised respiratory systems. Low / no VOC paint and flooring also contribute to indoor air quality. The owner has a robust resident education program about potential sources of VOCs that they have control over, such as particle board furniture and cleaning products. The project incorporates a high degree of accessibility for senior and disabled residents, and two elevators were added for resiliency. Low / no thresholds, removable under-sink kitchen, and bathroom cabinets transform adaptable units to accessible units, and universal design features throughout assist differently abled residents. A high number of roll-in and step-in showers, double handrails in corridors, and grab bars in all bathrooms promote aging in place. Pocket doors in bathrooms are a safety and accessibility feature. The site design creates a variety of outdoor spaces for residents while grounding the building in the town's emerging urban landscape. The front lawn and covered drop-off provides a welcoming front door for residents and visitors. To the east, the building creates a small courtyard for outdoor picnics and gardening. The raised beds are at different heights; some work best for those with walkers while others are better for residents using a scooter or wheelchair. The gardens are full and well used. The rear garden features a multitude of edibles along a small walking path. Aristolochia growing up a modern pergola is a contemporary take on the

a critical part of maintaining very high indoor air quality. Air sealing was a team effort and began with clearly denoting the air barrier on all sections and details. An integrated air sealing meeting held towards the beginning of the project was later revisited with contractors and builders present. Changes were made where necessary to address sequencing or constructability concerns to meet the Passive House target of 0.05 CFM50/SF.

- To create community is the goal of any housing project, but particularly so for seniors who may be less mobile. Site selection was therefore an important factor. The building is adjacent to a multitude of services to allow residents to connect to the existing community, and the design of shared spaces help create community within the building. The building is an armature for individual expression as well as collective gathering. For more mobile residents, an exercise room and walking path promote health and wellness.

classic Vermont porch. This large-leafed vine creates welcome dappled shade in the summer, and dies back in the winter to let the sun through. A new bocce court is centered inside the walking loop for gentle activity on long summer days.

Challenges: What were the greatest design challenges?

The design uses the parti of a Gothic cathedral to organize and conceive the building's diagram. A cathedral combines a series of cellular spaces and repetitive grids (the nave) with a unique and special space at the terminus (choir, altar, sacristy). Housing projects tend to be repetitive and box-like, primarily due to construction efficiencies and costs. A simple form has the added benefit of being easier to air seal and detail. That said, a simple box-like form creates a less vibrant streetscape. An 8-foot ceiling height is perfectly adequate for an apartment but can feel stifling in a larger community space. The cathedral diagram addresses these competing

goals, and segregating the shared community space from the housing lets each program piece be what it needs to be. Implementing this concept was a challenge. The front and rear ended up with different systems, detailing had to be carefully considered to marry different structural and mechanical systems into a cohesive whole. The rear of the building is regular and consistent, and the apartments stack above a screened parking garage. The steel moment frame designed to mitigate potential seismic shift differential supports an elevated concrete slab, and the hung garage ceiling allowed for deep insulation with inexpensive batts. The front of the building breaks this mold to animate the streetscape with varied roof forms and windows. Here the building sits upon a shallow insulated footing. The insulation necessary to meet Passive House comfort parameters required a shallow frost protected foundation. Small moves like this allowed costs to shift from one division to another without sacrificing performance. Despite budget

adjustments and other difficulties in the process, the original concept shines through. The great room and lounge volumes embrace a street-facing porch to reference grand old homes in Vermont, and these articulated volumes obscure the regular facades of the housing behind.

Collaboration: How did stakeholders, occupants, the design team, and / or others collaborate during the planning and / or design process?

Each aspect of Elm Place, including the original building program, the initial design competition, the Passive House design, and the health and housing design, was a collaborative process with input from staff, residents, energy consultants, planners, and care staff, to create a community responsive to its inhabitants, staff, and surrounding community and environment.

The owner benefited from The Enterprise Rose Architectural Fellowship underwritten by a national affordable housing funder from 2012 to 2014. During that time, the Rose Fellow

Opposite: The rear garden features a multitude of edibles along a small walking path
Left and above: The front lawn and covered drop-off provides a welcoming front door for residents and visitors

created a building program that articulated the design lessons learned to date regarding unit layout, program space, common area definition, maintenance, custodial and IT needs, and more. Creation of the building was a collaborative process including development, maintenance, operations and management staff, and a review and discussion of past building designs. The building program will evolve over time but is the starting place for the design of each new senior community.

The Elm Place development began with a smart growth site and a building program. In July 2014, Cathedral Square held a grant-funded design competition, soliciting proposals from area architects to create a design for a 30-unit senior community incorporating energy efficiency, sustainability, and walkability in Milton in northwest Vermont. Four finalists presented their design to a panel consisting of owner, staff, and members of the Milton community, including the town planner, at a daylong gathering. The winning design incorporated the core of the building program, communicated with the surrounding landscape, and proposed Passive House as the construction design. The owner's commitments to accessibility, energy efficiency, sustainability, durability, and green building are all incorporated in Elm Place, as a Passive House building is designed to use less energy. The decision to design to Passive House standards necessitated additional collaboration and planning, and the design team worked closely with a certified Passive House consultant as well as the local energy efficiency utility.

Left: Beyond affordability, the project creates a healthy and energy efficient environment that promotes wellness and allows residents to age gracefully within their community

Elm Place offers SASH® (Support and Services at Home), which is an evidence-based care coordination program that promotes healthy aging and wellness, with housing as the platform. SASH® programming (wellness programming, healthy living plans, walking groups, tai chi, chair yoga, and more) has documented positive health outcomes including reduced falls, reduced repeat hospitalizations, reduced social isolation, improved nutrition, improvements in controlled hypertension, immunizations, and access to primary care physicians. Many of Elm Place's design elements are a result of collaboration between the design team and the SASH® coordinators and wellness nurses. This includes an activity room with ample space for group exercise; a prominent stairway at the entrance (a visual cue to take the stairs not the elevator); garden beds at different heights to encourage gardening for all bodies; a wellness nurse office and conference room for private meetings; an outdoor walking loop with benches, attractive plantings, and a bocce court.

Outreach: What off-site outreach services are offered to the greater community?

Elm Place is a SASH® hub serving the greater Milton area. The site is host for the Milton SASH® panel that serves up to 100 persons, and Elm Place residents have the opportunity to become SASH® participants, which is a voluntary and free program. Medicare-eligible community members make up the remainder of the 100-person panel. The staffing includes 52 hours per week of team-based care coordination and 12 hours per week of wellness nursing. SASH® partners in the community include UVM Medical Center (health center adjacent to Elm Place), Age Well, Visiting Nurse Association, and Howard Center. These partners work with the care coordination team to support each individual participant according to the needs articulated in each individual's healthy living plan. The activities offered to

SASH® participants on a regular basis include but are not limited to: individual work on healthy living plans, tai chi, blood-pressure clinics, chair yoga, and a walking program. There are 100 persons on the Milton area panel, and there are many activities of all kinds per month. SASH® care coordination staff meet with community SASH® participants both at Elm Place and in their own homes. SASH® staff also help community participants with transportation in the event rural dwellers seek to come to Elm Place for group programs. This helps to combat social isolation that can accompany rural poverty.

Green / Sustainable Features: What green / sustainable features had the greatest impact on the project's design?

The key sustainable features are site selection, energy efficiency, and improved indoor air quality.

Primary motivations: What were the primary motivations for including green / sustainable design features in the project?

The primary motivations were to support the mission / values of the client / provider, lower operational costs, and improve the building for occupants.

Challenges: What challenges did the project face when trying to incorporate green / sustainable design features?

It was a challenge to meet the Passive House requirements while not compromising the performance or program of the building (apartment size, two elevators for resiliency, retaining common areas but making them more efficient in size). Upon deciding to pursue Passive House design and performance, the owner procured the services of a construction manager who reviewed the design and determined it would cost $1.1 million more to build than the project's initial cost estimate. Through an iterative process of value engineering, redesign, and additional cost estimating, the building was reduced by approximately 3400 square feet, decreasing the footprint and size of the common areas. Simplifying the wall assembly reduced construction costs without sacrificing performance.

Another challenge involved developing an affordable and reliable source of back-up heat, as the air source heat pumps are the sole means of heating and cooling. Given that Vermont is a cold climate area, and Elm Place is home for seniors who need and desire reliable heating and cooling, back-up heat and cooling is an important consideration. The air source heat pumps are reliable and efficient, but they do shut off at very low temperatures. As such, the building has to rely on the energy recovery unit for back-up heat. If the air source heat pumps go down, the mechanical ventilation system can deliver enough supplemental heat to allow the building to coast until the air source heat pumps can come back up. Education was provided for residents to understand how the air source pumps operate and how to use the thermostat. Private foundation funding received midway through construction, enabled the installation of a 20-kilowatt solar array on the roof, along with a generator for resiliency.

Technology: How is innovative / assistive / special technology used by the project to deliver care or services?

Elm Place incorporates several unique technologies to support residents' health, connect them to energy use and production, and to assist management of the building. Elm Place is a site for a telemedicine pilot program with Northwestern Medical Center located in St. Albans. The site is equipped with a large videoconferencing TV that connects to equipment in the offices at Northwestern Medical Center. The Elm Place wellness nurse facilitates

the appointment by providing the primary care doctor with the resident information, including blood pressure and temperature, and employs a special stethoscope that communicates to the remote doctor's stethoscope, allowing the doctor to listen to the resident's heart and lungs. After the visit is over, the nurse will print the after-visit summary and discuss how the resident can have a successful follow-up plan. The telehealth program allows residents to receive personalized care in their own home and saves travel time and logistics, which is helpful in bad weather or if the resident is ill or frail or lacks safe, affordable transportation.

The main lobby boasts a digital dashboard with a touch-screen menu providing real-time information on electric, gas, and water use; solar production; Passive House features; the ventilation system; the wall assembly and insulation; and the air source heat pumps. In addition, there is a calendar section that highlights residents' birthdays and events such as tai chi classes or van rides for shopping or social events. This resident engagement tool provides education about how the building operates, connects residents to energy use and solar production, and provides information about social activities occurring in the residence.

Elm Place has a direct digital control system that provides real-time information on the air source heat pumps, mechanical ventilation system, domestic hot water system, and the solar array, via the internet, to maintenance staff. They can remotely monitor building systems, tweak settings to improve operations, and diagnose problems identified by residents and on-site staff. The result is a significant savings in travel time and cost as well as more efficient resolution of resident building concerns. Sometimes maintenance staff diagnose problems before residents notice them.

Elm Place is an accessible housing community. All exterior doors have push pads for easy access by wheelchair and walker users, and super-scan technology so they do not close when people are still navigating the doorway or walking by. SASH® has partnered with private communications software company Patient Ping to ensure SASH® staff across the state are aware of their participants' admissions and discharges to hospitals, nursing homes, and home health in real time.

Jury Comments

Elm Place stood out to the judges for four main reasons. The first is that it serves the low-income community of Milton, Vermont. Second is the creative use of public / private financing for funding of the project reflected in the use of TIF districts, grants, and energy savings from sustainable design. Third, despite a target market for low-income senior housing, the design team / developer also made a commitment to sustainable design by following the Passive House standards. While costlier up front, this yields a long-term return to the project helping to keep it affordable. Means were provided for the residents to view and monitor their energy savings. Lastly, the community features a nice, simple design in a location within easy walking distance to services. With its massing, use of materials, and simple details for both interior and exterior design elements, a comfortable and attractive community was created for the residents.

Opposite top: The main lobby boasts a "digital dashboard" with a touch-screen menu
Opposite bottom: Community room
Photography: Carolyn Bates

Gensler

Fountainview at Gonda Westside
Playa Vista, California // Los Angeles Jewish Home

Facility type (year of completion): Independent Living; Assisted living; Assisted living—dementia / memory support (2016)
Target market: Upper
Site location: Urban; greenfield

Gross square footage of the new construction involved in the project: 400,677
Provider type: Faith-based non-profit

Below: A series of four distinct buildings on Jefferson Boulevard have a unique presence with sloping roofs and delicately curled slab edges

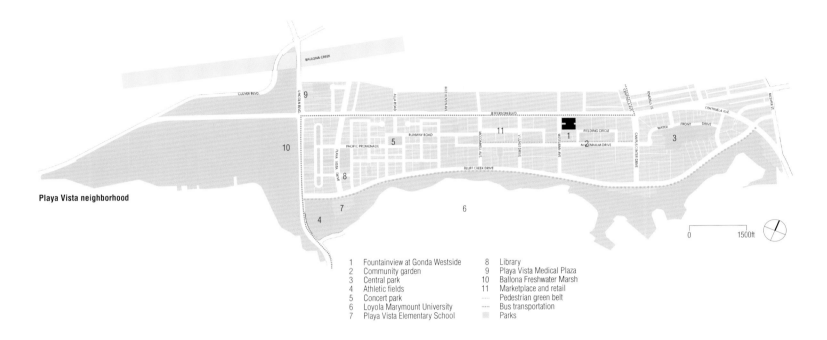

Playa Vista neighborhood

1	Fountainview at Gonda Westside	8	Library
2	Community garden	9	Playa Vista Medical Plaza
3	Central park	10	Ballona Freshwater Marsh
4	Athletic fields	11	Marketplace and retail
5	Concert park	-----	Pedestrian green belt
6	Loyola Marymount University	·····	Bus transportation
7	Playa Vista Elementary School	▪	Parks

Overall Project Description

Fountainview at Gonda Westside is a Continuing Care Retirement Community (CCRC) for active, independent living, located in the recently completed New Urbanism community of Playa Vista, California. This project aims to set a new standard for senior living communities by delivering high-quality care for the elderly with a focus on the needs of the whole person. It offers a place for seniors to enrich their quality of life through a physically and intellectually engaging lifestyle. Strategically located in the heart of Playa Vista, Fountainview offers seniors an opportunity to live in a multi-generational and urban neighborhood. The community is within walking distance to two different grade schools and Loyola Marymount University. Many students and the young families working in Silicon Beach call it home. The vision of Los Angeles Jewish Home is to not only benefit residents but also the community at large, and the architecture team conceived a design that encourages interaction between Fountainview residents and the Playa Vista community. It is designed to engage with the urban lifestyle of Playa Vista with walking paths and easy access to restaurants, retail, and recreational opportunities. Inside the project, multiple communal program elements build upon the active and engaging Playa Vista culture. The community includes 175 independent living residences, 12 assisted living apartments, 12 memory support apartments, a nursing facility within proximity, and a range of amenities to host a variety of educational and social experiences. Each residence is carefully designed to offer ample daylight, natural ventilation, and a strong connection with the outdoors. They are also equipped with an infrastructure that enables maximum use of e-health resources. The ground floor is anchored by a centrally located outdoor courtyard divided into two separate areas. A rich indoor and outdoor program offers a varied mixture of public, semi-public, and private spaces for the residents. A day-lit corridor wraps around the main courtyard connecting key public spaces together, including a theater, art studio, card room, spa, and large community room. Amenities were extended to a portion of the top floor to share the spectacular views of the nearby bluffs with all residents and guests. Anchored by a covered swimming pool and exercise pavilions, this rooftop amenity is designed as indoor-outdoor multifunctional space that can host a variety of functions and events. These spaces work together to foster an active and engaging atmosphere coupled with a second-floor terrace and numerous small, private garden spaces spread throughout the project. A separate front entryway for the memory support household is located on the ground floor of the project and the assisted living suite has an identical layout on the second floor. Each of the care suites are anchored by a large community room and dining space, and together they share a dedicated outdoor courtyard.

Los Angeles Jewish Home staff is accessible to residents, with operations offices located in the basement of the building offering integrated assisted living and memory support housing.

Project Goals

What were the major goals?

- To raise the standard for senior living communities by delivering a high-quality of care for the elderly and offering the seniors of Los Angeles a new model for living a physically and intellectually engaging lifestyle with

unparalleled access to cutting-edge technology and amenities. The project is designed for active aging and fully embraces the sentiment that 80 is the new 60. Today's 60-year-olds don't view aging as a time of physical decline. These actively aging baby boomers are looking for housing options to support their lifestyles and that allow them to live a long, purposeful life. Today's seniors are better educated than any of their predecessors, and as a population are well-connected and tech-enabled. As consumers, they are as savvy as these

characteristics would suggest. As a result, the U.S. active-aging population has discerning tastes and a hunger for good design. While the project has high-end features, its function as a CCRC for the Los Angeles Jewish Home required many unique design considerations.

- To encourage interaction between the residents of Fountainview and the local neighborhood, in line with the Jewish Home's vision to not only benefit residents but also the community at large. Taking note from the surrounding Playa Vista community, the facility's courtyards serve very important functions for Fountainview. Even high-end houses are quite close to each other, so the focus in these neighborhoods tends to be on the spaces in between. Because these courtyard gardens are part of so many homes in the Playa Vista neighborhood, they work towards the goal of creating a community that feels like home. Many circulation elements and corridors with access to the courtyards encourage residents to be outside and walk. Playa Vista is very walkable, and the design intent is to promote the walkability of the community.

- To reinforce the active and engaging Playa Vista lifestyle through multiple communal program elements inside the building. Residents have access to a rooftop pool and amenity deck where they can host events, as well as an exercise pavilion, full-service restaurant and bar with outdoor dining, two outdoor courtyards, a 99-seat screening room, art room, wellness center, spa, and game rooms.

Above: The central courtyard is the heart of the project where the multiple outdoor rooms and zones allow a flexible programming for activities

Innovations: What innovations or unique features were incorporated into the design of the project?

The design team created an innovative alternative to the typology of a typical, double-loaded residential corridor to meet the building program of 199 residential units on a tight site. A traditional double-loaded residential corridor carries residential units approximately 30 feet in depth on either side. Providing daylighting becomes difficult in units deeper than this. Along the corridor, units can vary in length from 30 feet for a studio, and up to 60 feet for a two-bedroom unit. Adding more units means adding more corridor and a longer building. This project required a different solution because of the limited site area and packed program. Rather than extending the length of corridor to add additional units and provide unit variety, the width is fixed at 28 feet and the depth of each unit varies between 50 feet for two-bedroom units and 30 feet for one-bedroom units. Deeper units are always adjacent to shallower units on one side. Every time this occurs, it creates a jog in the exterior and effectively produces another corner unit. Light penetrates deeper into the floor plate of a 50-foot-deep unit that has windows on at least two sides. This allowed the design team to break the barrier of the traditional 30-foot unit depth and gives seniors a bright environment that feels more connected to the outdoors because of the additional glazing. The effective unit layout and efficient use of circulation space means more square footage is available for the community-based program elements such as a rooftop amenity deck and the two outdoor courtyards.

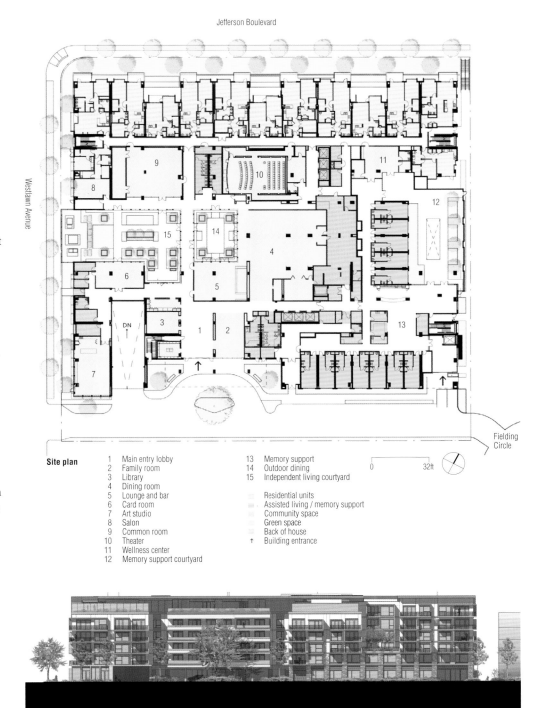

Site plan

1 Main entry lobby
2 Family room
3 Library
4 Dining room
5 Lounge and bar
6 Card room
7 Art studio
8 Salon
9 Common room
10 Theater
11 Wellness center
12 Memory support courtyard

13 Memory support
14 Outdoor dining
15 Independent living courtyard

Residential units
Assisted living / memory support
Community space
Green space
Back of house
↑ Building entrance

0   32ft

South elevation

Challenges: What were the greatest design challenges?

Los Angeles Jewish Home is a non-profit that wanted to host as many people as it could in this community. The desire for density required several unique design approaches to maintain a residential sense of scale. The challenge became an opportunity to use courtyards creatively and design more interesting units. The team considered the difficulty many senior residents face when moving out of large single-family homes into a dense community. Units have balconies that are private, but there is still a connection to neighbors. There are courtyards, large windows, awnings, and other features that create a single-family home feel, rather than one large facade. The team created an innovative alternative to the typology of a typical, double-loaded residential corridor to achieve this unique condition. Because of the effective unit layout and efficient use of circulation space, more square footage is available for the community-based program elements such as a rooftop amenity deck or the two outdoor courtyards. Aligning program elements in a way that promotes an active and engaging lifestyle is another design challenge that the team overcame in this dense community. Public program elements are thoughtfully arranged in a way that enhances their individual functions. For example, the theater is located next to the dining area and outdoor courtyard allowing it to function as a screening room. With all three program elements combined, the theater can play movies, host speaking engagements, or screen sporting events as part of a larger event that is hosted in the restaurant and outdoor courtyard. The pool was originally located on the sixth-floor roof due to space constraints. It is now a key feature combined with two exercise pavilions to form a flexible rooftop amenity deck. These flexible spaces can be converted into a large event space with a small catering kitchen and connections for outdoor grills. Many of the neighboring buildings utilize a traditional double-loaded corridor that results in a long facade with a minimal amount of relief along the street. In contrast, the unique unit layout of Fountainview creates a stepping facade that breaks down the scale of the building along the street. Along Jefferson Boulevard, four pairs of units read as distinct towers, and a shallower unit is placed between each of the towers, effectively pulling the facade back from the street creating substantial amount of relief. A dramatic overhanging roof is added to each of the towers to clearly define four separate elements, and each unit is articulated with features such as bay windows and balconies that help to further break down the scale of the building.

Collaboration: How did stakeholders, occupants, the design team, and / or others collaborate during the planning and / or design process?

Research is a large part of the design firm's culture. In conjunction with this project, the firm conducted a research study "Foundations of Design for Active Aging" to best understand the programmatic requirements of today's elderly demographic. The team worked with a professor of architecture and gerontology, an industry expert at the local university. Four trends emerged from the study and guided the design of Fountainview: connectivity, choice, independence, and wellness. Connectivity is the ability to maintain relationships with neighbors, coworkers, family, friends, and community members, both in person and online. Fountainview's design encourages connectivity between residents of Fountainview and the Playa Vista community and is designed to engage with the urban lifestyle Playa Vista offers with walking paths and easy access to restaurants, retail, and recreational opportunities. Multiple communal program elements inside the project also build upon the active and engaging Playa Vista culture, and access to outdoors encourages residents to go outside and walk. The building program was developed to foster a strong internal community for seniors of all different interests. Choice is the opportunity a person has to live in a location that fits their preferences, participate in activities they choose, and to make their own decisions about health care. The building spaces provide a strong framework for allowing residents to live the life they choose. From painting classes to group fitness, there are activities to keep resident's minds and bodies healthy and engaged with the program of their choice. Independence is relying on others as little as possible for personal care and getting around, including use of public transportation, ride sharing, and walking. The project's location in the urban Playa Vista community allows for mobile independence within a comfortable area. In much the same way that the community is attracted to the active amenity spaces offered, the community that lives in this building takes full advantage of the walkability and easy access to transit that the neighborhood offers. With a full-featured resident check-in system and emergency call technology, seniors also have the comfort of knowing that in the case of an emergency the staff from Jewish Home is directly accessible. Wellness is not only staving off disease but also managing long-term illness to lead a productive and fulfilling life. Residents at Fountainview have the benefit of accessing the Jewish Home's full range of services. The building has an on-site wellness center and residents also have access to assisted living and memory support apartments as well as the Jewish Home's off-site skilled nursing and rehabilitation facilities.

Opposite top left: Family room
Opposite top right: Courtyard
Opposite bottom: Rooftop amenity deck

Green / Sustainable Features: What green / sustainable features had the greatest impact on the project's design?

The key sustainable features are site selection, water efficiency, reduced solar gain / heat island-effect sunshades / planting, and maximized daylighting.

Primary motivations: What were the primary motivations for including green / sustainable design features in the project?

The primary motivations were to support the mission / values of the client / provider, make a contribution to the greater community, and improve the building for occupants.

Below: Ground-floor corridor
Opposite: Rooftop pool
Photography: Gensler / Ryan Gobuty

Challenges: What challenges did the project face when trying to incorporate green / sustainable design features?

Placing the project in a walkable Playa Vista neighborhood with easy access to grocery stores, retail, community gardens, and public green space means that residents can live a physically and intellectually engaging lifestyle every day without needing to get into their car. By understanding the importance of site selection up front, the client gave the design team an advantage on a successful path to incorporating sustainable design features. With the ideal site as a launching point, several other sustainable design features are incorporated that support the client's mission of providing the best possible environment for building occupants. Key features include a focus on maximizing daylighting while also reducing solar gain through passive shading

elements. The challenge is find an appropriate mix between these two competing strategies. By stepping the facade, the building form acts as a means of self-shading. For example, the four distinct towers along Jefferson Boulevard are each separated by a recessed facade that is shielded from direct sunlight as the building casts a shadow on itself. Large windows are added to the living spaces where shielded from direct sun exposure to provide daylighting. Every balcony has a both a swinging and sliding door that can be used to take advantage of the cool ocean breezes and provide outdoor access. Most of the units also have operable windows on two sides of the living space that create a cross breeze to passively ventilate the unit. Each balcony provides 10 feet of glazing, and balconies from the floor above offer passive shading for these opening.

Technology: How is innovative / assistive / special technology used by the project to deliver care or services?

Technology is used to strengthen community. Varying levels of support are offered to meet residents' needs and additional support can be offered as it is required. Because the community has independent living, assisted living, and memory support under one roof, residents have the comfort of knowing that they do not need to relocate to receive more support. This allows couples with varying needs to stay together and keeps the tight-knit community intact. Residents in the independent living units are encouraged and enabled to live an active lifestyle, and with the technology support offered, they have the comfort of knowing that help is nearby. The design team collaborated with the technology consultant on the installation of an emergency call solution throughout Fountainview. This is the first system of its kind installed on the West Coast. Los Angeles Jewish Home chose the unified platform to help differentiate the facility because it offers maximum scalability and the flexibility to add system enhancements over time to its current option of in-suite audio. Designed and UL-approved specifically for assisted living, this system enables staff to unobtrusively attend to safety while residents confidently enjoy an active lifestyle. Using in-suite audio, resident calls go directly to the right caregiver, saving time, prioritizing requests, and providing comfort to residents who know their needs will be met. Staff can later add discreet resident wristbands and pendants for check-in and wander management, utilizing the system's receivers and beacons to locate residents wherever they make the call. It can be configured to automatically alert staff when a resident leaves an area unauthorized, and in the memory care unit it offers the option to lock the doors to contain his or her movements. In the support suites, smart bed technology is

used to provide staff with a non-invasive health monitoring system. Tied into this same technology, a control system is provided at each bed that can perform everything from nurse calls to changing the TV channels.

Jury Comments

To understand the program requirements for today's aging demographic, the design firm conducted a research study "Foundations of Design for Active Aging." Four trends emerged from the study and informed the design: connectivity, choice, independence, and wellness. The jury felt these trends were all accommodated in the built design.

The location offers residents an opportunity to live in a truly multi-generational and urban neighborhood. The site was designed to engage with the community and provide access to local restaurants and retail via easy walking paths.

The creative building massing not only provides an interesting and well-articulated facade, but allows more daylight into larger units by staggering them with smaller apartments to create light-filled corner units.

The jury appreciated the opportunities to engage with the outdoors through multiple indoor / outdoor lounge and dining areas. The rooftop amenity deck provides pool and lounge areas as well as views of the surrounding hillside. This inviting space encourages socialization and supports a variety of events for residents and families.

The indoor common spaces are connected through corridors with views to the courtyard, bringing in lots of natural light and adding interest to circulation paths.

The jury felt that Fountainview at Gonda Westside was well positioned to engage with the community at large and designed to promote a healthy lifestyle through its inviting outdoor living spaces.

Wiencek + Associates Architects + Planners

Linden Park Apartments
Baltimore, Maryland // Somerset Development

Facility type (year of completion): Independent Living (2016)
Target market: Low income / subsidized
Site location: Urban

Gross square footage of the new construction involved
in the project: 6314
Gross square footage of the renovation / modernization
involved in the project: 178,964
Purpose of the renovation / modernization: Upgrade the
environment
Provider type: For profit

Below: Exterior with new addition
Opposite: Aerial view

Overall Project Description

Linden Park Apartments was originally constructed in 1967 as one of the earliest HUD 202-financed projects in the country to provide apartment living for seniors 62 years of age and older. Sited at the entrance to an historic, upscale Baltimore community, it was intended to provide opportunity and integration of incomes in the community, bringing people together. However, the property fell into a dire state of disrepair with malfunctioning elevators, outdated through-wall heating and air-conditioning systems, single-pane windows, poorly configured studio apartments, routinely failing water pipes, mold and asbestos issues, few functional common spaces, and a decrepit laundry room in the basement. In 2014, Somerset Development stepped in to lead the revitalization of this once vibrant 12-story property. The vision was to modernize all systems, making them energy efficient and state of the art, while transforming the exterior to appear like a new

building. The architect provided an innovative design that transformed the 1960s exterior by introducing a new vertical glass element in the corner units at the main elevation. The notches at the intersections of the three-wing "Y" were opened up with vertical glass, allowing light into the building and creating a bright experience in the interior common spaces on each floor. Original purple precast exterior panels were covered with new metal panel systems, totally redefining the building and bringing it into the current design age. The enclosure of previous under-building space allowed new amenities including a wellness suite, salon, library and computer lounges, fitness center, game and media room, catering kitchen, and a large community room divisible into smaller spaces to meet the varying needs of active seniors. Linden Park meets Enterprise Green Communities standards for energy efficiency by including new windows, domestic plumbing, stormwater management systems, and core

infrastructure systems that provide highly efficient central heating and cooling through a state-of-the-art water source heat pump system. This offers heating and or cooling in each unit at any time of the year. Utilities are paid by the building owners as residents have never had to bear this expense. All appliances are Energy Star rated and water-saving devices increase efficiency throughout. New ventilation systems with high efficiency starters circulate conditioned air throughout the building and provide fresh air to all units. The site was revitalized taking advantage of mature trees and creating new walking paths through the site that join with and encourage interaction with the surrounding community. Community gardens and landscaping, again, define a new vision for the site as does new entry signage, parking areas, a new and convenient drive-up drop-off location. Building and grounds lighting provide a new vision for the building creating an iconic neighborhood entry tower wall defined by specialty lighting. Linden Park's transformation redefines the building as a catalyst for the community, enabling the preservation of affordable housing, creating a greater neighborhood interaction, and allowing seniors to remain vital members of the community.

Project Goals

What were the major goals?

- To dramatically transform the dilapidated building. The building was completely transformed inside and out by modernizing the exterior, creating new functional interior spaces and updating all building systems. The architect stabilized the exterior facade and introduced dramatic corner window elements to break up the formerly monolithic building, creating a sense of openness in the community. Outdated panel systems were replaced and the under-building driveway enclosed with new glass enclosures and entryway.

- To preserve affordable housing for seniors. The project required 12 sources of funding and a unique organizational structure that would satisfy both the regulatory requirements of HUD 202 and the capacity requirements of debt providers and Low-Income Housing Tax Credit (LIHTC) investors. The developer secured the issuance of enhanced vouchers with the Housing Authority of Baltimore City (HABC) and HUD, which enabled achievement of two often mutually exclusive goals: increasing the project's affordability and shrinking its financing gap. The vouchers ensured that 165 very-low-income seniors would be able to remain in their homes during and after the renovation. The subdivision of the lot, consistent with the vision of the HUD Choice Neighborhoods planning effort for the area, was a creative way to provide an additional $600,000 in gap financing for the redevelopment.

- To allow seniors to age in place by providing necessary amenities and services. The low-income seniors at Linden Park Apartments have a unique set of service needs. The outstanding Resident Services Program provides programs, services, referrals, and amenities catering specifically to low-income seniors. Third-party providers also visit the site to provide physical, occupational, and mental health services as well as an ophthalmology, audiology, and podiatry check-ups. To provide these services and programs, the design created necessary spaces and Universal Design elements with a range of unit types to make the building more livable for seniors, eliminating the narrow hallways and adding features like grab bars in showers and by toilets. By adding several ground-floor units as well as a mix of units with tubs, showers, and roll-in showers, the design team paved the way for many of the building's residents to age in place by providing unique features suited for seniors at different stages of life. New amenity spaces include laundry and lounge areas on each floor, new multipurpose room with kitchen, library and computer lounge, fitness room, wellness center, quiet room, game room, hair salon, and a solarium overlooking landscaped gardens. On-site Zipcars, medical alert system, and community garden are available for resident use.

- To meet Enterprise Green Communities standards by converting the building's HVAC system from PTACs to an energy-efficient central water source heat pump system, showing the design and project team's responsiveness to environmental issues. All new windows, central boilers, and water-saving devices were installed. A new outside air intake system provides a significant improvement to air quality.

Innovations: What innovations or unique features were incorporated into the design of the project?

The architect provided an innovative design that transformed the 1960s exterior, breaking up the monolithic building, by introducing a new vertical glass element in the corner units at the main elevation. The notches at the intersections of the three-wing "Y" were opened up with vertical glass, and old purple precast panels were covered with new metal panel systems, totally redefining the building. The new design reorientated the front lobby and rear entrances by enclosing an under-building driveway that included construction of a new suite of offices, additional common area spaces, a wellness suite, and a salon. This innovative design included recreating a new building entrance that became a beautiful enhancement while improving the building's functional use. Several

dysfunctional apartments were reconfigured, changing the unit mix to reduce the number of extremely small efficiencies, increase the number of one-bedroom apartments, and adding four new two-bedroom apartments that increased the opportunity for aging in place with a live-in aide. The architect added new sitting areas and laundry facilities on each floor, versus previously having only one central laundry room. This allows for greater communal opportunities and interaction amongst residents, as well as providing greater convenience. Opening up the back of the building with a new solarium and patio allows residents full use of the interior and

Opposite: The architect devised a modern design that provided a renewed exterior facade by introducing floor-to-ceiling windows at the end of the building
Below: Interior lounge area

exterior of the building. The solarium provides a view to the community gardens. The architect incorporated Universal Design elements and a range of unit types and features to promote aging in place. Various amenity spaces recapture the previously unusable basement space, including a new game room and fitness center.

Challenges: What were the greatest design challenges?

To modernize and stabilize the 1960s brick facade the notches at the intersections of the three-wing "Y" were opened up with vertical glass and old purple precast panels covered with new metal panel systems. The new front entrance canopy draws people in while creating a new visual appeal from the street.

By reorientating the entrance and the under-building driveway the design maximizes the building's functional use for additional common areas, a wellness suite, salon, and management offices. By enclosing the driveway, the usable program space of the building was efficiently expanded.

To create a more functional lobby space the main entrance was separated from the service entrance, opening up the whole lobby area and allowing for sight lines to a newly designed solarium with views to the rear gardens. The space is brighter and flows easily from the lobby to all the first-floor amenity spaces while allowing the first-floor units to feel separate and secure.

As the entire 12-story building had one laundry room in the basement for all residents, the units were reconfigured and new common areas and laundry rooms added to each floor. The dark and tight elevator lobbies were reconfigured and opened up, introducing natural light and redefining circulation. New open lounge spaces were added adjacent to the new laundry facilities. Reducing the number of efficiency units also

allowed for more one-bedroom and two-bedroom units, furthering the building's aging in place goals by allowing several units suitable for those with live-in aides.

The complete renovation and modernization was done with tenants in place, including the reconfiguration of individual HVAC systems to a centralized system. The team worked together, along with a relocation specialist, to properly sequence the construction phases, including residents moving out of units into newly renovated units.

During the course of the renovation and after completing the second through twelfth floors, it was discovered that concrete columns were cracked and spalled on the first floor. In this unforeseen scenario, the usual response is to put shoring up every floor, from the first floor to the roof. This would have meant demolishing the newly renovated work on the second through twelfth floors, displacing residents to hotels; and $1 million in structural repair costs. The architects and structural engineers collaborated to come up with a solution to wrap the columns, allowing tenants to continue to remain in their newly renovated apartments, saving $700,000 and avoiding an eight-month delay in the schedule.

Collaboration: How did stakeholders, occupants, the design team, and / or others collaborate during the planning and / or design process?

Tenant-in-place renovation posed many challenges that required significant collaboration during design and construction. The team worked together with a relocation specialist to properly sequence the construction phases, including residents moving out of units into newly renovated units, mitigating scheduling conflicts and resident inconveniences, and ensuring that common area spaces were accessible during renovation. The team also worked closely with an interior design specialist who improved the design specifically as it relates to seniors, accessibility,

and functionality for aging in place. The team toured various senior communities, discussed design solutions that were unique to an existing building that did not initially have the necessary programmed spaces, and devised solutions to create an exemplary community.

Green / Sustainable Features: What green / sustainable features had the greatest impact on the project's design?

The key sustainable features are HVAC, water efficiency, reduced solar gain / heat island-effect sunshades / planting, and maximized daylighting.

Primary motivations: What were the primary motivations for including green / sustainable design features in the project?

The primary motivations for including green / sustainable design were to support the mission / values of the owner / developer, reduce operating expenses, and improve the quality of living for residents.

Challenges: What challenges did the project face when trying to incorporate green / sustainable design features?

Installing a new central heating and cooling system while maintaining occupancy in the building and decommissioning the existing PTAC system required maintaining the systems until renovated units were converted to the new system over a two-year phasing sequence. The sequencing required careful analysis and preparation to ensure that the electric load was not increased due to the prohibitive cost of upgrading the electrical systems. Meeting green standards and providing water-saving devices is challenging in Baltimore, as it requires being cognizant of Legionella contamination to the senior at-risk population. Low-flow showerheads had the potential to cause water to remain stagnant if the flow was too low, increasing the Legionella risk. The design team therefore had to ensure that the proper water flow was achieved.

Technology: How is innovative / assistive / special technology used by the project to deliver care or services?

The infrastructure to support a wireless medical alert system available throughout the entire building was installed during the renovation of Linden Park Apartments. The new system allows residents to have access to medical alert devices, such as pendants that residents can use to seek help when they have fallen, through a third-party medical alert provider at one third of the cost on the market. Linden Park residents also have access to SafeLink Wireless through the government's Lifeline Support Program. This program offers free cell phones and 250 free minutes each month for income-eligible customers. These cell phones can be used for general communication purposes and can be used to call 911 for help in case of emergency. Linden Park Apartments also offers a wide-ranging set of outstanding resident and social services to promote healthy living and aging in place. The property has two on-site Resident Services Coordinators who provide educational, recreational, and supportive programming opportunities for residents. The Resident Services staff help enhance the quality of life for residents through coordinating on-site programs and referrals. This includes the Eat Together Program that provides healthy meals four days a week at a very low cost, health and wellness programs and services, art classes, veterans program, computer training, financial literacy workshops, and a gardening club. A wellness suite, fitness center, and salon are also on site for resident use. The wellness suite hosts health providers who offer direct on-site health services to residents such as Baltimore Orthopedics & Rehabilitation and Step Well Podiatry. The Resident Services team organizes community building events such as summer barbecues, game and movie

nights, and holiday celebrations that help to prevent isolation and build community at Linden Park. The coordinators help connect residents to non-profit, government, and social service organizations for services that can include off-site education programs, off-site trips, health resources, home health aid agencies, utility, food or rental assistance for those in financial crisis, benefits assistance, and legal assistance. The coordinators have created valuable partnerships with organizations such as Action in Maturity, Maryland Institute College of Art, University of Maryland School of Pharmacy, Maryland Food Bank, and Baltimore Clayworks. Overall, the services provided through the on-site Resident Services staff working in conjunction with the management staff provide a safe and healthy community and a great resource to the residents of Linden Park.

Jury Comments

The jury was impressed with this very successful transformation of an existing affordable housing high-rise serving seniors in Baltimore. The project required a remarkable public / private partnership with multiple funding sources. The building

was brought up to modern standard even while keeping residents in place. The building exterior was completely modernized with the introduction of vertical glass elements and metal panels. A driveway under the building at ground level was enclosed to support the addition of more amenity and support spaces.

The building systems and interior spaces were completely redone using Universal Design principles. More natural light is brought into the building, and more common area and support spaces have been added. There is a welcoming entrance and lobby. Especially important was the creation of space for—and partnering with—outside organizations to bring a number of services on site. This will help support seniors who wish to age in place in a residence at Linden Park. This is a project that brings renewal to a neighborhood, while improving the lives of those who reside at Linden Park Apartments.

Previous page: Kitchen and living area
Above: Library
Opposite: Lobby
Photography: Eric Taylor Photography

Babcock Health Care Center

Winston-Salem, North Carolina // Salemtowne Retirement Community

Facility type (year of completion): Assisted living—dementia / memory support; Long-term skilled nursing; Short-term rehabilitation (2017)
Target market: Middle / upper middle
Site location: Suburban; greenfield

Gross square footage of the new construction involved in the project: 127,052
Provider type: Faith-based non-profit

Below: The Saal is surrounded by wide, sky-lit corridors where residents can sit and watch events and passersby. The wood paneling above the seats is oak reclaimed from the site.

Opposite: The perspective model view shows the long-term care entry at the front and the rehabilitation entry at the rear. Rehabilitation therapy spaces and common areas connect the rehabilitation unit to the household areas.

Overall Project Description

Salemtowne is a faith-based, non-profit Life Plan Community serving senior adults in Winston-Salem for more than 40 years. Founded by the Moravian Synod in 1972, Salemtown is home to 300-plus residents. Most of the community's facilities were built 20 or more years ago; many were outdated and not readily adaptable to the expectations and needs of current and future residents. The donation of a 58-acre parcel of land adjacent to the existing campus provided the opportunity for repositioning and expansion. Salemtowne identified a need in the community for high-quality short-term rehabilitation, as local hospitals were sending people to a neighboring city due to lack of available beds in Winston-Salem. Despite having an excellent reputation for nursing care, Salemtowne's existing skilled nursing building did not offer an opportunity to meet this need. Although only 15 years old, the building was outdated with semi-private rooms, no rooms with private showers, and an institutional feel.

Other needs included the existing assisted living, located in a 40-year-old building with many challenges. The community developed a 20-year master plan that responded directly to campus needs and a growing and changing marketplace. The plan envisions phased development, starting with a new health center to include rehabilitation, long-term care, and assisted living memory care (seen as more appropriate than the existing SN-licensed memory care). Future phases plan for additional assisted and independent living facilities and a complete renovation of the existing campus. Recently completed, the new 127,000-square-foot Babcock Health Care Center will eventually house up to 120 residents, including memory care residents. The center currently includes a 40-bed short-term rehabilitation skilled nursing designed on a hospitality model, three 20-bed long-term care skilled nursing households, and one assisted living memory care household. Common and support areas link all components. All rooms are private, with private baths that

include no-barrier showers. The center is designed for the addition of two future households and the households are designed for flexibility in case future needs change. The center has two separate entrances for short-term rehabilitation and for long-term care and memory care.

Project Goals

What were the major goals?

- To provide plenty of exposure to natural light and easy access to safe outdoor spaces. Studies have shown that where outdoor spaces are within sight of the staff, resident opportunities to actually go outside are greatly increased. Single-loaded corridors provide natural light and a view of the courtyard in each household. In addition, residents and staff can easily access their courtyard via one of two doors: the first is located near the household common areas, and the second is in the corridor located on the other side of the courtyard. In the memory care household, a keypad secures the door so that residents cannot wander outside alone.

- To provide a true homelike environment. Key to this goal was providing fresh, cooked-to-order food as well as a resident-accessible kitchen where residents can sit and relax. Each resident household has a large dining area, private dining room, living room, activity room, and sun room. The dining area is open to an accessible kitchen that backs up to the commercial kitchen that is open long hours and staffed by professionals who make fresh food to order. Residents can engage with the cook and staff and the accessible kitchen can be used for cooking-oriented activities that involve residents. A refrigerator and sideboard hold beverages and snacks. A prep kitchen located downstairs is used primarily for receiving goods and chopping vegetables, but all cooking is done in the individual kitchens.

Innovations: What innovations or unique features were incorporated into the design of the project?

The design needed to be two stories, yet a key goal was to create easy access to the outdoors, which meant no transverse hallways or elevators. A unique building cross section creates an on-grade courtyard for each household, even in the two-story portion of the building. The design eliminates as many institutional features as possible. Areas on the first floor provide space for back-of-house functions such as receiving and general food preparation. Instead of having to have medicine carts moving through the hallways, each room is equipped with a lockable, light-able medicine cabinet. A pull-down shelf under the cabinet provides a place for nurses to put their tablet to make notes. Located right at the doorway, nurses can complete their tasks with minimal disruption to the resident. In addition to the barrier-free shower design, resident bathrooms also include pull-down grab bars, based on research by Rothschild Foundation. Other innovations are related to the rehabilitation therapy unit, which, in addition to traditional equipment, includes a kitchen area so residents can retrain common tasks before returning home. A special private dining area is also available for therapists and residents to practice common dining tasks and movements in a more private space.

Moravian heritage and history provided a context for the exterior design as well as many of the interior features. For example, each household is named for and reflects a different era in the Moravian history of Winston-Salem. The signage at the entrance to each household is inspired by signage found at the historic Town of Old Salem, founded in 1766 by the Moravians and a major part of what eventually became Winston-Salem. At the entrance to each household is a welcome sign with each one featuring a different floral drawing found in a historic journal in the

- To provide a spa-like hospitality setting for short-term rehabilitation residents. The team created separation between the rehabilitation unit and the other households. Each area has its own front door on opposite sides of the building. In addition, the rehabilitation unit has its own living room and cafe where residents can go on their own or with visitors. The two-story living room has clerestory windows that provide a bright and airy atmosphere.

- To design for future needs and changes in need. Having previously invested in a facility that did not serve them well in the long term, Salemtowne was eager not to make the same mistake. The ability to expand or shift based on future need was critical. The design allows for the addition of two new households. In addition, the households are designed for possible future changes in use. All are similarly equipped and designed with the same amenities as well as private rooms with barrier-free showers. Thus, households are easily shifted based on need.

- To combine the intimacy of households with the benefits of shared amenities. Long-term households ring a central area similar to a town square with the Saal (a Moravian term for chapel or meeting place) as the focal point. Residents can exit their household to go to the salon, gift shop, dentist, or doctor's office, or simply sit in the light-filled space (provided by two 66-foot-long skylights) and enjoy the scenery. The Saal and spaces surrounding it are inspired by vintage storefronts and conservatories.

Moravian Archives and from archives at Winston-Salem's Museum of Early Southern Decorative Arts. Additional artwork also came from these archives. These linkages provide a connective tissue to the culture and the real history of Salemtowne's community.

Challenges: What were the greatest design challenges?

The original design was all on one story in order to meet the owner's goal for creating easy access to the outdoors. When it became obvious that a one-story scheme would drive site costs beyond the budget, the design had to be changed and the footprint reduced. The design team tested various options until, working closely with the contractor, they developed a plan to create two ground levels. This cross section allows each household to have an on-grade courtyard, even in the two-story section of the building. However, it also created its own challenges. Operationally, each care-type component needed to be co-located: all long-term care households on the same floor, all memory care on the same floor, and all rehabilitation on the same floor. Ultimately the team developed a plan that satisfied these needs as well as creating a logical, functional arrangement. Twenty rooms is a large number for a household design, especially given the goal of providing direct outdoor access from common areas of each household in a two-story building. As a result, corridors were longer than preferred. This is mitigated by making some corridors single loaded and by providing a sunroom at the farthest point in each household.

Collaboration: How did stakeholders, occupants, the design team, and / or others collaborate during the planning and / or design process?

The team worked closely with the administration, but also had a lot of input from staff, residents, and the board of trustees throughout the project.

This input was very important to the final outcome of the project. In addition, there was tremendous collaboration among the owner, contractor, development manager, and design team to accomplish the owner's goals within budget constraints. The bathroom design incorporates pull-down grab bars based upon research by Rothschild Foundation. This required permission from state authorities to approve as ADA enhancement. The interior design team worked with the Moravian Archives and the Museum of Early Southern Decorative Arts to find art and other items that would be meaningful within the building.

Outreach: What off-site outreach services are offered to the greater community?

The long-term care and memory care components of the project are to care for Salemtowne's internal population. However, the 40-bed rehabilitation unit is designed to meet a community need. Salemtowne has significant cooperation and support from local health care providers. In addition to partnering with the medical community (hospitals and other medical professionals), Salemtowne is developing partnerships with local colleges and universities to provide a unique environment for training students and undertaking research, implementing best practice programs based on that research, and partnering to create unique activities for Salemtowne residents.

Jury Comments

Babcock Health Care Center is the first phase of a master plan that is a great example of thoughtful planning to include future growth. The owner identified a need for a health care center and located it on a newly donated parcel adjacent to their existing community.

There are many things that the jury found noteworthy about this project. The plan is a very effective use of a larger household layout. This is achieved by the interconnected households that create interior courtyards and a linear commons space. The household plans are stacked in a two-level solution to reduce the footprint and preserve space on the site, creating the opportunity for future planned expansion. The courtyard areas provide secure opportunities for residents to enjoy the outdoors and natural light without long travel distance. The linear commons building is filled with daylight from a linear skylight structure that extends the length of the space. The skylight is a prominent feature that organizes the plan and links the highly functional neighborhoods.

The Moravian architecture featured in this project is simple, clean, and beautifully crafted. The design team made a strategic decision to use the reclaimed walnut and oak hardwood for the credenzas, trusses, and decorative barn doors, plus other features throughout the center. Other elements integrate work inspired from local craftsmen and elements borrowed from Old Salem, such as the welcome sign at the entrance.

Opposite top: Exterior
Opposite bottom: Resident room
Photography: Atlantic Archives, Inc. / Richard Leo Johnson

RLPS Architects

Edenwald Café

Towson, Maryland // Edenwald

Facility type (year of completion): Independent Living (2017)
Target market: Middle / upper middle
Site location: Urban

Gross square footage of the renovation / modernization
involved in the project: 4790
Purpose of the renovation / modernization: Upgrade the
environment
Provider type: Non-sectarian non-profit

Below: The design aesthetic of an urban farmers
market utilizes rustic and reclaimed natural-looking
materials throughout the renovated cafe
Opposite: Upper-level seating / private events

Overall Project Description

Edenwald's existing Garden Court Café had not received any renovations since it was built in 1999. The space was not user-friendly and residents had difficulties navigating the serving line when selecting foods. Another challenge was the ability of the food service staff to prepare healthy, nutritious meals that appealed to new residents—often younger seniors—arriving in the community. To provide fresh appeal, updates were needed not only to the physical structure but also to the types of foods and services offered. The resulting design took cues from a local farmers market, focusing on fresh foods (some locally sourced during the summer) and a wide range of options. A coffee shop, grab-n-go offerings, and a pizza station are new to the cafe, and complement a salad bar, deli, and hot entrée station. Another new dining experience to be offered is a patio dining component. The design aesthetic of an urban farmers market utilizes rustic and reclaimed natural-looking materials. Worn brick tile graces the entry and grill hood. The floors combine rustic wood-look tile with Old World tile medallions, and the coffee shop serving counter simulates reclaimed planks.

Project Goals

What were the major goals?

- The primary goals were to implement a fresh approach to food preparation, nutrition, and flavor diversity, and create an atmosphere that would reflect a new attitude toward the dining experience. The Edenwald Café was transformed to support food-service production changes allowing for healthier, locally sourced, made-to-order choices while simultaneously creating an appealing dining destination that resolves some circulation issues. The new open display stations, developed with a hospitality consultant, support these operational objectives in a vibrant and appealing atmosphere. The integration of ordering kiosks as well as the capability for staff or residents to place an order online and then pick up items at their convenience reflects Edenwald's commitment to a progressive, opportunity-packed lifestyle.

- To resolve circulation challenges, the contemporary cafe design is more open and allows for the necessary additional space between the food offerings. A seldom-utilized internal stair that connected the cafe to a mezzanine seating area was removed to achieve this. The mezzanine still provides a secondary seating area and is available for private parties, but access to the space is now from an existing elevator.

Innovations: What innovations or unique features were incorporated into the design of the project?

This design solution integrates innovative new software technology that ties the ordering system to the point-of-service and digital menus. Residents and staff can place orders from conveniently placed kiosks or their personal smart phones, tablets, or computers, and the system integrates those orders into the cooking line so food is ready at the precise time. The new technology aids the kitchen staff in planning menus, managing inventory, and providing quality food.

Challenges: What were the greatest design challenges?

The existing cafe was not user-friendly and presented the residents with challenges navigating the space, particularly while selecting food. The entire space was reconfigured to allow more open circulation space and to prevent long queues from forming at each station. The residents are encouraged to proceed directly to the desired food station rather than waiting in line just to select one food option. The salad bar had previously been designed as a "U" shape, where residents could only access food on one side, which made it difficult to reach all the food offerings. The new freestanding salad bar allows for circulation on all sides for easier access and increased efficiency over a single line formation. The menu offerings were limited by the cooking equipment and the ability to keep the food fresh and hot during meal times. Nearly all of the cooking equipment was replaced and upgraded during this renovation, with the exception of the existing hood, which was in good working order and remained in place. The new equipment uses up-to-date technology innovations to keep food precisely hot or cold for longer times. Food is now presented in an attractive open-kitchen display format. A new menu and ordering system, introduced in conjunction with the updates, allows residents and staff to place orders via a kiosk just outside the space or through a smartphone app.

The acoustics needed to be improved without losing the volume or scale of the space. A chief complaint from cafe patrons prior to the update was the poor acoustics of the existing space, which made it difficult to place orders or carry on a conversation. The new cafe space features a carpeted dining area to absorb the noise from general conversations. Fabric-wrapped acoustic panels cover the two-story open walls to absorb noise, but the hex-shaped design and bold colors contribute to the overall aesthetic. The pressed-tin ceiling panels also offer acoustic absorption.

Collaboration: How did stakeholders, occupants, the design team, and / or others collaborate during the planning and / or design process?

The design team worked with the community executive team as well as the kitchen staff members to define how the cafe should function and which new features to implement. The design team spent a day with the kitchen staff and observed how they worked and how the cafe functioned during meal times. This was followed by a group tour of an award-winning cafe at another Life Plan Community to further explore new ideas and envision the future potential for Edenwald. The executive team then undertook a survey of the residents to learn what might be improved in the new design. The design team developed a 3D model of the space and rendered it in full color to share the design with the staff and residents. This included a fly-through video as if walking through the space. The design team presented the design, function, and video to residents and their families during a town hall meeting. During this meeting the team responded to questions raised in the resident surveys and illustrated the resulting design concepts to address their concerns and ultimately provide a more functional and appealing dining experience.

Green / Sustainable Features: What green / sustainable features had the greatest impact on the project's design?

The key sustainable features are energy efficiency, improved indoor air quality, and reuse of existing building structure and / or materials.

Primary motivations: What were the primary motivations for including green / sustainable design features in the project?

The primary motivations were to support the mission / values of the client / provider, lower operational costs, and improve the building for occupants.

Technology: How is innovative / assistive / special technology used by the project to deliver care or services?

The new technology integrating the food ordering system to the point-of-service and digital menus aids kitchen staff in planning menus and managing inventory, while also providing enhanced ordering options through kiosks or web access.

Jury Comments

The jury noted the update of the existing casual dining space with better natural lighting, which was achieved mostly by simply removing a tree. The space is more interactive with the community, even vertically. It has the look and feel of a true market space with graphics and lighting, and there is an ease to how residents can flow through the space whether they are stopping to pick something up on the go or sitting down to meet with their friends over coffee. The freestanding kiosk as a point-of-sale brings technology to the space, while the farm-to-table menu gives it an old-fashioned feel.

Opposite top: The pressed-tin ceiling panels offer acoustic absorption

Opposite bottom: Residents can place orders on the kiosks or over their mobile devices

Above: The entire cafe was reconfigured to allow more open circulation space and prevent long lines from forming at each station

Left: Edenwald Café was transformed to create an atmosphere that would reflect a new attitude toward the dining experience

Photography: Nathan Cox Photography; Alain Jaramillo Photography

Perkins Eastman

Goodwin House Alexandria

Alexandria, Virginia // Goodwin House Incorporated

Facility type (year of completion): Assisted living—dementia / memory support; Long-term skilled nursing; Short-term rehabilitation (2017)
Target market: Middle / upper middle
Site location: Urban

Gross square footage of the new construction involved in the project: 108,371
Provider type: Faith-based non-profit

Below: With the new small house building and its reimagined garden courtyard, the campus buildings now create an intersecting element for social and resident interaction

Opposite: The design maximizes every square foot of outdoor space on this tight urban site, creating accessible areas for walking, gathering to chat with neighbors, relaxing, and gardening

A single house for assisted living memory support on the ground level offers residents their own dedicated courtyard garden. Key existing amenity spaces were relocated to this building at the public level to maintain and reinforce a strong sense of community. Both a new auditorium and courtyard are shared by the entire campus community, which totals 400 residents.

Project Goals

What were the major goals?

- To introduce a new culture of care embedded within a small house model, replacing existing single, double, and triple rooms with all private rooms. The team designed a new five-story small house with two houses per floor, supporting 10 residents. The open-plan design provides staff with a view of the front door, living room, den, and dining room. This allows staff to engage with residents while preparing meals, offering comfort to residents in other spaces or providing assistance. The open design also provides residents with greater choice for determining their own activities and social experiences.

- To knit together various campus buildings to create "one community." The new building, located in the original garden space, connects to the adjacent assisted / independent living buildings and now houses assisted living memory support and nursing, as well as a gallery / multipurpose space on the ground level. The concept for a stacked small house supported Goodwin House's goals. Placing it in the existing central garden made it easily accessible for all residents; adding the community-wide gallery / multipurpose room for large gathering events brings all residents into the building and allows frailer residents to participate at a greater level.

Overall Project Description

The existing community offered 271 independent and 41 assisted living apartments and 80 skilled nursing beds but had no remaining allowable area on the site. The last development project occurred 15 years earlier; this project doubled the independent living apartments, but did not increase dining capacity, choice, or variety. Additionally, the health care environment was even further behind on current expectations with a life care contract model. Both the lack of variety and choice in dining and an outmoded skilled care community negatively impacted Goodwin House's ability to serve current residents and to attract future residents. The client wanted change and this project was the initial step.

The client's initial goals included developing a strategic plan to rebalance and reinvent the independent living, assisted living, and health care components of the Life Plan Community, knitting together the various campus buildings to create "one community" that embraces long-term care and assisted living residents along with independent residents. Introducing a new culture of care embedded within a small house model sees the existing single, double, and triple rooms replaced with all private rooms, and dining options, which consist of a large, formal, underutilized dining room and a limited-capacity casual café, have been reconsidered, with operational inefficiencies addressed. The project is intended to improve the marketability of the independent living apartments to attract future residents and increase revenue stream.

This multi-phased reinvention relocates current licensed beds from a traditional model of care to a new culture of care within a stacked small house model in a newly designed building, central to other campus buildings. Each house (two per floor) supports 10 residents, whether assisted living memory support or nursing, shares a common kitchen, living room, and den.

Innovations: What innovations or unique features were incorporated into the design of the project?

Goodwin House Alexandria turns the standalone one-story wood frame small house into a five-story stacked model on a tight urban site. Design stacks the houses vertically and situates more than one house per floor while reinforcing fundamental features of the model such as scale, choice, and privacy. While the traditional one-story small house has a porch and front door, this model provides each floor with a lobby and then each of the two houses (apartments) with front doors and doorbells. More importantly, it balances hospitality and healing in an environment that supports residents' frailties and allows caregivers to efficiently care for them.

Challenges: What were the greatest design challenges?

The greatest design challenge was designing a new small house to fit within a tight urban site while maintaining the connection between health care and assisted / independent living residents. The original idea was to renovate the existing floor and floor above to maintain current census, but losing the residential apartments on the latter floor would greatly reduce revenue. Additionally, it wasn't possible to create a small house model on the existing 30,000-square-feet floor plates and the community was landlocked with no remaining allowable area. Although site constraints and other issues posed a technical challenge, the design challenge was to maintain community among all residents, with health care residents integrated into the fabric of the community. The selected site allowed for a physical connection to an existing building and improvements to the common areas allowed for the location of a large gathering space to be placed on the ground floor of the new health care building. The new site—a large, open, mature landscaped area with resident garden boxes and walking path—was considered a great asset. The small house model, the need to maintain a physical, programmatic, and service connection to the existing buildings, the goal to replace the quantity of outdoor space with quality outdoors experiences and the preference to not block views to the Washington, D.C. monuments all informed the design: a new five-story building that framed a new courtyard. With the small house model, activities such as dining, exercise, and arts occur in the house. Therefore, the large gathering events became an essential activity to reconnect skilled nursing residents with assisted / independent living residents throughout the community. Locating the gallery / multipurpose space in the new building was an important design decision. It communicated that the building was for the entire community (not just skilled nursing) and extended common areas around to a third side of the newly created courtyard. This placed the gallery / multipurpose space closer to residents with more assistive devices or needing assistance, improving its proximity and the likelihood of their involvement. The original garden was large with more planters than the residents used and no gathering areas or destination spaces. Few garden planters were adjacent to paths and uneven ground made it difficult for residents to traverse, especially those with assistive devices. The new garden design created accessible areas for walking and gathering, including raised planters, and offered more seating and choices for outdoor experiences within the courtyard and around the building. Residents helped to determine the correct number and size of garden planters.

Collaboration: How did stakeholders, occupants, the design team, and / or others collaborate during the planning and / or design process?

Goodwin House had three distinct goals for the planning study, one of which was directly related to the health care project. Board members, resident council, executive leadership, administration and nursing staff attended a series of small group workshops, which encouraged dialogue (collaboration) with those of different perspectives (due to title or responsibility to the organization), teased out the real priorities and goals, and distilled this into a concrete definition for the project. Exercises ranged from unwrapping definitions of descriptive language to touring other communities to inform decisions on how the number of residents impacts the impression of home within a house. Multiple scenarios incorporated all major goals, but addressed them with differing priority and cost implications. The team included a construction manager to estimate construction cost for each; a consultant who assisted in projecting operational cost differences between scenarios; and a finance consultant who modeled each scenario to incorporate construction and operations costs into a competitive financial feasibility. The process resulted in Goodwin House making informed decisions that balanced wants and desires with financial and operational models for informed decision-making.

Green / Sustainable Features: What green / sustainable features had the greatest impact on the project's design?

The key sustainable features are energy efficiency, improved indoor air quality, and maximized daylighting.

Opposite top: Small house living room
Opposite bottom: The resident room is furnished as a bedroom, including a small desk and shelving, which offers visual cues for wayfinding
Photography: Sarah Mechling

Primary motivations: What were the primary motivations for including green / sustainable design features in the project?

The primary motivations were to support the mission / values of the client / provider, support the mission / values of the design team, and improve the building for occupants.

Challenges: What challenges did the project face when trying to incorporate green / sustainable design features?

The primary challenge in meeting sustainability goals was site constraints. This prevented the design team from exploring more innovative measures such as thermal ice storage to reduce mechanical system cooling loads and an all-harvested-rainwater approach for irrigation. Due to those constraints, the program manager developed an approach to determining the feasibility of various sustainability measures and then managing expectations to create a roadmap for the entire team.

Technology: How is innovative / assistive / special technology used by the project to deliver care or services?

A ceiling lift track is present in all resident rooms and the lift is portable—a care partner can move it to any room. The track extends into the bathroom, passing the toilet, for access to the shower. This solution required a waiver that allowed designers to depart from standard Americans with Disabilities Act (ADA) requirements that are not senior-friendly; the toilet was moved away from the wall so caregivers can work on either side. Goodwin House plans to use special attachments, such as scales, to more easily monitor weight for those who are unable or find it difficult to stand on a scale. Ceiling lifts support better resident and care partner safety. A nurse call system is integrated with a wander guard system, which simplifies the number of devices and alerts to care partners. The system notifies the care partner assigned to that specific resident directly via a personal handheld

device and, if necessary, escalates the call to the next responsible person until the resident's need is addressed. Response times are tracked. Also, since devices are assigned to specific staff and the system notifies them directly, there is no need for overhead paging, alarms, or nurse call dome stations. Eliminating these elements in the environment removes some of the most institutional characteristics of a traditional nursing home. The use of electronic medical records allows care partners and nurses to be more mobile while maintaining comprehensive records for each individual. This also supports decentralization of medication storage and distribution to each resident's room, which further reduces staff time traveling and sees that residents receive proper and on-time medication.

Jury Comments

Goodwin House Alexandria is a strong solution to creating a vertical small house project on a tight urban site. The project also creates new linkages to existing uses on the campus. The neighborhoods each serve 10 residents. Each neighborhood has all the features of a well-designed small house project. The common spaces in each neighborhood make good use of natural light and views. The interior design is warm and residential with lots of use of wood trim. The resident rooms continue that look and feel. The rooms incorporate a barn-door entry to the bathroom and an unobtrusive ceiling-mounted track for a lift. The outdoor space that serves the residents who live in these neighborhoods is inviting and incorporates raised beds. Common area spaces that serve the whole campus are located at the first level of this building. This helps to create a strong link to the rest of the campus while making it easy and inviting for residents in this building to participate in campus-wide events. This is a well-designed multistory small house project that enhances an existing urban campus.

AG Architecture

Hillcrest Country Estates

Papillion, Nebraska // Hillcrest Health Services

Facility type (year of completion): Assisted living—dementia / memory support; Short-term rehabilitation (2016)
Target market: Middle / upper middle
Site location: Suburban; greenfield

Gross square footage of the new construction involved in the project: 281,019
Provider type: For-profit

Below: Rehab Cottage is designed to be a seamless connection of architecture between the existing campus and new buildings
Opposite: Courtyard at dusk

Overall Project Description

In the competitive senior living marketplace, where the lines are beginning to blur between quality for-profit and not-for-profit products, every provider is striving to find a competitive advantage. Creating an environment that elevates the quality of resident life is one factor that plays heavily in the decision-making process. Satisfied residents will stay and new residents will be easier to attract if the desired lifestyle is offered. Diverse amenities, comprehensive care options, and impeccable service play a critical role in achieving an exceptional experience for both the residents and provider. Hillcrest Country Estates wanted to complete its continuum of care rental community with new senior living choices that emulate the best aspects of a not-for-profit Life Plan Community campus. By adding a new residential component featuring an amenity-rich commons space, the community now provides the senior population in the Omaha, Nebraska

area with an alternative to heading South to resort-style communities in warmer climates. The Grand Lodge (264,000 square feet) provides additional independent living apartments and new assisted living and memory support units as well as a resort-style commons area full of vibrant amenities—a hospitality-inspired environment that entices area seniors to stay close to home in the Midwest. Furthermore, the addition of Rehab Cottage extends the level of care offered to seniors on campus as well as residents in the surrounding community. The efficiently designed rehabilitation center provides gathering and socialization spaces, a state-of-the-art rehabilitation gym and 22 private suites. The Grand Lodge and Rehab Cottage add the final pieces to a larger senior living campus plan that already offers a variety of living and health care options to area seniors. It provides residents with a new congregate living choice while offering additional amenities, services, and experiences that support a vibrant and active lifestyle.

Project Goals

What were the major goals?

- To elevate the lifestyle while maximizing operational efficiencies and improving resident satisfaction. While the addition of Rehab Cottage as well as the independent living, assisted living, and memory care units help to better position the community in the marketplace, the design of the commons area was integral to achieving the provider's goal to elevate the lifestyle on campus. The 36,000-square-foot commons offers numerous amenities, including exceptional dining venues and a floor dedicated to wellness. The team worked diligently to centralize the main production kitchen to service the bistro, ballroom, independent living fine dining, assisted living dining, private dining, and chef's table. In addition to the comprehensive amenity offering and centralized kitchen, the team explored efficiency of movement for residents and staff. The assisted living was designed so residents can access all services on one floor to avoid the difficulty of navigating an elevator core, which also saves time for staff. In memory support, the team created an accessible interior courtyard that is surrounded by buildings. This provides direct and easy access to the outdoors while addressing safety concerns. Looking at how space adjacencies impact resident satisfaction at every level of care was important throughout the design process.

- To provide a short-term rehabilitation center to serve campus residents and those in the surrounding community. The 17,019-square-foot building—the first rehabilitation cottage in Nebraska—is designed around a central service hub, the focal point being the rehabilitation gym. The team minimized resident steps to services by encircling the gym with suites on three sides. Interior spaces were designed to maximize efficiency while encouraging socialization.

Aerial context site plan

0   200ft

- To develop an architectural language that provides a fresh face to the campus while creating a seamless connection between new and existing structures. The architecture team was challenged to efficiently design a rehabilitation center to fit within the existing site constraints. The building had to be oriented to connect to existing site amenities and it had to serve as an architectural transition between the existing cottage typology and The Grand Lodge. While the existing cottage structures were done in a simple Craftsman style, the two-, three-, and four-story structures of The Grand Lodge are much larger in scale with a more hospitality-inspired entry sequence and contemporized materials palette to enhance the uniqueness of this new "main structure" on campus. As a result, Rehab Cottage utilizes a similar stone and fiber cement palette on familiar forms, such as projected window bays, but adds a layer of architectural detailing to create a seamless connection between the existing and new buildings. The building explores volume in the central rehabilitation gym and provides a similar entry sequence to The Grand Lodge, echoing its entry canopy.

Innovations: What innovations or unique features were incorporated into the design of the project?

This savvy for-profit provider has always focused on projects exploring cutting-edge concepts that maximize the wow factor while "baking in" the highest level of efficient service. From the centralized kitchen that efficiently services all food service components to simplifying movement for residents as they navigate the spaces, design decisions were made to deliver an exceptional experience for residents while supporting successful operations. While centralizing the main production kitchen required more square footage to access all the dining venues, the provider is pleased with the results as the efficiencies achieved made this a worthwhile investment. It services the bistro, ballroom, independent living fine dining, assisted living dining, private dining, and a chef's table. The commons area provides an amenity hub for all levels of care across campus. Quality of life is a priority throughout. Independent living and assisted living have direct connections to the wellness, dining, and entertainment spaces while the orientation of the building provides memory support with direct access to a courtyard to enhance this specialized resident experience. With this new project, wellness is a huge component of daily life for all new and existing

residents. The Oasis Aquatic & Fitness Center includes a saltwater pool, state-of-the-art fitness center, aerobics rooms, health center, retail salon, and 40-seat cinema. The surrounding grounds also include amenities such as a walking path and putting green. The community's wellness program is the most unique and robust program of its kind in the region, offering yoga, tai chi, exercise classes, and daily water aerobics in the saltwater pool—the first for a local retirement community. The provider invested in HUR fitness equipment—another first in the region—and the process involved traveling to Chicago to test the equipment. During HUR installation, the pneumatic hoses were concealed within the concrete floor for aesthetic reasons. In addition to these features, the fitness center offers personalized programs that are monitored electronically by a wellness director. The island oasis theme makes it a fun and comfortable place for residents to gather and socialize, in addition to exercise. Due to the number of retired military officers on campus, including several generals, an entire corridor within the Oasis floor was dedicated to honoring military service (the campus is within proximity of a military base). The Veterans Tribute is a museum space that offers an incredible mural depicting the action of each military sector that flanks walls of memorabilia displays, including items such as jackets, helmets, and awards. The intention of this amenity-rich commons area was to make residents feel like they are on vacation. The Grand Lodge offers a resort-style experience with a variety of wow factors unlike anything else in the area and it is designed to provide that experience to every resident.

Challenges: What were the greatest design challenges?

The excessive grade changes of the site posed numerous challenges. With no corner of the site at the same elevation, the team played with building heights, entry points, and adjacencies.

These challenges provided the opportunity to achieve the provider's desired "house on a hill" aesthetic. The team worked diligently to carefully orient The Grand Lodge on the site, develop an architectural language that complements the existing structures, and provide a fresh face to the campus. This was accomplished by considering the numerous viewpoints and approaches into the community. The goal was to create enticing views from these many angles. The independent living wings were each set at different heights and the commons area amenities were positioned on two separate stories. This also provided an opportunity to give residents in the existing independent living villas a direct connection to the amenity spaces at the lower level. The lower level also provides a secondary entry into assisted living and direct access to memory support. The drastic elevation changes allowed the team to create dramatic architectural statements and enticing outdoor amenities while capturing breathtaking views. The original intent of the parcel of land for Rehab Cottage was to accommodate a 14-bed skilled nursing cottage. The challenge was to design a rehabilitation center with gathering and socialization spaces, a state-of-the-art gymnasium, and 22 private suites to fit within the same site constraints. In addition, the existing skilled nursing cottages on the site are clustered around a central green space with a distinct connection between the buildings and the green space. Rehab Cottage needed to maintain this connectivity. The building was carefully positioned to achieve connectivity and provide rehabilitation residents with access to the green space. Inside, the efficient design features a centralized rehabilitation gymnasium. Daylight in the centralized gym was maximized by increasing the volume to allow for dormers and clerestory windows. Direct visual access to the green space was created on the north wall, while a translucent glazing detail on the south wall provides shared light between the gym and commons area.

Collaboration: How did stakeholders, occupants, the design team, and / or others collaborate during the planning and / or design process?

Early in the development phase, the provider conducted a community survey of seniors likely to move to a retirement community to measure the importance of certain amenities. This survey also included the community's Signature Villa residents already residing on campus. The results of that survey drove key decisions about the Oasis Aquatic & Fitness Center, which features the area's only saltwater pool for seniors. Another example is the Veterans Tribute, which was developed to honor veterans of all services since the community is located near a military base. A committee was formed with future residents who are veterans and their input solicited on what to depict, and how to organize the mural and shadowboxes. For Rehab Cottage, the team carefully evaluated the existing skilled nursing component to identify the strengths and weaknesses of its current service offering. Staff feedback was critical to this part of the process. The team identified the central hearth element as an important feature within existing facilities on campus. It serves as a strong organizational element and provides a sense of familiarity and consistency. Window seats were also identified as a familiar design element that residents enjoy.

Jury Comments

Hillcrest Country Estates is an expansion and addition to an existing community that enhances the common amenities for the independent living villas and adds a new dedicated short-term rehabilitation space. The expansion provides choice and adds variety to multiple dining venues, including a cafe and pub. A large, flexible multipurpose space is added with the intention to connect to the outside community for social events. Outdoor spaces include new courtyards with fire pit, linking the walking paths to the overall campus.

Above: The rehabilitation gym has overhead rails that help staff lift and transfer residents
Photography: Tricia Shay Photography; Admiral District

The most notable feature is the short-term rehabilitation gym. This addition creates a seamless connection of architecture between the existing campus and the new buildings. The special attention given to overhead rails that help staff lift and transfer residents creates a highly functional gym while reducing the possibility of staff injuries. Resident units are also equipped with lifts to support the staff with transfers into the toilet rooms.

RLPS Architects

Legacy Place Cottages

Allentown, Pennsylvania // Jah-Jireh Homes of America

Facility type (year of completion): Assisted living; Assisted living—dementia/ memory support (2015)
Target market: Middle / upper middle
Site location: Suburban; greenfield

Gross square footage of the new construction involved in the project: 26,855
Provider type: Faith-based non-profit

Below: Serving kitchen shared by both assisted living small houses
Opposite: Paired small houses

Overall Project Description

These residences are unique in both their mission and operations. Modeled after Jah-Jireh homes in Great Britain, Legacy Place is "wholly dedicated to accommodation and care of members of the community of Jehovah's Witnesses in a loving, spiritual environment staffed by brothers and sisters." Legacy Place Cottages provide aging members of the faith with a residence to support their physical needs as well as their lifelong spiritual practices. Phase one included a memory care small house and paired assisted living small houses. Each of the paired houses has its own living, dining, and support areas, while sharing services such as the kitchen, spa, and exercise room for operational efficiency. The layout maintains private zones where the residences are located, public zones containing the living, dining, and courtyard spaces, and service zones for deliveries, storage, and staff functions. Private resident spaces include small studios, large

studios, and one-bedroom units that are fully accessible so that residents can remain in their apartments as they age and need additional support. The open great room includes the living room with fireplace, dining room, and kitchen, and is organized to allow daylight to enter the space from both sides. This encourages residents to access the gardens through shaded porches and helps alleviate sundowning issues for residents experiencing dementia since the living spaces remain bright all day. Parlors in each small house provide a flexible space that serves as a quiet den, meeting room, and even an overnight room for guests. Situated in a residential neighborhood, the houses feature Craftsman-style detailing. The memory care small house takes advantage of the site topography with a daylight basement that allows much of the mechanical equipment to be located away from the living areas and easily accessible for service without disrupting residents. The remaining space is currently used for storage with plans and "rough-ins" for a future meeting

and worship space for members of the faith, and especially Legacy Place residents as they age and may have more difficulty getting to off-site locations.

Project Goals

What were the major goals?

- To provide a place for Jehovah's Witness members in the Allentown, Pennsylvania area to reside when they need assisted living or assisted living memory care, but where they will be cared for by, and reside with, members of their own faith (frequently referred to as brothers and sisters), and where they will remain in a familiar and comfortable environment they prefer. This was accomplished by local Jehovah's Witness members spearheading the project and it was designed and built with funds donated by members of the Jehovah's Witness community.

- To create a Jehovah's Witness-style care community similar to those already successfully functioning in Great Britain. This was accomplished by area-based Jehovah's Witnesses leading the effort with guidance from individuals running the original facilities in Great Britain. Funding for this project was exclusively private donations from members of the church.

- To keep a residential scale and feel to the residences. This was accomplished by creating small houses and locating the community in an already established residential neighborhood.

Innovations: What innovations or unique features were incorporated into the design of the project?

As the first Jehovah's Witness senior living homes in the United States, these small houses enable elders from the church to live with and be cared for by brothers and sisters in their faith. Legacy Place Cottages was designed and built with funds

donated by members of the Jehovah's Witness community. Designed to adapt to residents' changing, and likely increasing, care needs as they age, Legacy Place Cottages enables elders to remain in a familiar and comfortable environment. Artwork selections reflect their faith focus and the country kitchens in the assisted living small houses include built-in casework for members to store literature used for door-to-door ministry, daily Bible reading, and worship. Another unique feature of the assisted living small houses is the inclusion of an exercise room to support the needs of these more active and able residents. The small house design is perfectly suited to a residence dedicated to the care of older Jehovah's

Witnesses by members of the faith. The lifestyle of a Jehovah's Witness is different from that of most other religions and members are often uncomfortable within a traditional retirement community setting. Members do not celebrate holidays or birthdays and are ministry-oriented, often holding part-time jobs and spending the remainder of their time on church activities. Most important of all is the support that is provided to ensure each resident has a robust spiritual environment. The small house model reflects the leading-edge design and organizational structure that allows the fully staffed care partners, who are all Jehovah's Witnesses, to be completely engaged with the operation of the house as well as the lives of the residents. A spiritually qualified brother takes the lead in coordinating activities including daily text consideration, weekly family worship night, mid-week field service arrangements, and transportation to all meetings and assemblies. The country kitchens and family-sized tables are used for all meals where staff members and residents dine together. The small houses provide an intentional community that honors autonomy and privacy, as well as fostering opportunities for developing close personal relationships between residents, their families, and staff.

Challenges: What were the greatest design challenges?

Underground stormwater storage tanks are utilized beneath the parking areas and are part of an irrigation system that gradually distributes water back over the site. Another challenge was to locate the small houses in an existing residential community. To alleviate neighbors' concerns about a senior living community being built in their backyard and changing the look and feel of the neighborhood, 3D renderings were employed to show how the small houses would look from neighboring lots. Screening such as landscaping was employed to mitigate the views from neighboring lots. Situating multiple small houses on a tight site in a residential community was also a challenge. The two assisted living small houses were paired together sharing service areas so that they take up less area on the site and reduce costs. This does not diminish the small house concepts because the two assisted living homes still function independently.

Collaboration: How did stakeholders, occupants, the design team, and / or others collaborate during the planning and / or design process?

This project was led by the Jehovah's Witness community who used a similar model in Great Britain as the foundation for bringing this concept to the United States. To meld the programming goals with design concepts and site constraints, a mini design charrette was held, involving the programming / operations consultant, financial consultant, local civil engineer, construction manager, and board members who are all Jehovah's Witnesses. The desired outcome was an intentional care community enabling elderly Jehovah's Witnesses to continue their spiritual routine and live in an environment where their faith practices are understood and supported. The design team worked with the provider and a small house design consultant to define design standards and operational goals, and to incorporate "lessons learned" from existing small houses for Jehovah's Witnesses in Great Britain. The small house principle of allowing universal workers to be completely engaged with the operation of the house as well as the lives of the residents aligns well with the faith-based goals for the residences. The future meeting space in the daylight basement of the memory care small house is envisioned as a resource for residents to continue their spiritual journey as they age and may be unable to travel to an off-site Kingdom Hall.

Green / Sustainable Features: What green / sustainable features had the greatest impact on the project's design?

The key sustainable features are site design considerations, energy efficiency, and maximized daylighting.

Primary motivations: What were the primary motivations for including green / sustainable design features in the project?

The primary motivations were to support the mission of the provider, lower operational costs, and improve the building for occupants.

Jury Comments

The jury felt the Legacy Place Cottages were very nicely planned with well-appointed spaces. There is ample natural light streaming into the common spaces throughout the day. The exterior of the memory care and assisted living cottages create a welcoming street appeal, and the front porches look very inviting. The jury appreciated the paired assisted living houses that allow for efficiencies in food service and delivery of care.

Most rooms in the memory care suites have sightlines to the washrooms from the head of the bed, and the single resident rooms have large windows, making the rooms feel bright and comfortable. The assisted living suites are well appointed with built-in cabinetry. As the open-concept common spaces are clustered at one end of the house, the jury wondered about noise throughout the area. The presentation photos didn't show the ability for the residents to access secure outdoor courtyards.

Opposite top: All assisted living resident rooms are equipped with kitchenettes and space for a small table and chairs so residents can maintain some of their independence and entertain guests in the privacy of their rooms
Opposite bottom: The great room allows daylight to stream into the main living space throughout the day
Photography: Nathan Cox Photography

Wattenbarger Architects

The Plaza at Waikiki

Honolulu, Hawaii // MW Group, Ltd.

Facility type (year of completion): Assisted living; Assisted living—dementia / memory support (2016)
Target market: Middle / upper middle
Site location: Urban

Gross square footage of the new construction involved in the project: 117,548
Provider type: For-profit

Below: Living room
Opposite: The site is located along Ala Wai Canal and Makiki Stream with the entire site raised approximately 42 inches to elevate it out of the flood plain

Overall Project Description

The Plaza at Waikiki was constructed to provide much needed assisted living and memory care support for local residents of Honolulu. While many senior living housing projects on the island focus on the high end of the market, The Plaza at Waikiki was conceived and designed to support middle and upper-middle income residents. The eight-story structure contains 125 assisted living and memory care units, designed to support a total of 153 residents. The project site is only 4 feet above sea level, requiring all parking to be above grade. In addition to the entrance lobby, the first two floors contain parking, mechanical, and back-of-house services. An elevator from the entrance lobby goes directly to the third floor, which contains all of the resident amenities and support functions for the building. Floors four and five are dedicated to serving residents with Alzheimer's and memory care needs. The two memory care neighborhoods are self-contained with their own

dedicated living, dining, and activity spaces, and each floor serves approximately 33 residents. Floors six, seven, eight, and a wing on floor three contain 79 assisted living apartments. The third floor contains an activity room, dining, living room, bistro, theater, and a large exterior lanai.

Project Goals

What were the major goals?

- To design an affordable, attractive, and secure assisted living and memory care community on one of the busiest streets in Honolulu, with one foot on the edge of the most expensive developed land in Honolulu—Waikiki Beach— and the other in a transitional neighborhood still populated by homeless encampments and commercial businesses with bars on the windows.

- To achieve affordability by maximizing density through reducing the living unit size and maximizing common use amenities—

residents want to live there because of the rich community environment; by using a cost-effective structural system—precast concrete frame with proprietary floor support system, which is pre-assembled off site, reducing construction time and cost; by providing a rental model that is affordable for retired teachers, police, state employees, and middle-income seniors.

- To achieve attractiveness by making the building attractive from the inside out as there was no budget for expensive cladding. Precast concrete spandrels and columns and color transitions emphasize modulation within the facade, and limited high-quality materials and elements are at key focal points where they can have the greatest impact. The design maximizes views to Diamond Head, the ocean, mountains, and Ala Wai Canal from living units and common areas. Street-level pedestrian amenities and landscaping is consistent with Waikiki Special District Design Guidelines.

- To achieve security, a landscaped, elevated outdoor amenity above the two-level parking structure includes shade structures, seating, and activity space that can be independently used by residents and has the flexibility for organized activities. The reception is located on the third level, which is accessed via a staffed secure street-level lobby.

Innovations: What innovations or unique features were incorporated into the design of the project?

The Plaza at Waikiki required a number of unique design considerations to accommodate the difficult site, and the need to keep the project affordable. The site is located along Ala Wai Canal and Makiki Stream and has an average elevation of only 4 feet above sea level. Although the first floor is primarily parking, the entire site was raised approximately 3.5 feet to elevate it out of the flood plain. This helped keep costs

Site plan

Above: Shaded pavilion

Photography: David Franzen

down, by avoiding the need for flood insurance and expensive construction requirements at the first floor, and it improved the overall safety of the building. One of the biggest costs associated with the project was the structural system necessary to support an eight-story building. To stay below the high-rise threshold and avoid the cost of implementing the associated requirements, floor-to-floor heights were limited. Given the high cost of post-tensioned concrete construction, a number of alternate structural systems were explored. Ultimately a precast structure integrating proprietary DELTABEAM® was selected. The DELTABEAM® structure, which consist of an inverted steel T, has a thin profile that avoids the loss of floor-to-floor clearance typically encountered with precast inverted "T" construction. The Plaza at Waikiki was one of the first buildings in the United States to use the system. This required significant coordination with the precast designer, DELTABEAM®, and the City of Honolulu to design and validate. Total savings on the structure reduced project costs by approximately $1.5 million, and the system enabled construction to be completed three months earlier than conventional construction, generating additional cash flow, supporting the financial model.

Challenges: What were the greatest design challenges?

The Plaza at Waikiki site is situated 4 feet above sea level and within a flood plain. It was critical to reduce the high cost of flood insurance and to maintain a safe environment. Removing the flood insurance requirement was critical to achieving the project goal of affordability. In order to accomplish this, the site has been raised by approximately 3.5 feet and Letter of Map Revision filed with the Federal Emergency Management Agency (FEMA). Given the height of the building, raising the site by 3.5 feet threatened to push the building into the high-rise category. Cost impacts of high-rise construction would have had a negative impact on the ability to control costs and maintain affordability. Because raising of the site was voluntary and represented a significant life safety improvement, meetings were held with the fire and building departments. The solution implemented the majority of the high-rise provisions that the Honolulu Fire Department felt were most critical to life safety, but which recognized the raising of the adjacent grades for fire truck access, therefore avoiding classification as a high-rise building and realizing significant cost savings.

Collaboration: How did stakeholders, occupants, the design team, and / or others collaborate during the planning and / or design process?

This project is unique in that the owner / operator of the assisted living / memory care community was also the general contractor and the major equity partner in the venture. The architect and owner had collaborated on four previous assisted living / memory care projects and had accumulated a significant amount of data through post-occupancy evaluations. That evidence-based information was used to inform all phases of the project development. In this scenario, function, budget, and affordability were tested throughout the process and the prior 10-year working relationship made it possible for the team to continuously fine-tune the project, which was completed on time and under budget in one of the most volatile and expensive construction environments in the United States.

Outreach: What off-site outreach services are offered to the greater community?

The Plaza at Waikiki participates in the following community outreach events: Honolulu Walks; Children and Youth Day; Senior Fair; Age-Friendly Communities; University of Hawaii; It's Just Aging, an intergenerational collaboration with 'Iolani School for teaching aging sensitivity; National Public Health Week.

Green / Sustainable Features: What green / sustainable features had the greatest impact on the project's design?

The key sustainable features are energy efficiency, water efficiency, and maximized daylighting. Water and electricity are expensive in Hawaii. In addition to energy-saving appliances and low-flow fixtures, The Plaza at Waikiki installed a solar hot water system and photovoltaic panels to significantly reduce energy consumption and operational costs.

Primary motivations: What were the primary motivations for including green / sustainable design features in the project?

The primary motivations were to support the mission / values of the client / provider, make a contribution to the greater community, and to lower operational costs.

Challenges: What challenges did the project face when trying to incorporate green / sustainable design features?

The project made efforts to incorporate sustainable products where possible, but most materials were imported. Availability and cost of products presented a challenge and the project did have to make compromises. The cost of documentation and certification was the biggest barrier to pursuing a formal LEED certification.

Technology: How is innovative / assistive / special technology used by the project to deliver care or services?

The Plaza at Waikiki uses the following systems to enhance care delivery: PointClickCare software for electronic medical records, and Sagely interactive app for organizing activities in the community including taking attendance and linking families to residents.

Jury Comments

The Plaza at Waikiki provides an affordable alternative for retired middle and upper-middle income seniors in a busy urban environment. It is situated between an affluent shopping, dining, and entertainment area and a developing neighborhood across the waterway, providing views of Diamond Head and the Waikiki skyline. Because the site is within a flood plain the designers raised the building 3.5 feet and placed the residential living areas on the third floor over a two-story parking structure, accessed by a secure street-level elevator lobby. This increases the sense of security for residents while also allowing better views.

The interior amenity spaces are light and bright with a simple, modern, but warm aesthetic. The roof terrace is beautifully landscaped and provides ample opportunity for residents to enjoy the outdoors in a comfortable, safe environment. In order to achieve affordability, building costs were controlled by maximizing density and utilizing a thin-profile precast structural system to reduce the building height and save on construction time and cost. The jury agreed that this building met the owner's goals for creating a safe, affordable, urban-living option for seniors.

The Woodlands at John Knox Village

Pompano Beach, Florida // The Woodlands at John Knox Village

Facility type (year of completion): Long-term skilled nursing; Short-term rehabilitation (2016)
Target market: Middle / upper middle
Site location: Urban; greyfield

Gross square footage of the new construction involved in the project: 124,777
Provider type: Faith-based non-profit

Below: Visitors' entrance
Opposite: Community-facing entrance

700

by the open layout of the kitchen, dining, hearth, and sunrooms. The design of The Woodlands was influenced by the modern International Style that draws from the past architectural era of Southeast Florida. A touch of playfulness in the building shape, along with colorful Florida-inspired pastels, help embody the feeling of having fun and being lighthearted. The building's interior continues this theme throughout the space, creating a comfortable, warm, and welcoming place for The Woodlands' residents to call home.

Project Goals

What were the major goals?

- To change the quality of life for the elders in a skilled nursing environment, and to integrate the skilled nursing elders into the community, not relegating them to the back of the campus. The quality of life for John Knox Village skilled nursing elders has been impacted in a dramatic way. Stories have continually emerged about the impact on elders and staff since they moved in. Currently being documented, fulfilled staff and elders are eager to share their stories with others and reinforce the culture being created at John Knox Village. The previous building at John Knox Village was the stereotypical institutional model of care with side-by-side companion rooms, hard sterile surfaces, and loud noises and odors. The community has seen an increase in visitors of family and friends because of the warm and inviting environment. The elders of The Woodlands, once hidden at the back of the campus, now reside in the newest environment on campus with independent and assisted living residents, staff, and visitors interacting in the environment as a part of their daily routine. The community commons floor was provided to offer a second dining venue for the campus as well as multipurpose, therapy, and spa

Overall Project Description

The Woodlands is a new 144-unit seven-story skilled nursing Green House® Project community, nestled into a beautifully wooded site on the John Knox Village campus in Pompano Beach, Florida. Thoughtfully planned to protect elders' privacy, honor their personal choices, and assure their dignity, the design of The Woodlands has eliminated the institutional feel of traditional nursing homes and created a residence, which is the fundamental philosophy of the Green House® Project. The building, one of Florida's first Green House® projects, contains 12 Green House® homes above a unique community commons area on the first floor. Along with the elders of The Woodlands, the main floor serves the needs of all residents of John Knox Village, their visitors, and the John Knox Village staff, providing socialization spaces to the entire community and promoting the idea of "one community sharing life together." The commons area includes the Palm Bistro, Rejuvenation Salon & Spa, Wellness Center,

rehabilitation services, and Life Enrichment Center, reserved for social activities, gatherings, and other events and occasions. The bistro, which caters to health-conscious individuals wanting fresh gourmet salads, soups, sandwiches, and wraps, offers an inviting second dining option for the campus. The building's lobby has two prominent entry points; one along an inviting porte-cochere on the north, and the second at the end of a beautiful, landscaped courtyard to the south. The six upper floors of The Woodlands are home to the skilled nursing Green House® homes. Each floor consists of two homes with 12 elders living in each. The private bedroom suites each contain personal bathrooms, and surround a hearth living room, open kitchen, and dining room. Large windows throughout the homes afford elders with both the physical and mental benefit of visual access to the outdoors. Window configurations vary, and window treatments are thoughtfully customized for the unique rooms in each home. Sunlight filters through the entire home, afforded environments. Interaction with the rest of the community has increased significantly over the old environment. Skilled elders also have access to a higher level of rehabilitative therapy, spa / salon, and fitness environments. Green House® homes' elders are empowered to be independent. Access to the entire home includes outdoor balconies, and more service-related spaces are allowed. This empowerment is enhanced with the ability to frequent the first-floor amenities utilized by the rest of the campus. Smaller environments strengthen the relationship between caregivers, elders, and visitors. The Green House® model epitomizes the goal of resident-centered care.

Innovations: What innovations or unique features were incorporated into the design of the project?

The building's design was influenced by the modern International Style that draws from the past architectural era of Southeast Florida. A touch of playfulness in the building's shapes with colorful Florida-inspired pastels help embody the feeling of playfulness, having fun, and being lighthearted. The building's interiors continue this theme throughout the space. The integration of the community commons on the ground floor promotes the idea of "one community sharing life together." Situated below six floors of skilled nursing residents, the commons were designed for all John Knox Village residents, off-site visitors, and staff. The commons has resort-like amenities consisting of the Palm Bistro, Rejuvenation Salon & Spa, Wellness Center, Life Enrichment Center, and rehabilitation services. Because each resident is unique, diversity in the design of the elder room was important. The solution by the design team was to provide four distinctive window configurations in each home: corner bay window; shared bay window (back-to-back); single bay window; and no bay window with a larger window

instead. This provides an individual private living space worthy of each elder's personality. This also gives the multi-story exterior facade more variety, supporting a look that is less institutional and more residential. Designed with a direct relationship to the outdoors, each home has large floor-to-ceiling windows that look out onto a beautiful, landscaped courtyard and the site's natural asset—the woodland area. Adjacent to the open dining and hearth rooms is a well-positioned screened-in porch that provides the elder an opportunity to experience the sea breezes without having to leave the home. For those with the ability to leave, centralized elevators are positioned for ease and convenience, which connect the residents to the ground floor. From there, the building's featured landscaped courtyard and park-like woodland area are only a few steps away.

Challenges: What were the greatest design challenges?

The design team studied multiple site options on the campus for location of skilled nursing homes while also addressing this initial site. Philosophical discussions about providing care, home, and integration of the skilled nursing elders into the community started to take place with the different sites, setting the stage for discussions about which site best suited the goals and concepts emerging. The site leverages the existing woodland area, as opposed to the master plan, which involved removing all existing trees. The wooded site was a unanimous selection by everyone on campus.

As the first skilled nursing Green House® in Florida, the team developed a strategy to educate and advocate for this new philosophy of care (although Florida had recently adopted nursing regulations that differentiated between traditional and household designs). The design team proactively addressed this with local and state

officials. A two-part presentation addressing the philosophy of care and resultant environments was assembled by the design team and the Green House® organization. The first presentation was to the leadership of the Agency for Health Care Administration in Tallahassee. Plan reviewers, surveyors, and directors received the information in a positive manner and directed the team to present the same information to the staff involved in the project in the Miami office. Local building and fire code officials in Pompano Beach were engaged to discuss aspects of this new model of care. Though this effort was hugely beneficial in getting buy-in from all of the regulatory stakeholders, it did not eliminate all challenges.

Collaboration: How did stakeholders, occupants, the design team, and / or others collaborate during the planning and / or design process?

The design team worked with residents, staff, and board leadership throughout the design and construction process. Residents engaged in bringing the Green House® model to campus and were excited to see the project through to completion, participating in design meetings even after their terms on boards and committees had expired. Campus presentations to residents, family members, and staff not directly involved in the project were conducted to elicit input on current needs and desires, as well as inform about them this new model of care. Collaboration with state and local building officials throughout the design and construction process helped to ensure the design intent was maintained, not allowing the design to regress to what was familiar and comfortable. This collaboration was accomplished through presentations, dialogue, and review processes at every level from senior leadership to front line surveyors and inspectors, which greatly minimized any issues that arose. The Pompano Beach community requires collaboration with their architectural review board, which required multiple design review meetings

to address the community's needs. Collaboration with a neighboring city was also needed to coordinate the efforts of local fire protection agencies in responding to emergencies. This proved to be very challenging since the requirements had not yet been fully defined and required collaboration between mayors of the two cities and their associate staff to address the needs of the elders. The Green House® was a part of the design team at every step, bringing its skills and industry experiences for the team to adapt into the John Knox Village way.

Green / Sustainable Features: What green / sustainable features had the greatest impact on the project's design?

The key sustainable features are site design considerations, improved indoor air quality, and maximized daylighting.

Primary motivations: What were the primary motivations for including green / sustainable design features in the project?

The primary motivations were to support the mission / values of the client / provider, make a contribution to the greater community, and improve the building for occupants.

Challenges: What challenges did the project face when trying to incorporate green / sustainable design features?

The project faced challenges across a number of areas. Civil challenges included the small undeveloped wooded site, erosion control challenges, and stormwater retention. Landscaping challenges were the local landscaping requirement to record tree species and size values for removal, replacement, and retention; extensive native landscaping and integration with site lighting; and irrigation water from non-potable source. Architectural challenges included providing alternative transportation, such as bikes and efficient car parking spaces, on a retirement community

campus; the white TPO roof membrane; creating a recycling area in the building; specifying interior and exterior materials and finishes with recycled content and regional manufacturing; and using low-emitting materials. HVAC challenges consisted of using water-efficient fixtures to reduce potable water use; high-efficiency HVAC units and energy recovery units; occupancy sensors and LED lighting; meter measurement at equipment and electric panels; providing outdoor make-up air and increased ventilation air for high indoor air quality and monitoring of systems; and providing individual light and thermostat controls. Other challenges included waste recycling, IAQ construction methods, designated non-smoking in building, and creating green policies for owner (such as cleaning and pest control). For the team, overall, the challenge was to achieve Innovation in Design credits for various items (as LEED Accredited Professionals). The project achieved LEED Gold.

Top: Reception and lobby
Bottom: Kitchen and dining area for residents to build meaningful relationships
Photography: C.J. Walker Photography, Inc.

Jury Comments

This new multistory addition follows the principles of neighborhood or small house design but in a vertical application. Multiple neighborhoods per floor with easy flow from one to the other allows for both a close-knit neighborhood but also for more interaction between residents from different houses. The placement of amenity spaces on the first floor with a new dining venue will attract residents from other parts of the campus, thereby creating the sense of an internal neighborhood and being inclusive of the entire John Knox Village, breaking down the barriers between old and new.

Hord Coplan Macht

Brightview Bethesda
Bethesda, Maryland // Brightview Senior Living

Facility type (year of completion): Assisted living—dementia / memory support (2019)
Target market: Middle / upper middle
Site location: Urban; greyfield

Gross square footage of the new construction involved in the project: 121,272
Provider type: For-profit

Below: The area is served by a free public circulator bus which, in addition to public transportation, gives senior residents and their families easy access to the community at large

Opposite: The urban site in downtown Bethesda offers a central location with convenient access to public transportation and a variety of community resources

Building massing allows for a number of rooftop lounges and amenities both at the second-floor and eighth-floor levels. The rooftop decks, restaurants, cafes, and gyms on the eighth floor, as well as many apartments will have commanding, uninterrupted panoramic views of both downtown Bethesda and surrounding parks.

Project Goals

What were the major goals?

- The design team was challenged to meet a number of client goals in the implementation of this project. As the first urban, standalone assisted living and memory care community in the owner's portfolio, this eight-story project needed to be a multi-generational, sustainable, accessible, secure senior living community that complemented the vibrant Bethesda Arts & Entertainment District in which it is located.

- Strategically located in Bethesda's Woodmont Triangle, this community was designed to be welcoming to the surrounding community while providing a secure home for seniors. This is achieved by locating amenities such as the coffee shop, salon, and theater at street level, and the dining room, pub, and multipurpose room at roof level. The street-level amenities are open to both the public and residents while the roof-level amenities are more private, yet attractive to family members.

- Located at a transitional location between 17-story high-rise multi-family buildings to the south, and three-story low-rise apartment buildings to the north, the design of the building is boldly contemporary and quietly respectful. The use of metal panels and expansive glazing confirms its urban bona fides, while the careful application of masonry and wood detailing acknowledges its primary function as a homestead. Walking the line

Overall Project Description

The project is strategically located in Bethesda's Woodmont Triangle, an area that is home to a number of exciting multi-family developments, both mid-rise and high-rise, as well as desirable retail, restaurants, and small businesses at the street level, which create a dynamic mixed-use environment. The project will be a vibrant addition to this mix, bringing a multi-generational element to the community. The building was designed to be distinctive among senior living communities and serves as a departure from the traditional design styles predominant among suburban buildings. The site's location in Woodmont Triangle is an amenity it itself. The neighborhood is well known for its excellent restaurants, entertainment, and arts scene. Residents will be surrounded by restaurants, specialty shops, and retail service providers. Grocery stores, a movie theater, library, and more, allow residents to continue an active life as part of their community instead of isolation. Embracing its urban location, the building facades

are designed to be clean and modern with large windows and varying materials, heights, and setbacks. A large-scale art feature spans the height of the building. The street level features commercial retail uses accessible to residents and the general public. This serves to activate the street and further energize the image of Bethesda as an exciting place to live, work, and play. This entry level also provides access to the assisted living community located on the upper levels. Required parking is strategically placed on two levels, out of sight behind and below the street-level retail uses. Community amenities include dining facilities, fitness and multipurpose rooms, and theater. The design creates opportunities for courtyard / patio space to be located on the second-floor roof of the garage below, and at the seventh floor. The second floor features the Wellspring Village® memory care suite, which takes advantage of the roof over the parking garage at the rear of the building to create a secure outdoor courtyard for resident use.

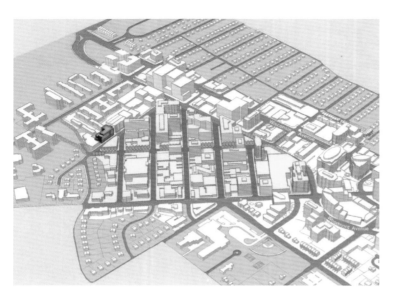

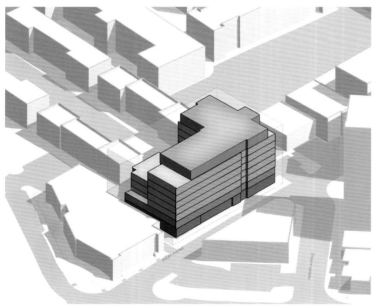

Top: Brightview Bethesdsa is strategically located in Woodmont Triangle, which is home to mid-rise and high-rise multi-family developments as well as retail, restaurant, and small business establishments

Bottom: The location was ideal but the site was limited in size

Opposite: The building facades are designed to be clean and modern with large windows and layered materials, heights, and setbacks

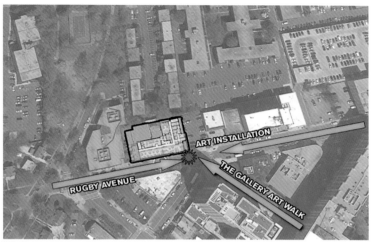

Site plan

RUGBY AVENUE

ART INSTALLATION

THE GALLERY ART WALK

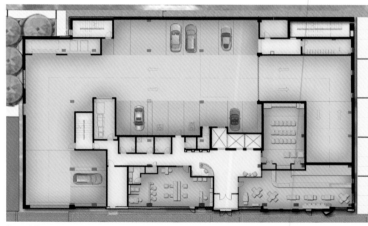

Second-floor plan

Basement plan

Ground-floor plan

between these opposite, yet equally important, characteristics was a challenge met head on by the design team.

- As an important addition to the downtown Bethesda arts and entertainment scene and being located at the pinnacle of an established public art walkway, the owner was determined to incorporate artistic elements into the design and programming of the community, for the mutual benefit of residents, employees, and the general public.

- The owner set a target of LEED Gold to follow up on the success of another project in their portfolio (the first senior living project in Maryland to be awarded LEED Gold status in March 2012). LEED has evolved in the ensuing five years and the owner wanted to make sure their projects were still at the forefront of providing highly sustainable environments for their residents and employees. This project is on track to attain LEED Gold.

- Due to the owner's desire for residents to be able to remain and thrive in their apartments for as long as possible, accessibility requirements were given a very high priority. Fifty-three percent of the apartments and all of the common spaces are designed to be fully accessible. These accessible features were designed to be non-obtrusive, intuitive, and attractive, in order to maintain the homelike ambience of the residence.

Typical floor plan

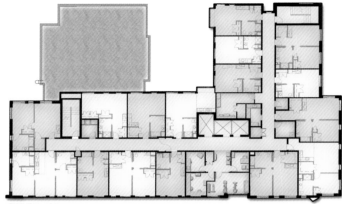

Fifth-floor plan

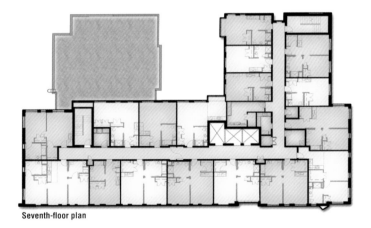

Seventh-floor plan

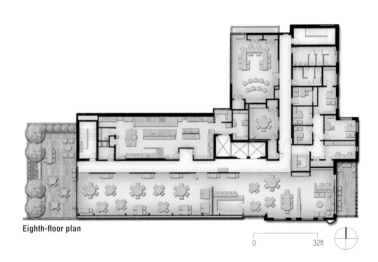

Eighth-floor plan

0   32ft

- The owner's goal is to incorporate the latest wireless technology for safety, security, entertainment, communications, and operations into the design of the project. This allows staff to spend less time performing routine tasks and more time interacting with residents.

Innovations: What innovations or unique features were incorporated into the design of the project?

The architectural design for this eight-story building is inspired by its surroundings and has been thoughtfully conceived to place the varied community uses at their optimum locations. It is envisioned to be distinctive among senior living communities as a departure from the more traditional design styles predominant among suburban and rural communities. The building facades are designed to be clean and modern with large windows and layered materials, heights and setbacks. The massing is carefully articulated to further express the facades in three component parts: base, body, and crown. Elevational features such as smooth masonry, variegated panel finishes, extensive fenestration, and a soaring roof line align the building with the urban context of its neighbors in Woodmont Triangle. The design creates three opportunities for private courtyard and patio areas. One is a secure healing garden for the Wellspring Village® memory care residents on the second floor. The other two are adjacent to the dining room and the pub / lounge on the eighth floor and provide residents with spectacular rooftop views.

The L-shaped plan also allows for multiple gathering spaces and amenities both at the street level and at the eighth floor. The rooftop amenities on the eighth floor, the fitness center on the seventh floor, as well as many apartments have commanding, panoramic views of downtown Bethesda to the south and Battery Lane Urban Park and National Institutes of Health to the north. Inside, the dining room and pub are surrounded with floor-to-ceiling glass and a dramatic, sweeping ceiling that allow residents to enjoy the view at all their meals.

Challenges: What were the greatest design challenges?

This project is located on a very tight 0.48-acre infill site in downtown Bethesda. By comparison, a project for the same owner of similar size and scope was recently completed on a more suburban 6.36-acre site. Challenges included creating a more vertical program that maintained connectivity and efficiency without duplication, while accommodating parking, providing secure and private outdoor areas, maintaining security and a homelike environment, and connecting to the urban arts scene surrounding the project in an interactive, meaningful, and safe way. The building is organized in a way that the Wellspring Garden floor takes advantage of the roof of the parking garage to create an outdoor secure healing garden for residents. This floor houses the memory care residents in a secure yet comfortable setting. The building wraps and surrounds a central healing garden to create a secure outdoor respite. The garden features comfortable senior-friendly seating, carefully selected plants, ample shade, and a soothing water feature. The security enclosure is a custom-designed fence featuring tinted and clear glass panels and trellis work. Security of residents is paramount and is maintained by having a centrally located street-level receptionist who doubles as a concierge and monitors access to the elevators, garage, coffee shop, and spa.

Compared to a typical suburban site where surface parking is the norm, this project incorporates two levels of covered structured parking at street level and below grade. Although this added considerable construction cost, the result is a well-lit, protected, and secure garage for residents and employees, sheltered from the elements. Locating parking within the building provides short and comfortable travel distances for seniors.

By strategically locating those aspects of the owner's program that could be shared with the general public at the street level, the project created opportunities for local small business to be embedded in the community. The coffee shop and salon / spa will prioritize services to residents and also be open to the public. The street-level theater and cafe are optional venues for local film festivals, lectures, poetry readings, and presentations, which are part of the Bethesda Art Walk. These will be highlighted by a custom Vine of Life artwork installed on the building facade and that also serves as a beacon and a marquee for events.

Collaboration: How did stakeholders, occupants, the design team, and / or others collaborate during the planning and / or design process?

The location of the project provided a unique opportunity to highlight the downtown Bethesda Art Walk. In collaboration with local professional artist Sally Comport, the owner commissioned a striking seven-story tall artwork to be installed on the facade of the building at the apex of the Art Walk where it intersects Rugby Avenue. As described by Comport, a translucent tinted, illuminated substrate is overlaid with laser-cut veneer allowing the cut shape to define the image of a deconstructed vine associated with life-affirming growth and seasonal change. A digital display is integrated into the metal cut design.

Right: The rooftop amenities on the eighth floor

Above top and bottom: The dining room and pub / lounge on the eighth floor have commanding, panoramic views of downtown Bethesda to the south and Battery Lane Park and National Institutes of Health to the north
Renderings: courtesy of Hord Coplan Macht

Other collaboration with the local community involves the inclusion of local small businesses, a spa, and coffee shop. These establishments, along with the community theater, open up the possibility of hosting future community events.

Outreach: What off-site outreach services are offered to the greater community?

The project is located in the designated Bethesda Arts & Entertainment District, which hosts cultural events such as film and arts festivals, dance activities, exhibits, block parties, and other events. The project's 75-foot-tall illuminated public art installation is located at the apex of the Bethesda Art Walk, a pedestrianized walkway that features galleries, sculptures, water features, the works of local painters, photographers, and other artists. The area is served by a free public circulator bus, which, in addition to public transportation, gives senior residents and their families easy access to the community at large. The first-floor cafe and theater are designed to provide an attractive venue for poetry readings, book signings, art exhibitions, and music and film presentations, providing residents with opportunities for fine and performing art experiences. The independent first-floor salon and coffee shop also provide opportunities for outreach to support local small businesses that serve as a link to the Woodmont Triangle neighbors and community at large.

Green / Sustainable Features: What green / sustainable features had the greatest impact on the project's design?

The key sustainable features are energy efficiency, improved indoor air quality, and maximized daylighting. Excellent indoor air quality was a priority of the design team to ensure the most comfortable, healthy environment for residents and staff. It has long been a priority of the owner to focus on health and wellness and this project is no exception. Low VOC paints, adhesives, and sealants were selected to help reduce off-gassing of building materials. The building has also been designed to monitor carbon dioxide levels, and plans are in place to maintain air quality during construction. Prior to building occupancy, an air quality test will be performed to check for common pollutants such as particulate matter, volatile organic compounds, and carbon monoxide to ensure the maximum concentrations have not been exceeded. Maximizing daylighting was also a significant driver of the overall building design. More than 77 percent of regularly occupied spaces in the building have access to daylight within an acceptable and comfortable range. The focus was placed on providing adequate daylight in the bedrooms of all residences as well as common spaces, such as the dining room, lounges, activity, and fitness areas, which are all regularly occupied. Access to plentiful natural light has been shown to have a variety of human health benefits, including increased productivity, decreased healing time post-surgery, and improved circadian rhythms. Increased daylighting also reduces energy use from artificial lighting in certain spaces. It has always been a priority of the owner to create energy efficient buildings. This helps reduce building operating costs and the overall energy demand and greenhouse gas emissions. The team selected a very efficient VRF mechanical system designed to be controlled by individual occupants for comfort and efficiency. Careful consideration was taken to choose almost exclusively LED light fixtures and bulbs in both residential and common areas. Excellent materials were selected for the building envelope including insulation and windows.

Primary motivations: What were the primary motivations for including green / sustainable design features in the project?

The primary motivations were to improve the building for occupants, support the mission / values of the client, and lower operational costs.

Challenges: What challenges did the project face when trying to incorporate green / sustainable design features?

The team chose an urban site in downtown Bethesda with the goal of being in a central location with easy access to public transportation and a variety of community resources. The location was ideal, but the site was limited in size. The project team explored creative solutions to incorporate all the desired features of the building. There was very little extra space on site for features such as a courtyard, stormwater management system, and amenity space, which were all important for the community. Having a courtyard with outdoor space for residents was extremely important, so it was added on the second floor instead of the ground-floor level. Stormwater management was also a key design aspect because of the nature of the urban site, so an extensive green roof was added to manage stormwater on site, help reduce heat island-effect and the heating and cooling loads of the building.

Technology: How is innovative / assistive / special technology used by the project to deliver care or services?

Innovative technologies are used to deliver up-to-date, efficient entertainment, security, and services to the residents. In addition to providing Wi-Fi throughout the community, the project is equipped with the Eversound wireless headphone system, designed specifically for senior living. It enables wearers to hear clearly and comfortably, whether or not they have hearing loss, and can connect to any audio source allowing residents to be included and engaged. The community also has an in-house TV channel that broadcasts customized events and information to residents and staff. Other technologies include wireless emergency call systems that interface with the wireless pendants worn by residents; centrally monitored perimeter latches and discreet cameras; LED night-lights, some with sensors, to assist with cueing residents to bathrooms in the memory care apartments; and touch screen tablets for medication and resident care.

Jury Comments

Brightview Bethesda is a distinctively designed senior living community in Woodmont Triangle, with a conscientious departure from the traditional senior housing design styles. There are many elements in this project that the jury found noteworthy. The project approach includes significant enhancements to the community, residents' families, and, of course, the residents. Public art installation on the facade and an engaged streetscape are clearly elements that go above and beyond the required programming for a traditional senior housing project. The street-level amenities engage the community with a very prominent cafe and salon. Multiple programmed spaces scattered vertically in the building create variety in social venues and take full advantage of the city views. The top-floor terrace offers more private amenities, including a gathering space, dining room, and outdoor patio that has spectacular panoramic views.

The jury saw this bold departure as a commitment to the community, and an investment in the larger arts district of this rich urban environment within which the community resides. The connection to the community is not only physical as demonstrated in a pedestrian walkway but includes cultural events organized by the residents such as film festivals, block parties, and other events.

Memory care is positioned over the podium taking advantage of outdoor space created by the garage structure below. The L-shaped plan of the assisted living floors provide for views and plentiful natural light.

c.c. hodgson architectural group

The Seasons at Alexandria
Alexandria, Kentucky // Baptist Life Communities

Facility type (year of completion): Assisted living—dementia / memory support; Skilled nursing—dementia / memory support; Long-term skilled nursing; Short-term rehabilitation (2018)
Target market: Middle / upper middle
Site location: Suburban; greenfield

Gross square footage of the new construction involved in the project: 152,605
Provider type: Faith-based non-profit

Below: Central chapel courtyard
Opposite: Concept sketch

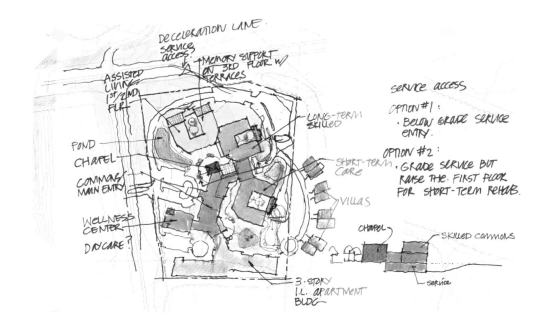

The following handwritten labels appear on the sketch:

DECELERATION LANE
SERVICE ACCESS
ASSISTED LIVING 1ST/2ND FLR
MEMORY SUPPORT ON 3RD FLOOR W/ TERRACES
LONG-TERM SKILLED
POND
CHAPEL
COMMONS MAIN ENTRY
SHORT-TERM CARE
WELLNESS CENTER
DAYCARE?
VILLAS
3-STORY I.L. APARTMENT BLDG

service access
OPTION #1:
• BELOW GRADE SERVICE ENTRY.
OPTION #2:
• GRADE SERVICE BUT RAISE THE FIRST FLOOR FOR SHORT-TERM REHAB.

CHAPEL
SKILLED COMMONS
service

Overall Project Description

Baptist Life Communities is a provider of senior housing in Northern Kentucky that offers a continuum of care at four locations, including the Convalescent Center building in Newport, which is 60-plus years old. The Seasons at Alexandria will be a replacement for this old center and is currently under construction on a new site in Alexandria, Kentucky. The beds from the old center will be transferred to the new site. The scope of the project includes 50 personal care assisted living suites, 16 personal care / memory care suites, 38 short-term rehabilitation beds, 48 skilled beds, 30 skilled memory care beds, and one skilled observation bed. The amenity spaces include a great room, living, dining, and kitchen in each of the eight households, a central living room on each of the personal care floors, a personal care dining room and community room, a complete physical and occupational therapy rehabilitation center including a residential suite for training, a beauty salon, and a welcome center.

Administrative functions are grouped in an office suite on the ground floor, with other support staff offices on the second floor. A second phase of the development is a chapel / conferencing center, wellness center, and an independent living apartment building with commons / amenity spaces. The site is located at the intersection of AA Highway and the U.S. Route 27 connector and slopes from north to south. The site parti is a hillside town designed to look like a "collection" of buildings grouped around a central plaza anchored by the chapel building. The collection of buildings is seen as the site is approached from the northern highway Turning south to the main driveway, the plaza and several more building forms add to the "grouping," as would have occurred over time. The "outdoor room" created by the plaza gives the sense of having arrived at the center of this hillside town. The buildings are tethered together with a C-shaped circulation path designed as a single-loaded corridor that forms the edge of the plaza, allowing the circulation

path to always have natural light and views to the plaza in one direction and the courtyards in the other direction. This circulation spine also provides the foyer entry point into each of the various households. This ground-floor public traffic is separated from the service traffic on the second floor, which is where the central kitchen and laundry are located. From the service entry at grade, a service elevator is used to access the kitchen as well as provide other service functions. The food service circulation comes out of the second-floor kitchen, travels through the single-loaded corridor to the household elevators and then distributes down to the first floor, including service to the serving kitchen at the personal care dining room. The future phases will tie into this circulation pattern providing connectivity throughout all of the buildings of the "town."

Project Goals

What were the major goals?

• To learn from two recurring themes that emerged from a visioning workshop conducted as a kick-off for the project: "unique" and "state of the art." State of the art implies current state. It is a slice through the current state of what is happening in senior living, and it can be trend driven. The visioning workshop discussion can be categorized with four concepts, or goals, which crystalized into a statement of what The Seasons at Alexandria is: "A special place," "Engaging programs," "Alive community spirit," "Origin in faithfulness." A strategies matrix was developed early on in the charrette that captured how "unique" and "state of the art" translated into design criteria to achieve the concept goals. "A special place" focuses on the design challenge of place making and creating a special place. "Engaging program" focuses on the unique elements of the households. "Alive community spirit" and

Site plan

"Origin in faithfulness" further describe the design criteria to achieve uniqueness as well as meet challenges.

- To utilize the Integrated Project Delivery (IPD) system. One tool in this process was for the development team, including the owner, to develop a values matrix (in an A3 format) that captured and defined measurements of value. This became the guiding tool in decision-making through the implementation phases.

Innovations: What innovations or unique features were incorporated into the design of the project?

Since this project is a replacement of an old dysfunctional convalescent home, the staff and board approached the project with the philosophy that the visioning of the project must be rooted in innovation and uniqueness. The client group was used to struggling in a non-supportive environment and at first had difficulty envisioning an ideal environment that would support innovation. This was the start of the culture change journey for the client. Since

they were creating an entirely new building, everything about it was unique: moving from an institutional medical model building to purpose-built household models; moving from a central nurse station configuration to a residential great room plan; moving from a non-descript urban site with no sense of arrival to a community designed with place-making principles; and moving from a community room-turned-chapel for services to a purpose-built chapel that anchors the plaza and marks the sense of arrival. In order to support the culture change process and infuse the design process with collaborative consensus building, a two-day charrette process built upon the visioning statement. The charrette process serves as a way of quickly generating potential design solutions while engaging the interests of a diverse group of client representatives such as staff, board members, community members, and residents as appropriate. It involved six architects, 18 staff, two board members, three consultants, and five community leaders including the Mayor of Alexandria. The format of the charrette directly related to the visioning workshop, which resulted in the following visioning statement: The Seasons at Alexandria is a special place with engaging programs and an alive community spirit with its origin in faithfulness. While the replacement and enhancement of the existing Convalescent Center (phase one) was the initial driver of the project, the design program addressed in the charrette included future phases for independent living and associated common areas. The potential for portions of future phases to be located on adjacent land was also considered.

Challenges: What were the greatest design challenges?

There were two major challenges for the project: the site and the culture change journey for the client and architect. The approximately 11-acre site was ideally located from an accessibility and market standpoint since it was at the intersection of a key highway and local connector. But none of the context of the area surrounding the site contributed to its attractiveness from a design viewpoint. The "aha moment" came with realizing the design driver would be creating a community, essentially creating a place, a town, a special place—as the visioning statement would articulate. The challenge was to apply place-making principles to the development of the design.

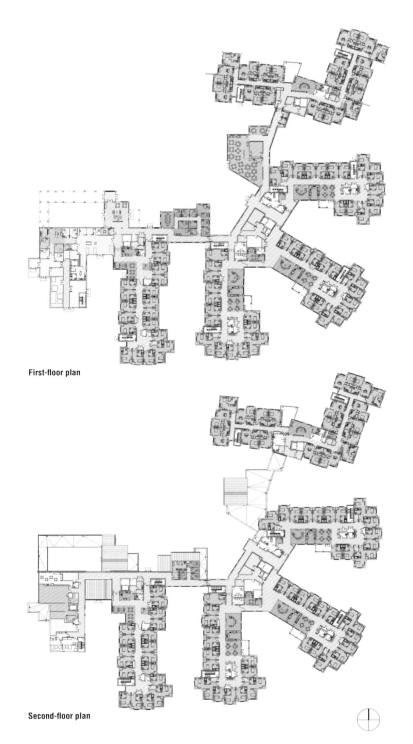

First-floor plan

Building services
Building utility and services
Circulation
Living spaces
Resident services
Resident suite

Second-floor plan

Above: Massing refinement sketch
Opposite: Chapel view

The strategies matrix focused a section on addressing how to translate place-making principles into the design of the project. Since the client was used to operating in a dysfunctional old building, the leap to a new way of doing things, which entailed a great deal of change, was a major culture change process. The workbook *A Tale of Transformation: Four Stages to Tell the Story* by LaVrene Norton of Action Pact was used. The development team viewed the video to kick off their culture change journey. They have continued to move through a process of bi-weekly "transition planning" during the construction of the project in order to prepare for creating the new culture and implementing it when they move into the new building. For the architect, engaging in the IPD process was a culture change process in itself. The "throw-it-over-the-wall" design approach of design / engineering / construction specialists and sub-consultants working in isolation from each other is the common way of being trained.

The architect talking to sub-contractors, or the owner communicating directly with the contractor rather than through the architect, are engrained in the standard AIA documents. Breaking out of the isolated, adversarial, lack-of-trust mentality is a culture change. It requires training of team members to engage in this different delivery method. Training was conducted in target-value design, lean construction techniques and tools, multiple A3 problem-solving sessions, engaging in study action teams, and continually conducting retrospectives throughout the process.

Collaboration: How did stakeholders, occupants, the design team, and / or others collaborate during the planning and / or design process?

The collaboration during the project is highly unique because the team used an IPD method that combines ideas from integrated practice, lean construction, and target-value design, along with powerful collaboration tools such as Building Information Modeling (BIM) and cloud

technology. While IPD is more commonly used in large-scale institutional projects, it is unique to the senior living design practice. A multi-party agreement is used in IPD in which primary team members include the architect, engineers, key technical consultants, general contractor, key subcontractors, and owner. An IPD system seeks to align interests, objectives, and practices through a team-based approach in a process where all disciplines in a construction project work essentially as one firm. Rather than each participant focusing exclusively on their part of construction without considering the implications on the whole process, the IPD method brings all participants together early with collaborative incentives to maximize value for the owner. This collaborative approach allows informed decision-making early in the project where the most value can be created. This IPD process was particularly important in The Seasons at Alexandria because of the tight financial and budget parameters,

Left: Building exterior
Above: Dining room

plus the unusual aspect of beginning a Life Plan Community with the health care component. Every team member worked hard to develop the trust and commitment within the team throughout the various IPD training sessions. They had to stretch their collective creativity as the project ran into many rocks in the road that at times seemed insurmountable. But on the day of ground breaking, the team agreed that they wouldn't have gotten to this day if not for using an IPD process that created a climate of trust and commitment that motivated the team to work collaboratively to make The Seasons at Alexandria happen.

Green / Sustainable Features: What green / sustainable features had the greatest impact on the project's design?

The key sustainable features are energy efficiency, improved indoor air quality, and maximized daylighting.

Primary motivations: What were the primary motivations for including green / sustainable design features in the project?

The primary motivations were to support the mission / values of the client / provider, lower operational costs, and improve the building for occupants.

Technology: How is innovative / assistive / special technology used by the project to deliver care or services?

Within an IPD mode, a fully integrated BIM model has been developed to benefit potential construction conflicts, streamline construction sequencing and staging, improve safety, and simulate and analyze the building and its systems. This included the low-voltage systems typically relied on for patient monitoring and care programs. This virtual design provides new benefits every day, allowing owners and clinical staff to virtually visit each space while still in the design development phase. This allows for course correction and tweaking of the final layout to maximize the resident and staff experience. With a robust IT infrastructure, campus-wide Wi-Fi, and a deployed PointClickCare electronic medical records, The Seasons at Alexandria is on the cutting edge of resident-centered care technologies and positioned to adapt to changing software and hardware challenges emerging in today's industry.

Jury Comments

This new campus design for The Seasons at Alexandria reflects excellent massing, use of the site, and compact relationships between the community elements. The jury was impressed with the values-based and methodical process that guided the ultimate design of this community. That process led to the Italian-village inspiration for the design. The resulting clustering of the buildings ties the community elements together in thoughtful, creative, and efficient ways. Outdoor spaces are created by the building locations. There is abundant natural light within the living areas. The current trends in household design are evident and thoughtfully applied.

The central chapel courtyard serves as a focal point, for it emphasizes the faith-based mission of this community, and ultimately ties the project together. This is a strong example of a successful collaborative planning process with a well-executed design outcome.

Opposite left: Design inspiration
Opposite right: Village green model
Above: Central courtyard model

Renderings: courtesy of c.c. hodgson architectural group

c.c. hodgson architectural group

EmpathiCare Village
Miami, Florida // Miami Jewish Health

Facility type (year of completion): Skilled nursing—dementia / memory support (2020)
Target market: Middle / upper middle
Site location: Urban

Gross square footage of the new construction involved in the project: 265,932
Provider type: Faith-based non-profit

Below: Aerial view

Overall Project Description

In 2015 Miami Jewish Health celebrated its Diamond Jubilee 75th anniversary serving Miami and the region in providing quality senior living options along with a variety of community care services. Miami Jewish Health is now moving forward with its vision for the next 75 years and beyond. This vision includes a new master plan for the Miami campus that will incorporate several phases of new construction, allowing the organization to continue enhancing and growing its ability to provide high-quality residential options for all levels of senior care along with community outreach programs. These new facilities and campus plan will enhance Miami Jewish Health's ability to provide top-quality services to the greater Miami area, as well as amplify its role in the region as a leader in gerontological services and research. The new master plan is based upon providing key additions to the campus and repurposing and improving the existing buildings and open landscape areas that make up the fabric of the campus. One major goal is to enhance the ambience of the overall campus by reducing surface parking and providing more decked parking. This will allow the addition of more lush, green, open spaces and extend the beauty of the existing open courtyards in the north side of the campus to the south areas that are currently occupied by surface parking. The first phase of construction is planned for EmpathiCare Village, a new memory care center that will provide a revolutionary approach to resident care, making the campus a leader in this critical field of service. The design approach creates a secured "village," designed to provide neighborhood residential settings along with a variety of amenities for residents that emphasize the rhythms of daily living and familiar settings. Programmatically, EmpathiCare Village consists of residential households, cultural and therapeutic wellness spaces, offices for administration, and a research institute. In addition, a three-level parking structure replaces the current parking on the site. This approach will provide residents with a full range of stimulating indoor and outdoor experiences and options that are much more similar to a residential or hospitality lifestyle versus a hospital-like environment.

Project Goals

What were the major goals?

- To create a strong future for Miami Jewish Health that aligns with the current and future needs of the residents and patients its serves and establishes the vision for the next 75 years. This was achieved through an intensive collaborative process with senior administration and staff to redefine the essence of Miami Jewish Health moving into its next 75 years of service. Through an intensive charrette process and working with memory care specialists, the vision for the initial phase of the master plan was to create EmpathiCare Village. This visionary concept for memory care in a holistic setting provides household living within a context of interior and exterior support spaces that reaffirm therapeutic patterns of daily living. The second phase of the master plan includes creating the Miami Jewish Health Institute for Gerontological Studies. Future phases include a year-round indoor garden atrium and a hotel to support the Institute and guests receiving treatment at Miami Jewish Health.

- To master plan the main Miami campus, which is the traditional home of Miami Jewish Health, in a way that maximizes the strengths of the existing campus while providing new and cutting-edge services for the people it serves. This was addressed by building on and maximizing the charms and strengths of the original elements of the campus. Seventy-five years ago, the Douglas Family Estate was donated to establish Miami Jewish Home.

The original home and gardens were more than 100 years old, and the original elements of the campus became the centerpiece of the central courtyard around which the campus grew. Over time, however, expansion and the demand for parking changed the feeling of the outer portions of the campus as surface parking lots dominated. The master plan is designed to recapture and extend the ambience of the original campus through the addition of parking decks that allow for the creation of new internal courtyards, including the EmpathiCare Village central court, bringing the lush garden landscape theme back to the overall campus.

- To provide, in the initial phase of development, a level of memory care second to none in both the care model and the architecture to support and augment that care model. This involves the realization of the EmpathiCare Village concept. The overarching theme is to provide a secure, therapeutic environment for residents with dementia by creating a secured "village." The residential households surround individualized courtyard spaces emphasizing the indoor / outdoor therapeutic connections by providing cultural, social, and therapeutic wellness spaces. This stimulating yet secure environment encourages more natural patterns of daily living for residents, their families, and caregivers as they move throughout the day from the households to the various amenities.

Innovations: What innovations or unique features were incorporated into the design of the project?

The most unique feature is the translation of the vision of a new and innovative concept in providing memory care. While there have been previous models that have sought to provide some memory care amenities using visual and architectural cues, such as the Hogeweyk community in Holland, EmpathiCare Village provides a much richer program of therapeutic

Ground-floor plan

opportunities in a more authentic environment. Programs ranging from dance and music therapy in the theater, visual arts programs and gallery spaces, gardening and pet therapy, and brain gym activities are provided in settings that correlate to storefronts and shops that one would encounter in daily life. The cafe and common house are additional examples of the social interaction opportunities the village affords as well. Opportunities for interaction with family members, staff, and visitors in a safe and supportive secure environment can lead to a much richer experience for residents where there is a world of possibilities beyond being only in their room or the shared great room of each household, like so many memory care facilities are limited to today. Another innovative design feature is the careful and elaborate separation of the service areas and the resident areas. Service corridors are hidden and all material movement including food, supplies, and trash occur behind the scenes making for a much calmer, quieter, and positive resident, family, and staff experience.

Challenges: What were the greatest design challenges?

One of the major design challenges was to provide all the elements that are part of the vision of EmpathiCare Village within the overall campus in a way that achieved the proper balance of security, privacy, and user integration. EmpathiCare Village had to provide the shared amenities that the entire population of the campus can take advantage of, while providing a secure environment, as well as replacing the surface parking necessary to make the project viable. The balancing of all these constraints was achieved by composing the architecture and entry sequences to provide a series of paths of secure movement from parking deck, new entry drop-off courtyard, and entry pavilion connected to the rest of the campus. This system, plus the servicing through the parking deck and into the hidden service corridors, was a complex design challenge that called for a clarity of diagramming and ultimately an architectural sequence that wove all the various complex circulation demands together. A second challenge was to create a secure environment for EmpathiCare Village (and the rest of the campus), while satisfying the urban design goals of making the campus a more appealing neighbor to the surrounding community. Over time, the campus had grown within a continually evolving urban neighborhood. In order to remain secure, a series of perimeter walls were constructed to contain the surface parking lots. In the new master plan approach, the design vision was to minimize the perimeter walls and utilize the buildings and perimeter park areas to create a more positive street environment all around the campus. For Miami Jewish Health and the City of Miami, this approach is a win-win as security is maintained but a more positive urban streetscape is achieved.

Collaboration: How did stakeholders, occupants, the design team, and / or others collaborate during the planning and / or design process?

The design process for the project was and continues to be extremely collaborative and interactive. The process began with a series of meetings with senior administration and staff to get to the heart of the vision of the institution moving forward and to establish the goals for the master plan of the campus and the initial phases of implementation. The group of design professionals, senior administration, and staff formulated the essence of a new care model for the organization, creating the EmpathiCare model and shepherding all design decisions to support it. The next steps included a two-day charrette bringing together all stakeholders, including administration, staff, residents, and family members, along with the design team, to define the goals and programs of the future of the organization and formulate the strategy to create the buildings' components and typologies to implement the vision. The iterative design continues through the master planning and formulation of the special area plan submitted to the City of Miami and to the design of EmpathiCare Village.

Outreach: What off-site outreach services are offered to the greater community?

Miami Jewish Health is a major provider of outreach services to the local community. Its traditional main campus includes a PACE (Program of All Inclusive Care for the Elderly) center that provides social and medical services to the surrounding local community. The Rosomoff Pain Center provides pain therapy to patients from all over the world. The main campus also provides a variety of educational and wellness support programs for area residents. These and other outreach programs serve more than 200 local residents in the immediate surrounding neighborhoods each month.

Green / Sustainable Features: What green / sustainable features had the greatest impact on the project's design?

The key sustainable features are site design considerations, energy efficiency, and rideshare, such as carpooling and Zipcars.

Primary motivations: What were the primary motivations for including green / sustainable design features in the project?

The primary motivations were to support the mission / values of the client / provider and of the design team, and to make a contribution to the greater community.

Jury Comments

As part of a larger senior living community and health center, this new assisted living / memory support addition follows the principles of neighborhood or small house design. The neighborhoods, while separate from each other, have shared central back-of-house spaces and exterior garden spaces. Even the upper floor neighborhoods can access the garden space. The location on the campus, although remote, has a connection to community-wide amenity spaces and health center, thus creating the sense of being inclusive of the entire community and breaking down the barriers between old and new.

Top and bottom: Courtyard
Renderings: courtesy of c.c. hodgson architectural group

Hord Coplan Macht

Frasier Meadows Retirement Community Independent Living Additions and Renovations

Boulder, Colorado // Frasier Meadows

Facility type (year of completion): Independent Living (2019)
Target market: Middle / upper middle
Site location: Suburban
Gross square footage of the new construction involved in the project: 250,715 (13,555 addition)

Gross square footage of the new renovation / modernization involved in the project: 41,370
Provider type: Faith-based non-profit

Below: The new independent living building occupies the northeast corner of the campus adjacent to a major arterial road into downtown Boulder
Opposite: Front entry

Overall Project Description

Located within the small city of Boulder, Colorado, this retirement community's identity is informed and given shape by the front range of the Rocky Mountains that rise a few miles west of campus. The well-known Flatirons peak formation dominates the view in that direction. The culture of the area combines the rough-hewn virtues of a healthy outdoor life, the benefits of a university town, and a progressive social and environmental outlook. The community was originally opened in 1960 as a single, large, five-story bar running north / south. The campus has been built out over 50 years in a number of styles. Along with the physical campus, the spirit of the community has developed over the years as well, embracing the ambience of the healthy Boulder lifestyle. Residents are physically, intellectually, and socially active, and are accustomed to involvement in campus decision-making. A devastating flood damaged more than 50 percent of the campus

in 2013, but without fatalities. However, a large one-story assisted living building was a complete loss. The current project includes a new 98-unit five-story apartment building on the site of the damaged assisted living building, a renovation and addition to the independent living commons, and a renovation and addition to the Wellness Center. There is also a fifth-story Sky Lounge being renovated.

The project is intended to restore community income to pre-flood levels by adding up-to-date independent living apartments to make up inventory losses from unit combination over the years. Dining is upgraded to multiple venues and multipurpose space accommodates large and small gatherings and programs. New opportunities for community outreach include performances, an expanded clinic, and an upgrade of the wellness program to current best standards, including replacing the small existing swimming pool. Leveraging the work being done in multiple

locations on campus, the project creates more coherence in the building's exterior and interior, particularly at the main entrance and the east Foothills Parkway side of campus. The project also addresses the concerns and needs of the current residents as expressed by a number of special resident committees. An updated visual brand will exemplify the unique values of the community and city, and the owner's goal is to achieve LEED Gold certification and to become the first senior living community to receive WELL Building certification.

Project Goals

What were the major goals?

- To develop an architectural vocabulary that resonated with the values and culture of the community and Boulder at large. This vocabulary had to be able to harmonize with the architecture of the original 1960 building while providing more character and visual appeal. The final design vocabulary mixes mid-century modern with the more natural materials and detailed compositions of Prairie style. Flat roofs minimize height and substantial overhangs reduce solar gain. The walls are clad mainly in locally manufactured brick or the local sandstone of the Flatirons. The owner felt that the simplicity of the basic geometry related best to the underlying frontier flavor of Boulder. The design was well received by the city as a suitable approach to building materials and composition in the area.

- To fit the 98 large independent living apartments on the former assisted living site without encroaching on the central green space or impacting the surrounding neighborhoods of Boulder more than necessary. The need to raise the first habitable floor above the flood plain and strict city height limits, measured from below the elevation of the lowest floor, dictated that four occupiable floors could be achieved only if the floor-to-floor heights were

10 feet 3 inches. The large units required full 9-foot-high ceilings in the main spaces to be competitive in the local market. The extremely tight floor / ceiling assembly was achieved by using long-span composite concrete decks for the floors bearing on the corridor walls and exterior walls. This also allowed for flexibility in unit customization and future reconfiguration because no bearing walls or shear walls occur within the individual units' perimeter. HVAC was carefully coordinated with dropped ceiling zones in secondary unit spaces. Ventilation and exhaust was all run vertically. The ceiling of the parking garage needed to be fully insulated because the flood plain regulations dictated

that the garage be completely open. Various strategies were developed to ensure that the waste piping coming from the building above was held as tight to the ceiling as possible.

Innovations: What innovations or unique features were incorporated into the design of the project?

This will be the first retirement community to seek certification from the WELL Building program. The owner chose to be the pilot project for applying WELL Building to senior living because the certification aligns very well with the values of the Boulder area. This program is relatively new and similar in approach to LEED certification, however, rather than sustainability it measures

the building's direct effect on the health and welfare of the occupants. WELL Building gives the project access to evidence-based design recommendations for issues that have previously been decided primarily by intuition and assumptions. WELL Building certification promotes a model of wellness that is holistic, in accordance with the latest understanding of the connections between mind and body, healthy diet, cognition, and so on. Its requirements are very detailed and measurable, based on current scientific studies and the work of a dedicated research lab associated with the WELL Building program. WELL Building has influenced the design of this project in diverse ways, in many instances serving to validate the instincts of the architect or owner. For example, WELL Building awards points for the provision of high-quality views and easy access to nature. The size and proportions of the independent living porches was affected by WELL Building values, allowing more extensive use of the porches for outdoor living.

Challenges: What were the greatest design challenges?

One of the challenges was leveraging the new construction and renovation to create a more unified and coherent appearance for the campus as a whole. Given that less than 20 percent of the campus building mass will be included in the project, this goal focused on the two most prominent areas of the community: the main entrance on the west side of the community, and the east edge of campus bordering Foothills Parkway, a major arterial leading into downtown Boulder. Because the taller existing independent living buildings are mainly aligned along the west side of campus, the new five-story independent living building will dominate the east side of campus. This new building will become the face of the community most often seen by the general public as they drive along Foothills Parkway. The goal of appearance unification is therefore easy

to achieve on the east side. At the main entrance, this goal is more difficult to achieve. While the commons area around the main entrance is included in the project, it sits in front of the much taller and longer mass of the original 1960 portion of the building. This building is well maintained but is a bland example of 1950s International Style design. The solution to the main entrance is based on using the simple wall of the existing building as a neutral background. The renovated commons block and new arts and education addition were designed to be more articulated and sculptural. The effect was heightened by a minimal connection vertically down from the renovated Sky Lounge on axis with the new main entrance, making the new style of the addition and renovations vertically bracket the mass of the 1960 building.

Another challenge was to respect the view of the Flatirons and enhance the campus's relationship with the peak formation. The view is a defining aspect of Boulder and this campus has one of the better vantage points. A number of straightforward strategies were employed at the commons renovation and addition. Because it is located on the west side of campus, it has an unrestricted view. Existing walls were opened up to be mainly glass, and the entry sequence was completely reoriented to directly face and focus on the mountains. The new independent living building is located on the east side of campus, however. The mountains are so large that they can be seen over the existing independent living building unless you are close to the building's east face, but a conventional double-loaded-corridor apartment building would have a large minority of apartments facing east. Also, a conventional layout would create a huge wall between the existing single-family homes east of Foothills Parkway, completely blocking their view. The building was therefore arranged as three east / west bars disconnected above the first floor.

All but the lowest, most westerly apartments can see the mountains clearly from porches rotated towards the view. The neighbors have views between the three towers rather than a totally obstructing wall of building.

Collaboration: How did stakeholders, occupants, the design team, and / or others collaborate during the planning and / or design process?

The culture of the Boulder area values inclusiveness and community-based decision-making. This led to the inclusion of several residents as permanent members of the design team, attending all design meetings. A significant number of resident committees addressed various design issues and reported to the design team at intervals, and the design team also reported on progress during monthly meetings open to all residents.

Outreach: What off-site outreach services are offered to the greater community?

To date, the community's outreach has consisted of semi-regular events to which the public was invited, and various classes that included some non-resident guests. Once the current project is complete, the owner plans to expand and regularize outreach. This includes establishing a membership outreach program that allows non-resident area seniors to take regular advantage of some of the amenities such as wellness, classes, and spa services; serving both resident and non-resident seniors in the enlarged clinic; and expanding the range of potential offerings that will be open to the public in the new multipurpose space. In partnership with local service providers, the owner will establish a home care service that helps ensure non-residents released from the community's short-term rehabilitation have proper follow up and aid in completing their healing at home. Participation numbers are not yet available for the initiatives, but a main goal of the programs is to promote significant and regular community integration.

Technology: How is innovative / assistive / special technology used by the project to deliver care or service?

Drone technology was employed to allow future residents to understand the view from their future apartments. WELL Building certification was pursued to incorporate evidence-based design features to enhance wellness.

Jury Comments

The new independent living addition to the 1960s campus brings the varied architectural styles into a more cohesive whole. The buildings are designed to take full advantage of the views toward the mountains to the West, with almost every unit afforded a view. The new outdoor dining terrace is a nice addition providing social space with access to views and bringing daylight into the interior. The mountain views are also important to the town of Boulder and the building design was modified to accommodate interior-view corridors of nearby residences.

The jury appreciated the more intuitive entry sequence and that the design of the new building raised the residential portions above the 100-year-old flood plain, avoiding the possibility of future damage by placing them above a new open-air parking garage. The daylight brought into the multipurpose room through clerestory windows is a nice feature not often found in similar large multi-use spaces. The jury agreed that the new wellness center is the centerpiece of the expansion and supports the community's focus on health and well-being. Being the first senior living community to participate in the WELL Building program underscores Frasier Meadows' commitment to the physical, mental, and cognitive health of its residents.

Opposite top: Front entry
Opposite bottom: Dining terrace
Renderings: courtesy of Hord Coplan Macht

Perkins Eastman

Shenyang Senior Living
Shenyang, China

Facility type (year of completion): Assisted living; Assisted living—dementia / memory support; Hospice; Long-term skilled nursing; Skilled nursing—dementia / memory support (2020)
Target market: Middle / upper middle
Site location: Urban; greyfield

Gross square footage of the new construction involved in the project: 1,598,000
Provider type: For-profit

Below: Shenyang Senior Living is centered within a vibrant mixed-use development offering aging adults a lively and diverse intergenerational community
Opposite: The entrance to the Life Plan Community embraces the traditional layout of the Chinese home in which the entry sequence creates layers of space

Overall Project Description

According to the United Nations, China's population is aging more rapidly than almost any other country in recent history. The U.N. predicts the population aged 65 years and older will increase from 100 million in 2007 to more than 350 million by 2050. According to Richard Jackson in "The Aging of China" (2010), growth in China's senior population is occurring at a time of rapid increase in urbanization and industrialization, which have weakened the traditional family support network. Additionally, the one-child policy, low mortality rates, and increases to modern health care contribute to the growing senior population and their needs. The government is keenly aware of this population's challenges and has charged developers to address the aging population by creating new housing options for seniors mainly in urban environments.

Shenyang Senior Living is a result of this change and is sponsored by a Chinese utility company.

Shenyang is the capital and largest city in China's northeast Liaoning province. To address the growing number of seniors within this region, the cultural need for intergenerational connectivity, and the shift to urban environments, Shenyang Senior Living is centered within a vibrant mixed-use development offering aging adults a lively and diverse community. The project is on 37-plus acres of land and incorporates nearly 1,600,000 square feet, and the site design links the project to the city's adjacent park system. The program consists of a Life Plan Community featuring 316 independent living residences; 204 residences for assisted living, memory support, skilled care, rehabilitation, hospice, and community club house; 938 active adult residences; 250 market-rate housing apartments; a K–12 school with daycare; retail, mixed-use, and medical office areas. The retail, mixed-use, school, and daycare enhance the new internal community and offer amenities to the greater adjacent community.

Project Goals

What were the major goals?

From the beginning of the design process, three main goals are woven into the design: connecting people, connecting nature, and connecting culture.

- To create a diverse intergenerational community, the design connects the site to the city's adjacent park system, providing residents from within the community and adjacent neighborhood the ability to connect. Amenities within the park are enhanced and new amenities are incorporated into the project. Programmatically, varied housing types (senior living, active adult, and market rate) further encourage intergenerational connectivity. The housing is collaged into neighborhoods with varied amenities and programs providing unique destinations. Retail, office, medical, and a school with daycare offer community resources within close proximity to the Life Plan Community. The school with daycare is adjacent to the community and physically linked to encourage connectivity.

- The Chinese symbol for long life represents connection to the elements found in nature and a sustainable lifestyle. This symbolic meaning is emulated throughout the site and building design. The landscape and amenities within the adjacent park are woven into the site plan resulting in a series of pocket parks hosting various activities and breaking down the scale of the large site. The design within these pocket parks echoes programs, native landscape, and water features found in the park system. Sustainable balance occurs with limiting the amount of paved surface by providing pervious paving systems and by locating most parking underground. Within the building design, spaces have visual and physical connectivity to the outdoors. Patterns and materials found in nature are incorporated

within the architecture and interior design. Biophilic design principles were introduced and embraced as a standard and directive for design and sustainability. Within the senior living community four distinct private gardens are woven into the site: a wellness garden, recreation garden, meditation garden, and traditional Chinese garden. Additionally, an enclosed four-season garden becomes the heart of the seniors community offering outdoor enjoyment throughout the year with lush landscape and koi pond.

• China is changing and developing quickly, and while new traditions are born, ties to traditional cultural activities and events remain important. The site design provides spaces for traditional outdoor markets, exercise and dance, tai chi, performances, holiday gatherings and parades, and socialization. Program spaces are purposefully located to promote passive and active interaction between people, culture, and nature. Within the Life Plan Community, the entrance embraces the traditional layout of the Chinese home in which the entry sequence creates layers of space. The gateway leads to the ceremonial forecourt, entry pavilion, and grand hall. The four-season garden, tea room, wellness center, card rooms, Chinese buffet dining, and karaoke room embrace the lifestyle. Special attention was given to provide large enough spaces indoor and outdoor to accommodate Chinese New Year events and traditions, along with other holiday functions. Each apartment unit faces south following building codes, cultural expectations, and feng shui principles. A feng shui master provided detailed design requirements for the apartments and club center layouts.

Innovations: What innovations or unique features were incorporated into the design of the project?

Typically, developments in China are monster blocks of sameness with little differentiation between buildings and outdoor space. Breaking the scale of the development into a collection of neighborhoods provides uniqueness and a sense of place within a very large development. The development is divided into three neighborhoods: market-rate housing with commercial, retail, and a K–12 school; active adult housing with commercial, retail, and designated medical office space; and senior living community with club center, independent living, assisted living, memory support, and skilled care. Within the senior living neighborhood, the design provides distinct identities for each component of the continuum. Variation of building massing and heights brings distinctive character to the urban community, while providing visual differentiation between market, active adult, and independent and assisted living. A family of cohesive materials is used throughout the site to further articulate each building's distinctive character.

Challenges: What were the greatest design challenges?

Local Chinese codes and requirements push the design direction toward a layout that has little or no variation and variety. These codes and requirements include challenging allowable area requirements, south exposure requirements, specific clearance and firetruck access and turning radius, sun and shade studies, and large parking counts. Most codes in China have not identified senior housing as a building type. The success of the site design was to develop and create a sense of place addressing the scale of the site and the size of the buildings. This is accomplished by creatively placing the buildings to meet sun study requirements and create pocket parks that assist in breaking down the scale of the development.

Collaboration: How did stakeholders, occupants, the design team, and / or others collaborate during the planning and / or design process?

The development team consisted of a 60 / 40 split of a Chinese utility company and a privately owned Japanese development, management, and investment group. Regularly scheduled meetings in Northern China, with all parties present, assisted in moving the project along. Additional meetings also occurred in Japan to understand their management and operational style for delivering care. The design team consisted of domestic and international planning, architecture, interior design, and landscape team members based in the United States and China. Additionally, local design institutes were included to provide architecture, interior design, MEPFP, structural, landscape, and civil services. A feng shui consultant was also part of the team. Communication was key to the success of the project to date. Collaborative work sessions between all team members in China and the U.S. were conducted at in-person meetings as well as via WebEx. BIM software offered ease of coordination between team members.

Jury Comments

Shenyang Senior Living is a mega-scale master planned senior living community to address the growing population in China. Despite the proposed community of more than one million square feet, the design team maintained its focus on sensitive, design principles: connecting people, connecting to nature, and connecting culture. Respect for the Chinese culture is evident in the entry of the community with the traditional arrival sequence through the organization of spaces, and the scale of the forecourt, entry pavilion, and grand hall. The garden room becomes an essential common gathering space that will serve the residents throughout the year. The double-height space connects various programmed amenities to one another visually and creates to link to the outdoors.

The master plan organizes the various resident types and levels of care to create overlapping neighborhoods that relate to three distinct user groups. These different resident populations converge, making places for natural

intergenerational experiences. The market-rate housing is positioned on the edge closest to the public areas and retail spaces. The active adult housing is in a more private location. The senior living levels of care are positioned within the community with a sense of security. The active adult towers are designed to maximize precious daylight. The assisted living towers are designed to adapt, allowing flexibility and aging in place. In this instance, studios are designed to be combined to meet the changing market demands.

Opposite: Chinese senior resident dining is quickly evolving from the traditional practice of cooking at home to a mix of dining practices that include communal dining

Opposite: A four-season enclosed garden becomes the heart of the community, offering outdoor enjoyment throughout the year with landscape features and traditional Koi pond

Renderings: courtesy of Perkins Eastman

The Trousdale Assisted Living and Memory Care

Burlingame, California // Peninsula Health Care District

Facility type (year of completion): Assisted living—dementia / memory support (2018)
Target market: Middle
Site location: Suburban; brownfield

Gross square footage of the new construction involved in the project: 139,209
Provider type: Non-sectarian non-profit

Below: Trousdale has a mix of stucco and wood-veneer paneling on the exterior

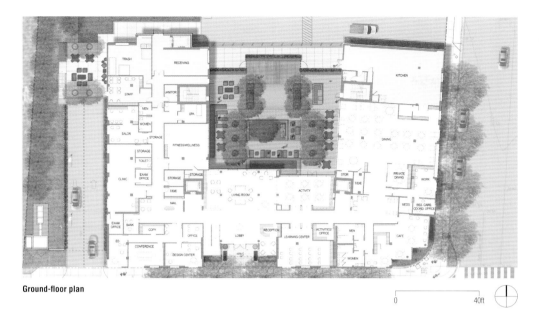

Ground-floor plan

0   40ft

Overall Project Description

Peninsula Health Care District (PHCD) Trousdale provides a model for accessibility and patient-centric care that all health care districts strive for when serving aging populations. Health care districts such as PHCD are public entities that provide community-based health care services to residents in their jurisdiction. As a part of this responsibility, the Trousdale project was undertaken by PHCD to address the growing need for quality care among the aging population of San Mateo County. Located at the corner of two prominent thoroughfares in Burlingame, California, this assisted living and memory care facility is designed to be flexible, contextual, vibrant, and focused on the local community. The six-story residence comprises 101 assisted living and 24 memory care units designed to give the district and Eskaton, its operator, the ability to change the unit mix based on future market demand. To invest in the well-being of PHCD Trousdale residents, the facility employs various design elements that provide a connection to the greater PHCD community. These amenities include a community room, learning center, multiple dining venues, cafe, wellness center, clinics, and activity rooms. The assisted living and memory care units are designed with large picture windows and balconies, blurring borders between the facility and surrounding site to build on and connect residents to the landscape. These windows provide views into a large courtyard with a built-in barbecue, water feature, wellness area, and dog run bringing activity into the center of the facility. To accommodate memory care residents, the urban context dictated that those programs be placed on an upper floor with their own large terrace, limited corridors, and many open common spaces.

Project Goals

What were the major goals?

- PHCD Trousdale is designed to be flexible and community oriented, and to achieve a contemporary / residential feel while meeting Eskaton's "livable design standards."

- To execute Eskaton's desired flexibility, PHCD Trousdale is designed with a unit mix that changes over time. All of the unit plans are designed to be combined in different variations. For example, two studios can become a one-bedroom, or a studio and one-bedroom can be combined to form a two-bedroom and vice versa. Each floor is designed with a modular layout that can flex between assisted living and memory care with minor renovation. This level of flexibility means that Trousdale can adapt to various market demands and increase accessibility by providing better rates for residents. The entire ground floor is programmed as a common space that is designed to adapt to various programmatic needs including hosting events. Building a connection to its surroundings, a ground-level wall of transparent glass blurs the divide between inside and out, creating visibility from the interior to the landscaped courtyard. The building also includes a learning center and cafe open to the greater community.

- Located in a rapidly growing area with new housing development, the design team worked to create a modern and contemporary look that maintains a residential feel. A mix of materials on the exterior, including stucco and wood-veneer paneling, bring a refined tone to the facade while protruding sunshades and overhangs add additional functionality and accent the design direction.

- These design goals were met to achieve Eskaton's Livable Design Seal of Approval program. This program is available to signify the excellence in adaptability required for a facility to provide long-lasting value to its residents. Although this program is traditionally only available to home builders and residents of single-family homes, this was the first time it was applied to a purpose-built senior living community.

Below: Ground-floor common spaces are designed to be transparent so the community can see through to the internal courtyard
Right: The cafe sits at the prominent corner of the site and will be a beacon for the community
Renderings: courtesy of SmithGroupJJR

Innovations: What innovations or unique features were incorporated into the design of the project?

Serving the San Mateo community, PHCD Trousdale incorporates numerous flexible design innovations that meet Trousdale's programmatic needs now and into the future. Both the unit mix and the function by floor provide adaptability. With its various floor plan configurations, the project unit count can accommodate from 92 to 136 units. This stand-out feature required careful mechanical and plumbing planning. The team was able to solve this with stubbed-out plumbing so that modifying units is merely cosmetic and requires no mechanical labor. The project was expanded to meet the maximum unit count of 136 units even though it will open with 125 units. In addition to unit plan flexibility, each floor is designed with a modular layout that can flex between assisted living and memory care with minor renovation. Demolishing six assisted living units will convert a floor to memory care; likewise adding in walls for those units on a memory care floor converts it to assisted living. The flexibility of PHCD Trousdale's design understands and adapts to the ever-changing, ever-aging health care market offering PHCD Trousdale and its residents the space they need to thrive.

Challenges: What were the greatest design challenges?

The greatest design challenge stemmed from the City of Burlingame's planning code. It required that 60 percent of the building's street frontage have zero setback, meaning it had to go up to the sidewalk. There was little opportunity for massing changes on the facade, protrusions such as overhangs and sunshades were not possible, and there was limited room for planting. To overcome this, the design team worked with the City to lessen those requirements when possible and designed a new facade that was exactly

60 percent to the lot line. One other design challenge was implementing the below-grade parking. Having below-grade parking meant that the parking and all of the structure attached had to line up with the spaces and units above. In addition, the surrounding seismic zone meant that there was a large amount of shear walls at the building perimeter, further limiting massing changes and openings at the facades.

Collaboration: How did stakeholders, occupants, the design team, and / or others collaborate during the planning and / or design process?

Due to the planning code challenges, the planning and design process was highly collaborative between the owner (PHCD), the operator (Eskaton), the City of Burlingame planning department, and the design team. The entire team worked with the City early on to push the boundaries of the 0-foot lot-line setback. After much discussion between all parties, the City agreed to allow protruding sunshades over the lot line as long as they were demountable. These changes to the code smoothed out the design process and lead to a better building as a result.

Green / Sustainable Features: What green / sustainable features had the greatest impact on the project's design?

The key sustainable features are energy efficiency, water efficiency, and maximized daylighting.

Primary motivations: What were the primary motivations for including green / sustainable design features in the project?

The primary motivations were to support the mission / values of the client / provider and of the design team, and to make a contribution to the greater community.

Technology: How is innovative / assistive / special technology used by the project to deliver care or services?

PHCD Trousdale uses an innovative lighting system to improve patient comfort. The lighting system is designed to integrate "responsive light bulbs." These tunable light bulbs communicate wirelessly and can be controlled by iPhone or iPad to adjust a room's color temperature. These responsive light bulbs learn a patient's living habits over time and adjust to align with a patient's circadian rhythm. The lighting system is also capable of responding to its environment, automatically dimming and brightening according to the natural light in a room. Early studies show this system may help residents fall asleep faster and reduce daytime drowsiness.

Jury Comments

The jury appreciated that the Trousdale Assisted Living and Memory Care project was aiming to serve the low- to middle-income aging population of San Mateo County on this tight urban site. The community-based health center on the ground floor serves the residents throughout their neighborhood. The jury was also interested in the flexible construction design that allows for changing suite configurations with minimal disruption and renovation. The exterior of the building blends in well with the local community and looks like other apartment buildings in the surrounding area. The 24-resident memory care house uses a niche in the building to create a secure outdoor patio to encourage residents' independence; the jury did not know how much the balconies in some of the suites would get used. The cafe on the corner of the property is a nice addition that invites the neighbors in.

CJMW Architecture

Well-Spring Resident Activity Center + Expansion

Greensboro, North Carolina // Well-Spring Retirement Community

Facility type (year of completion): Independent Living (2018)
Target market: Middle / upper middle
Site location: Suburban; greenfield
Gross square footage of the new construction involved in the project: 27,260 (27,474 addition)

Gross square footage of the renovation / modernization involved in the project: 34,800
Provider type: Non-sectarian non-profit

Below: Aerial view of the Well-Spring campus
Opposite: The exterior facades of dining (right) and resident activity center (left) merge and complement existing campus architecture

Overall Project Description

Well-Spring, a single-site Life Plan Community, started out like many communities 25 years ago with relatively modest common areas, including a small multipurpose room, single dining room, very small bar, and arts and crafts room. Well-Spring has experienced significant growth in its independent living population in recent years and felt it was time for a major upgrade of community amenities. An extraordinary component of this expansion is a 338-seat auditorium designed specifically for seniors. Instead of the typical flat-floor multipurpose room, Well-Spring wanted a space where all members of the audience would be able to see and hear as well as possible, and with the ambience of a high-quality performing arts venue. This will be a space where residents can participate in and attend educational talks, performances, resident / staff meetings, and more. The theater can accommodate up to 63 wheelchairs. Acoustics and systems were

specially designed to suit this population and its needs. Another key part of the project is re-envisioning the community's dining services. Where before there was one traditional dining room with wait service, Well-Spring will now add a bistro with open kitchen and a market-stall service approach for casual dining. The bar will be relocated and expanded to bring people out of their rooms and into a more sociable environment. Site considerations dictated the theater be located on the same level as the primary dining and commons areas, leaving space below for resident activities, including art studios and a woodworking shop. Because the theater will draw people from within the Well-Spring community as well as those outside it, a new entrance / drop-off point, as well as parking will be added as part of the project. The scope includes only the dining renovation, new resident activity center, new entry, and drive. No other common spaces are affected, and no living spaces were part of this project.

Project Goals

What were the major goals?

- To provide an arts and activity center for Well-Spring to be used for multiple purposes such as music, drama, digital projection, musical theatre, dance, and lectures. The venue needs to be high quality in order to fulfill Well-Spring's vision of the center as a community gathering and event spot. It needs to be suited for a senior population, both in terms of acoustics and mobility / access, as well as to a non-senior population. The architect, drawing on previous experience designing performing arts venues, gathered a design team that included acousticians and theater design consultants and engineers, all of whom had previously collaborated on multiple arts projects. The team's collective knowledge formed a base for additional study and research to investigate issues such as how to best address the acoustic needs of seniors, what is the right slope given multiple mobility levels, and the number of wheelchairs that can fit into a 338-seat theater. While the true test will come once the project is completed and in use, significant study went into its design.

- To focus on the common areas and dining. Previously, the common areas were divided and compact, with little clear space for flow or movement. Places where residents could gather were few and finding areas for internal or external functions, including memorial services, was difficult. Commons spaces were more distinct and single purpose (for example, the bar area was a small and separated room, and dining areas were closed in with walls) so residents tended to pass through corridors, from point to point at specific times and for specific reasons. Many of the existing corridors were narrow and did not function well when used by people with a range of mobilities.

The addition of the resident activity center and the need to connect it to the main commons areas, as well as the addition of a new covered drop-off / entry at the front of the new addition provided an opportunity to improve flow and resolve space problems. With numerous people needing to move through the same space on a variety of pathways, the design team studied numerous options, ultimately designating the central open space as a "landing spot" and providing lounge and casual seating where people can stop and linger, chat, or reorient themselves once the group has gathered. From this point, residents can filter into the dining area, follow a generously wide corridor

(approximately 11 feet) to the resident activity center, stop into the newly expanded and relocated bar, or cross a bridge to go directly to independent living.

Innovations: What innovations or unique features were incorporated into the design of the project?

Overall, the concept of this type of theater / assembly space is a new one for Life Plan Communities. The design is unique in its attention to mobility, sight lines, acoustics, and sound systems for a senior population. The design team—all experienced in designing spaces for performing arts—had to approach the design of this space with new eyes and new ways of thinking in order to tune it to this specific population.

For example, HVAC supply air in most assembly spaces comes from the ceiling, however, ceiling supply can create uncomfortable drafts and contribute to background noise—both problematic for a senior population. To avoid these problems the team designed a plenum supply system in which a concrete box below the seating serves as a gigantic duct into which conditioned air is introduced at a low velocity. Under each seat, a 6-inch vent allows the air to slowly seep out, avoiding both noise and drafts. Acoustics and hearing are also a major focus in the design of the dining spaces, with sound-absorbing finishes and a loop system under the floor in the large "special occasions" section of the bistro (a room designed for meetings and special events with up to 70 people attending).

Challenges: What were the greatest design challenges?

The first challenge was to provide a great view of the stage from every seat while accommodating many seniors with mobility limitations. Using 3D modeling and specialty software to evaluate sight lines, the team tested multiple options, varying seating locations, slope, aisle lengths, number of fixed versus semi-fixed versus wheelchair seats, as well as considering exit points, stage access, and mobility considerations. The team also incorporated input from Well-Spring leadership and staff throughout the study period. Ultimately, the plan includes 26 non-fixed seats, 20 semi-fixed seats, and another 17 fixed seats that can be removed easily for wheelchair access. The slope and placement of wheelchair spots provide clear sight lines for those in wheelchairs as well as those sitting around and behind them. The second challenge was to create a logical sequence and series of spaces to organize people coming from multiple directions into the new dining spaces and auditorium. To facilitate flow through the common area and into the resident activity center, the team studied multiple options for connecting the center to the existing building. Placing the center atop a ridge and at the end of the existing building provided an opportunity to reconfigure the central spaces on the main level. Existing corridors were narrow and much of the traffic was dependent on a grand stair coming up from the lower floor. Corridors are strategically expanded, a bridge will connect directly across the atrium to other second-floor spaces, and several new pre-function areas where groups can gather and rest before or after events are carved out. A third challenge was to design the acoustics and sound system of the auditorium for an audience that includes many members with hearing impairments. Normally in such a venue, the room would be tuned to be multipurpose, with variable acoustics to allow different types of uses / events while maintaining good acoustic quality. In designing the acoustics for this specific population, however, the team had to take into account that not only will most users have some type of impairment, but that the level of impairment will vary widely. The room includes a hearing loop in the floor that broadcasts a signal directly to modern-day hearing aids. For those people who are hearing-impaired but do not use a hearing aid, or those who have hearing aids but do not use the loop system, the space was made to be acoustically absorptive, minimizing reverberation that would interfere with speech intelligibility. The room was also designed to eliminate distracting background noise from HVAC systems and outside noise. This strategy is designed to make the amplified sound system function as well as possible for a broad range of users.

Collaboration: How did stakeholders, occupants, the design team, and / or others collaborate during the planning and / or design process?

Well-Spring put together a small, focused resident committee including people with performance and / or performance management experience or with construction expertise. The design team met with this committee at the outset of the project and key decisions were vetted by the committee throughout the design process. In addition, the design team worked extensively with staff to determine critical design factors. For example, in considering options for slope / non-sloped floor and the degree of any slope, staff told the design team that a majority of residents are able to walk up and down handicapped ramps but not steeper slopes. The team therefore knew a sloped floor was possible but that the slope would have to conform to that of a handicapped ramp (1:12) versus the steeper slope (1:8) allowable by code in assembly spaces. Dining chairs can often become a lightning rod for residents who dislike change, so the interior design team developed efficient and effective ways to involve the residents in the selection so that people feel they have had a voice in the process. For this project, the team sourced samples of the chairs under consideration and brought the truck load (literally) to the community. The chairs were left for several days for people to test and residents filled out response cards on which they could simply circle options as well as write more detailed comments. One fascinating finding was that while in current interior design (especially in hospitality) using multiple fabrics on one chair is considered a luxurious, upscale look, to many residents who remembered the Great Depression and the following years, it was a reminder of not having enough money to recover the entire chair in the same fabric at once.

Outreach: What off-site outreach services are offered to the greater community?

Well-Spring views the theater as an opportunity to engage with the community by hosting lectures, musical events, plays, and so on. It will increase opportunities for Well-Spring residents to connect with staff and students from the local university as well as with the larger community outside Well-Spring. Well-Spring plans to host educational programs that appeal both to residents and the larger community, providing intellectual stimulation.

Jury Comments

A thoughtful addition to a successful existing campus, the Well-Spring resident activity center and dining expansion brings an important connection with the outside community as well as exciting new social options for residents. These new dining and pub venues, purposefully situated around the main entry, provide an authentic pretheater experience for residents and their families, as well as encouraging engagement with off-campus friends and visitors. The design of the theater reflects diligent study of the needs of seniors allowing them to easily negotiate the space and enjoy musical or theatrical performance. Not only are the aisles short and wide for ease of circulation, there is plenty of open seating to accommodate wheelchairs and assistive devices. The low-slope ramps make all parts of the theater, including the stage, accessible to patrons or performers who are mobility challenged.

In addition to accessibility, considerations were made to improve the experience for those with hearing impairments through an induction hearing loop installed around the perimeter of the room. Specialty lighting was designed to provide floor-illuminating fixtures in circulation paths to aid mobility for residents with visual challenges. Spaces were also created below the performance hall to support the performing and visual arts with practice rooms and an art studio. The jury felt that this addition was worthy of note because it promotes social interaction for residents and engagement with the overall community in a state-of-the-art space designed specifically to serve the needs of older adults.

Opposite top: The bistro design opens up resident choices for dining
Opposite bottom: The Special Occasions room is designed to function as a dining destination and fill an upscale need on campus, as well as serve community meetings and celebrations
Renderings: courtesy of CJMW Architecture

Design for Aging
Knowledge Community

DFAR14 INSIGHTS AND INNOVATIONS // STUDENT DESIGN AWARDS // ROB MAYER: A LOOK BACK

DFAR14 Insights and Innovations

By Emily Chmielewski, Perkins Eastman Research

About the Design Competition and Insights Study

In 2017, the American Institute of Architects Design for Aging (DFA) Knowledge Community conducted its 14th biennial Design for Aging Review design competition (DFAR14). In total, there were 53 submissions; the jury recognized 25 of these for an award or publication. Six projects received an award of Merit; five projects received Special Recognition; and 14 projects were recognized for publication within this book.

Projects submitted to DFAR14 and recognized by the jury include:

Merit projects:
- Brightview Bethesda
- North Ridge at Tacoma Lutheran
- Rose Villa Pocket Neighborhoods & Main Street
- The Cottage at Cypress Cove
- The Seasons at Alexandria
- The Summit at Rockwood South Hill

Special Recognition projects:
- Abiitan Mill City
- Caleb Hitchcock Memory Care Neighborhood at Duncaster Retirement Community
- Elm Place
- Fountainview at Gonda Westside
- Linden Park Apartments

Published projects:
- Babcock Health Care Center
- Cuthbertson Village Town Center Renovation
- Edenwald Café
- EmpathiCare Village
- Frasier Meadows Retirement Community Independent Living Additions and Renovations
- Goodwin House Alexandria
- Hillcrest Country Estates
- Legacy Place Cottages
- Shenyang Senior Living
- The Burnham Family Memory Care Residence at Avery Heights
- The Plaza at Waikiki
- The Trousdale Assisted Living and Memory Care
- The Woodlands at John Knox Village
- Well-Spring Resident Activity Center + Expansion

The data collected through the DFAR14 design competition adds to the information gathered by the 13 previous cycles conducted since 1992. This report, DFAR14 Insights and Innovations Study, provides a more comprehensive look at statistics, patterns, and concepts impacting the senior living industry and design community. Summarized in this chapter, the study's findings reflect the changing demands and emerging concepts shaping today's senior living industry.

The Insights Study also supports the American Institute of Architects' goal of promoting best practices by going beyond typical post-occupancy evaluations that focus on one building or design concept. By analyzing data from the 53 design competition submissions, this study investigates many sites across the nation and multiple design objectives, thereby presenting a more thorough explanation of state-of-the-art design solutions to help designers and providers improve the quality of design and the industry as a whole.

In addition to identifying best practices and emerging ideas in senior living, the Insights Study provides a benchmark from leading-edge design solutions to help designers and providers "raise the bar" on the quality of design provided to the industry. The study also enhances the awards process by describing what about the 25 jury-recognized submissions makes them unique and what can be learned about the state of the industry, now and as we look to the future.

To share the insights learned from the study, this chapter is organized into four sections. First, "Insights and Innovations" highlights interesting findings from the analysis of the DFAR14 submissions. Next, graphic summaries in the "Project Statistics" section report basic project information about the submissions. The "About the Jury-Recognized Projects" section provides an overview of the applicants' narratives about what was critical to their project's success, a breakdown of amenity spaces, and summaries of applicants' self-described challenges and innovations. The final section, "Project Themes," conveys the most common themes expressed in the jury-recognized entries. Starting with the most prevalent, each theme is reviewed and then illustrated by "In Their Own Words" select excerpts from the submissions, which highlight how the related projects address the common theme. Throughout this report, comparisons to previous design competitions (DFARs 9, 10, 11, 12, and 13) are provided, when possible.

Insights and Innovations

Analysis of the DFAR14 submissions revealed several interesting things about today's senior living industry, which may add to the forecasts of the trends for tomorrow. Reviewing the charts created for the "Project Statistics" section of this report reveals there were more for-profit providers than in years past, and that projects' target markets are now more likely to be geared toward middle / upper-middle income than upper income. More suburban, and fewer rural sites, were submitted this year. The average number of parking spaces per resident was less for both urban and suburban projects. There were more new construction projects compared to the last cycle, and more greenfield project sites. In terms of resident payments, there was more private pay and less Medicaid / Medicare payments.

There were smaller residential unit sizes across most of the care-level / facility types. The submitted Independent Living projects had fewer studio units and more one-bedrooms, whereas Assisted Living projects reported more studios and fewer one-bedrooms. Residential units in Long-Term Skilled Nursing and Short-Term Rehab projects were almost exclusively private rooms.

In the "Project Themes" section of this report, several new themes were described by the jury-recognized DFAR14 submissions: homelike environments; addressing the current market / repositioning to be competitive; designing for flexibility and aging in place; and a focus on wellness / active living. In addition, several projects noted their use of biophilic design principles, as described in the theme of Connection to Nature. This theme saw a significant increase, from 76% of DFAR13 jury-recognized projects to 92% in DFAR14, and included such features as access to outdoor spaces, extensive daylighting, and views.

The theme of promotion of sense of community also saw a significant increase, from 31% in DFAR13 to 52% in DFAR14. This is indicative of the industry—and indeed the world's—increased focus on the impact of social isolation,

as evidenced by the U.K.'s recent appointment of a Minister for Loneliness.[1] In addition to site-specific relationships, the jury-recognized DFAR14 submissions continue to create connections to the greater neighborhood, including being within walking distance to public transit and / or public services and amenities, or providing outreach services to members of the greater community. Some facilities / campuses even open their doors to the greater neighborhood, allowing the public to access their amenities and services.

The common themes analysis further found a shift in design layout and aesthetics. An evaluation of the DFAR14 jury-recognized projects' Household floor plans revealed more layouts with defined public-to-private hierarchies, with 53% of the DFAR14 floor plans arranging resident rooms away from common areas (compared to 35% in DFAR13), as opposed to ringing around the common areas. In terms of aesthetics, the jury-recognized projects maintained the trend of approximately 70% being classified as having a contemporary style, both inside and out. The remaining 30% were categorized as having a mixed style, incorporating both contemporary and traditional design elements, with DFAR14 being the first cycle to have no projects classified as solely traditional in style.

Another insight from the DFAR14 analysis echoed findings in the DFAR13 analysis: There is still a disconnect between green motivations and impactful green features (refer to the charts in the "Project Themes" section on Ecological Sustainability). The analysis showed a major reason for a project to be green is to improve building occupants' health / well-being, with 50% of the DFAR14 jury-recognized submissions indicating this as one of their top three motivators. However, contrary to this, improving indoor air quality is still being reported as having a relatively low impact, at only 29% (a marginal increase from 26% in DFAR13). These two statistics seem out of line with one another considering the major effect indoor air quality has on seniors' health.[2] If occupant health / well-being is a strong motivator for being green, then senior living projects ought to pay more attention to improving indoor air quality for building occupants.

There is also a disparity in the number of projects that self-report having ecologically sustainable features (96% of the DFAR14 jury-recognized projects) versus the 28% that actually discussed this concept within the submission narratives (less than DFAR13's 38%). An increase was seen, however, in the number of jury-recognized projects that are or are registered to be certified as ecologically sustainable by an independent organization (e.g., LEED, WELL Building), with DFAR14 at 32% compared to DFAR13 at 26%.

The content throughout this report, in addition to the above insights, should enable you to make more informed decisions, explore new innovations, and feel inspired. From benchmarking against the industry statistics presented herein to understanding the common themes and trends, this report can help you with your next senior living project.

Project Statistics

The application form for DFAR14 consisted of two parts: an initial entry form completed by all applicants, and a secondary form distributed only to those the jury recognized. Accordingly, some of the following charts are derived from data from all 53 projects submitted to DFAR14, whereas others include data only from the 25 jury-recognized projects. Each chart notes the data set used for analysis. This differs from previous cycles in which the data presented herein from five previous design competition cycles (DFARs 9, 10, 11, 12, and 13) was derived from all of the projects submitted to the DFAR competition, unless otherwise indicated.

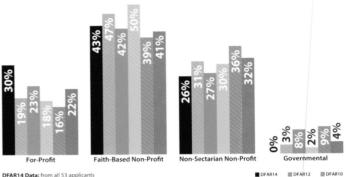

Provider Type

DFAR14 Data: from all 53 applicants

■ DFAR14 ■ DFAR12 ■ DFAR10
■ DFAR13 ■ DFAR11 ■ DFAR9

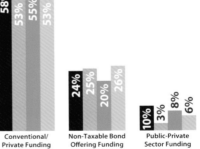

Average Funding Sources

DFAR14 Data: from the 25 jury-recognized projects only

■ DFAR14 ■ DFAR12
■ DFAR13 ■ DFAR11

Target Market

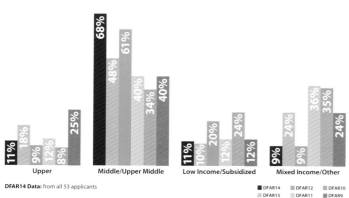

DFAR14 Data: from all 53 applicants

■ DFAR14 ■ DFAR12 ■ DFAR10
■ DFAR13 ■ DFAR11 ■ DFAR9

Site Location

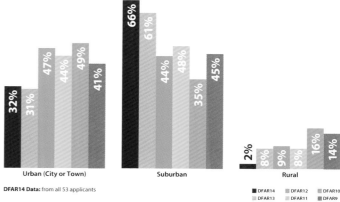

DFAR14 Data: from all 53 applicants

■ DFAR14 ■ DFAR12 ■ DFAR10
■ DFAR13 ■ DFAR11 ■ DFAR9

LPC/Part of a LPC

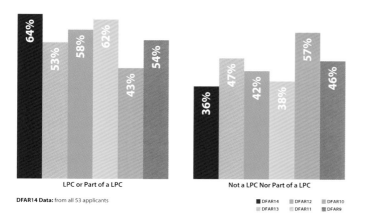

DFAR14 Data: from all 53 applicants

■ DFAR14 ■ DFAR12 ■ DFAR10
■ DFAR13 ■ DFAR11 ■ DFAR9

Average Number of Parking Spaces Per Resident, by Site Location

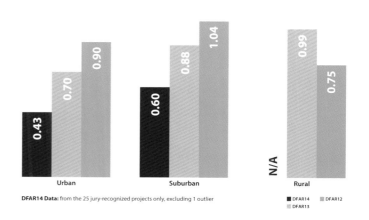

DFAR14 Data: from the 25 jury-recognized projects only, excluding 1 outlier

■ DFAR14 ■ DFAR12
■ DFAR13

Facility Types

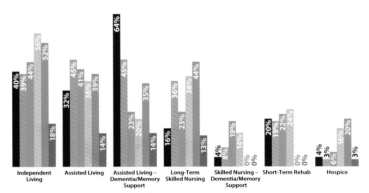

	Independent Living	Assisted Living	Assisted Living – Dementia/Memory Support	Long-Term Skilled Nursing	Skilled Nursing – Dementia/Memory Support	Short-Term Rehab	Hospice
DFAR14	40%	32%	64%	16%	4%	20%	4%
DFAR13	39%	45%	45%	36%	8%	19%	3%
DFAR12	44%	41%	23%	23%	19%	22%	6%
DFAR11	56%	36%	20%	38%	14%	24%	16%
DFAR10	52%	39%	35%	44%	0%	0%	20%
DFAR9	18%	14%	14%	13%	0%	0%	3%

DFAR14 Data: from the 25 jury-recognized projects only
Note: Under DFAR9 and 10, Dementia/Memory support was not specified as AL or SN populations. Accordingly, for this chart, all entries are listed as AL-DMS for simplicity. Similarly, Short-Term Rehab was not an option listed under DFAR9 and 10.

Legend: DFAR14, DFAR13, DFAR12, DFAR11, DFAR10, DFAR9

Purpose of the Renovation

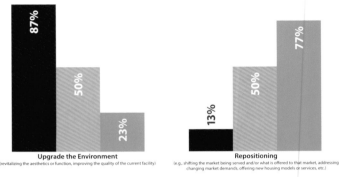

	Upgrade the Environment (revitalizing the aesthetics or function, improving the quality of the current facility)	Repositioning (e.g., shifting the market being served and/or what is offered to that market, addressing changing market demands, offering new housing models or services, etc.)
DFAR14	87%	13%
DFAR13	50%	50%
DFAR12	23%	77%

DFAR14 Data: from the 25 jury-recognized projects only (8 projects)

Legend: DFAR14, DFAR13, DFAR12

Projects by Construction Type

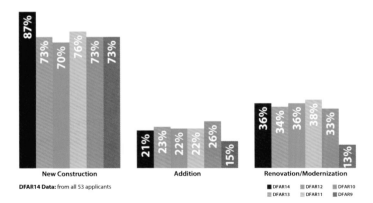

	New Construction	Addition	Renovation/Modernization
DFAR14	87%	21%	36%
DFAR13	73%	23%	34%
DFAR12	70%	22%	36%
DFAR11	76%	22%	38%
DFAR10	73%	26%	33%
DFAR9	73%	15%	13%

DFAR14 Data: from all 53 applicants

Legend: DFAR14, DFAR13, DFAR12, DFAR11, DFAR10, DFAR9

Project Size (GSF), by Construction Type

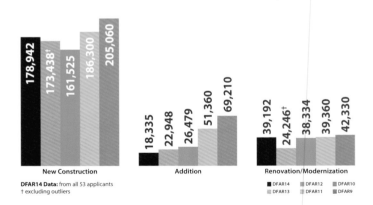

	New Construction	Addition	Renovation/Modernization
DFAR14	178,942	18,335	39,192
DFAR13	173,438†	22,948	24,246†
DFAR12	161,525	26,479	38,334
DFAR11	186,300	51,360	39,360
DFAR10	205,060	69,210	42,330

DFAR14 Data: from all 53 applicants
† excluding outliers

Legend: DFAR14, DFAR13, DFAR12, DFAR11, DFAR10, DFAR9

Project Costs

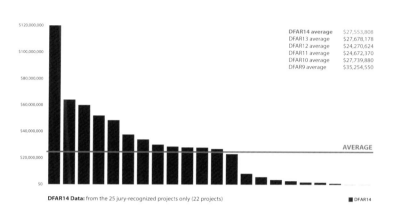

DFAR14 average	$27,553,808
DFAR13 average	$27,678,178
DFAR12 average	$24,270,624
DFAR11 average	$24,672,370
DFAR10 average	$27,739,880
DFAR9 average	$35,254,550

AVERAGE

DFAR14 Data: from the 25 jury-recognized projects only (22 projects)

■ DFAR14

Average Cost Per Gross Square Foot, by Site Location

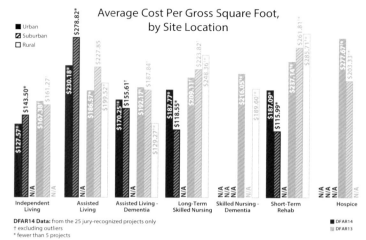

■ Urban
▨ Suburban
□ Rural

DFAR14 Data: from the 25 jury-recognized projects only
† excluding outliers
* fewer than 5 projects

■ DFAR14
▨ DFAR13

Average Cost Per Gross Square Foot, by Facility Type

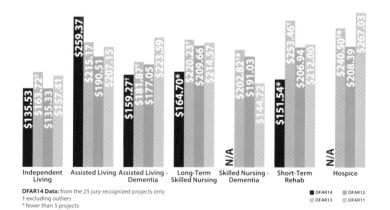

DFAR14 Data: from the 25 jury-recognized projects only
† excluding outliers
* fewer than 5 projects

■ DFAR14   DFAR12
  DFAR13   DFAR11

Residential Unit Distribution – Independent Living

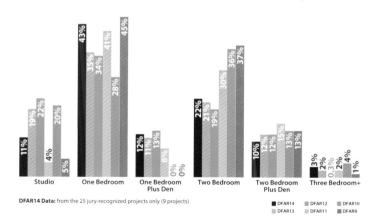

DFAR14 Data: from the 25 jury-recognized projects only (9 projects)

■ DFAR14   DFAR12   DFAR10
  DFAR13   DFAR11   DFAR9

Average Residential Unit Size (NSF) – Independent Living

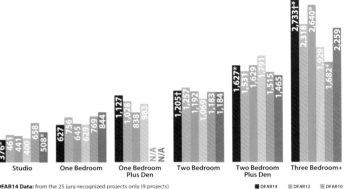

Studio: 376*, 461, 441, 400, 658, 508*
One Bedroom: 627, 756, 645, 629, 769, 844
One Bedroom Plus Den: 1,127, 1,028, 838, 983, N/A, N/A
Two Bedroom: 1,205†, 1,257, 1,192, 1,069, 1,183, 1,184
Two Bedroom Plus Den: 1,627*, 1,531, 1,629, 1,791, 1,515, 1,465
Three Bedroom+: 2,733†*, 2,318, 2,640*, 1,929, 1,682*, 2,259

DFAR14 **Data:** from the 25 jury-recognized projects only (9 projects)
† excluding outliers
* fewer than 5 projects

Legend: DFAR14, DFAR12, DFAR10, DFAR13, DFAR11, DFAR9

Average Residential Unit Size (NSF) – Assisted Living

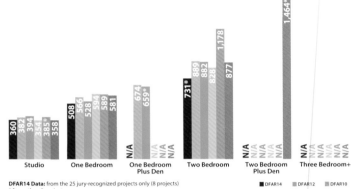

Studio: 360, 382, 394, 354, 385*, 358
One Bedroom: 508, 565, 528, 594, 589, 581
One Bedroom Plus Den: N/A, 674, 659*, N/A, N/A, N/A
Two Bedroom: 731*, 869, 882, 828, 1,178, 877
Two Bedroom Plus Den: N/A, N/A, N/A, N/A, 1,464, N/A
Three Bedroom+: N/A, N/A, N/A, N/A, N/A, N/A

DFAR14 **Data:** from the 25 jury-recognized projects only (8 projects)
* fewer than 5 projects

Legend: DFAR14, DFAR12, DFAR10, DFAR13, DFAR11, DFAR9

Residential Unit Distribution – Assisted Living

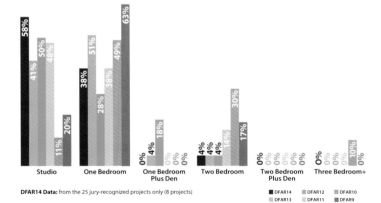

Studio: 58%, 41%, 50%, 48%, 11%, 20%
One Bedroom: 38%, 51%, 28%, 38%, 49%, 63%
One Bedroom Plus Den: 0%, 4%, 18%, 0%, 0%, 0%
Two Bedroom: 4%, 4%, 4%, 14%, 30%, 17%
Two Bedroom Plus Den: 0%, 0%, 0%, 0%, 0%, 0%
Three Bedroom+: 0%, 0%, 0%, 0%, 10%, 0%

DFAR14 **Data:** from the 25 jury-recognized projects only (8 projects)

Legend: DFAR14, DFAR12, DFAR10, DFAR13, DFAR11, DFAR9

Residential Unit Distribution – Assisted Living Dementia/Memory Support

Private Room: 91%, 93%, 87%, 84%, 80%, 80%
Semi-Private Room: 9%, 5%, 5%, 8%, 20%, 20%
Shared Room: 0%, 2%, 8%, 9%, 0%, 0%

DFAR14 **Data:** from the 25 jury-recognized projects only (16 projects)

Legend: DFAR14, DFAR12, DFAR10, DFAR13, DFAR11, DFAR9

Average Residential Unit Size (NSF) – Assisted Living Dementia/Memory Support

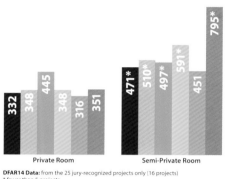
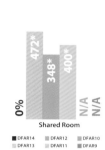

Private Room
332 | 348 | 445 | 348 | 316 | 351

Semi-Private Room
471* | 510* | 497* | 591* | 451 | 795*

Shared Room
0% | 472* | 348 | 400* | N/A | N/A

DFAR14 Data: from the 25 jury-recognized projects only (16 projects)
* fewer than 5 projects

■ DFAR14 ■ DFAR12 ■ DFAR10
■ DFAR13 ■ DFAR11 ■ DFAR9

Average Residential Unit Size (NSF) – Long-Term Skilled Nursing

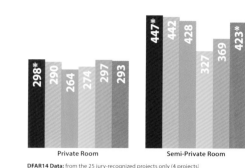
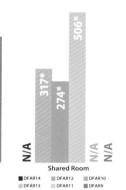

Private Room
298* | 290 | 264 | 274 | 297 | 293

Semi-Private Room
447* | 442 | 428 | 327 | 369 | 423*

Shared Room
N/A | 317* | 274* | 506* | N/A | N/A

DFAR14 Data: from the 25 jury-recognized projects only (4 projects)
* fewer than 5 projects

■ DFAR14 ■ DFAR12 ■ DFAR10
■ DFAR13 ■ DFAR11 ■ DFAR9

Residential Unit Distribution – Long-Term Skilled Nursing

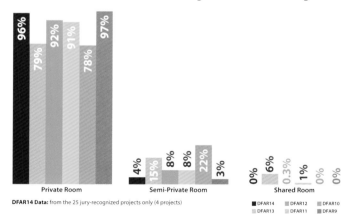

Private Room
96% | 79% | 92% | 91% | 78% | 97%

Semi-Private Room
4% | 15% | 8% | 8% | 22% | 3%

Shared Room
0% | 6% | 0.3% | 1% | 0% | 0%

DFAR14 Data: from the 25 jury-recognized projects only (4 projects)

■ DFAR14 ■ DFAR12 ■ DFAR10
■ DFAR13 ■ DFAR11 ■ DFAR9

Residential Unit Distribution – Long-Term Skilled Nursing Dementia/Memory Support

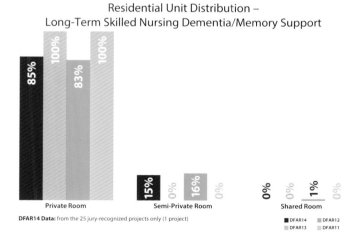

Private Room
85% | 100% | 83% | 100%

Semi-Private Room
15% | 0% | 16% | 0%

Shared Room
0% | 0% | 1% | 0%

DFAR14 Data: from the 25 jury-recognized projects only (1 project)

■ DFAR14 ■ DFAR12
■ DFAR13 ■ DFAR11

Average Residential Unit Size (NSF) – Long-Term Skilled Nursing Dementia/Memory Support

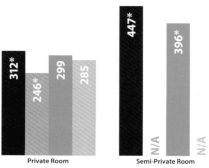

Private Room: 312* | 246* | 299 | 285
Semi-Private Room: 447* | N/A | 396* | N/A
Shared Room: 0% | N/A | 339* | N/A

DFAR14 Data: from the 25 jury-recognized projects only (1 project)
* fewer than 5 projects

■ DFAR14   ■ DFAR12
■ DFAR13   ■ DFAR11

Average Residential Unit Size (NSF) – Short-Term Rehab

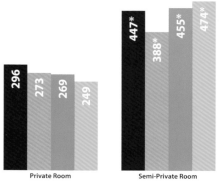

Private Room: 296 | 273 | 269 | 249
Semi-Private Room: 447* | 388* | 455* | 474*
Shared Room: 0% | 422* | 413* | N/A

DFAR14 Data: from the 25 jury-recognized projects only (5 projects)
* fewer than 5 projects

■ DFAR14   ■ DFAR12
■ DFAR13   ■ DFAR11

Residential Unit Distribution – Short-Term Rehab

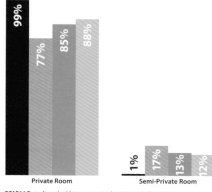

Private Room: 99% | 77% | 85% | 88%
Semi-Private Room: 1% | 17% | 13% | 12%
Shared Room: 0% | 6% | 2% | 0%

DFAR14 Data: from the 25 jury-recognized projects only (5 projects)

■ DFAR14   ■ DFAR12
■ DFAR13   ■ DFAR11

Residential Unit Distribution – Hospice

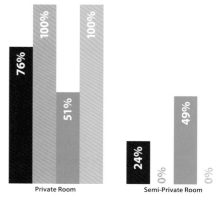

Private Room: 76% | 100% | 51% | 100%
Semi-Private Room: 24% | 0% | 49% | 0%
Shared Room: 0% | 0% | 0% | 0%

DFAR14 Data: from the 25 jury-recognized projects only (1 project)

■ DFAR14   ■ DFAR12
■ DFAR13   ■ DFAR11

Average Residential Unit Size (NSF) – Hospice

Private Room
350*
472*
384*
311

Semi-Private Room
650*
N/A
475*
N/A

Shared Room
N/A
N/A
N/A
N/A

DFAR14 Data: from the 25 jury-recognized projects only (1 project)
* fewer than 5 projects

■ DFAR14 ■ DFAR12
■ DFAR13 ■ DFAR11

Average Resident Gender Breakdown

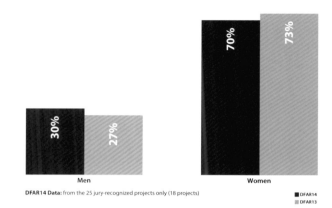

Men
30%
27%

Women
70%
73%

DFAR14 Data: from the 25 jury-recognized projects only (18 projects)

■ DFAR14
■ DFAR13

Average Accessibility of Independent and Assisted Living Units

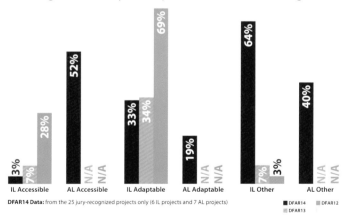

IL Accessible
3%
7%
28%

AL Accessible
52%
N/A
N/A

IL Adaptable
33%
34%
69%

AL Adaptable
19%
N/A
N/A

IL Other
64%
7%
3%

AL Other
40%
N/A
N/A

DFAR14 Data: from the 25 jury-recognized projects only (6 IL projects and 7 AL projects)

■ DFAR14 ■ DFAR12
■ DFAR13

Average Resident Cohabitation Status

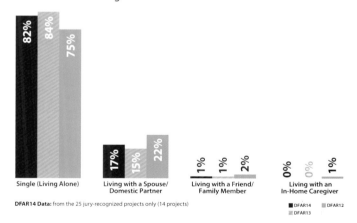

Single (Living Alone)
82%
84%
75%

Living with a Spouse/ Domestic Partner
17%
15%
22%

Living with a Friend/ Family Member
1%
1%
2%

Living with an In-Home Caregiver
0%
0%
1%

DFAR14 Data: from the 25 jury-recognized projects only (14 projects)

■ DFAR14 ■ DFAR12
■ DFAR13

Source of Resident Payments

Private Payment	Medicaid/ Medicare Payment	Government Subsidy Payment	Other
84%	3%	9%	5%
65%	19%	11%	6%
64%	23%	7%	6%
72%	17%	3%	7%

DFAR14 Data: from the 25 jury-recognized projects only (16 projects)

■ DFAR14 ■ DFAR12
■ DFAR13 ■ DFAR11

About the Jury-Recognized Projects

The 25 DFAR14 projects recognized by the jury varied greatly, in both scale and scope, ranging from residential buildings to common cores with amenities for residents and sometimes the greater community. However, when the projects with residential components were asked what was more critical to the success of their project—either improving common spaces and amenities or improving units / private spaces—82% stated the common spaces were more important. This is higher than DFAR13's 71%, and significantly greater than DFAR12's 41% and DFAR11's 38%.

Critical to Project Success: Improving Common Spaces

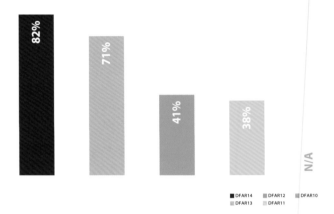

82%	71%	41%	38%	N/A

■ DFAR14 ■ DFAR12 ■ DFAR10
■ DFAR13 ■ DFAR11

Average Resident Age

Independent Living	Assisted Living	Assisted Living – Dementia/ Memory Support	Long-Term Skilled Nursing	Skilled Nursing – Dementia/ Memory Support	Short-Term Rehab	Hospice
73	83*	86	88*	N/A	82*	N/A
71	79*	84	87*		79*	

DFAR14 Data: from the 25 jury-recognized projects only
* fewer than 5 projects

■ DFAR14 ● Age Designed to Support
⊘ Age Upon Entry

Fitness / wellness continues to be a growing trend for the industry, though the types and quantities of fitness / wellness spaces described by the jury-recognized DFAR14 projects are fairly consistent to past DFAR cycles.

Both large-scale and more intimate small-scale gathering spaces are common for learning, meeting, and / or activities spaces, as are activity / game rooms and activity kitchens.

Fitness / Wellness Amenities

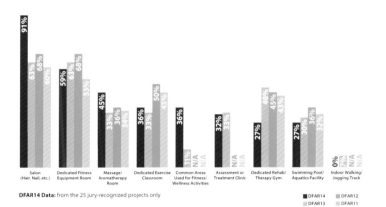

Salon (Hair, Nail, etc.): 91%, 63%, 68%, 60%
Dedicated Fitness Equipment Room: 59%, 63%, 68%, 53%
Massage/ Aromatherapy Room: 45%, 33%, 36%, 34%
Dedicated Exercise Classroom: 36%, 36%, 33%, 50%, 45%
Common Areas Used for Fitness/ Wellness Activities: 36%, 11%, N/A, N/A
Assessment or Treatment Clinic: 32%, 33%, N/A, N/A
Dedicated Rehab/ Therapy Gym: 27%, 48%, 45%, 43%
Swimming Pool/ Aquatics Facility: 27%, 30%, 36%, 32%
Indoor Walking/ Jogging Track: 0%, 7%, N/A, N/A

DFAR14 Data: from the 25 jury-recognized projects only

■ DFAR14   ▨ DFAR12
▨ DFAR13   ▨ DFAR11

Learning / Activity Amenities

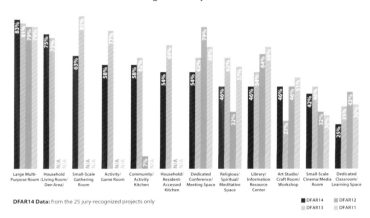

Large Multi-Purpose Room: 83%, 81%, 79%, 73%
Household (Living Room/ Den Area): 75%, N/A, N/A, 73%
Small-Scale Gathering Room: 63%, N/A, N/A, 73%
Activity/ Game Room: 58%, N/A, N/A, 77%
Community/ Activity Kitchen: 58%, N/A, N/A, 62%
Household/ Resident-Accessed Kitchen: 54%, 7%, N/A, N/A
Dedicated Conference/ Meeting Space: 54%, 62%, 79%, 68%
Religious/ Spiritual/ Meditative Space: 46%, 32%, 62%, 57%
Library/ Information Resource Center: 46%, 54%, 64%, 68%
Art Studio/ Craft Room/ Workshop: 46%, 27%, 46%, 31%
Small-Scale Cinema/Media Room: 42%, 32%, N/A
Dedicated Classroom/ Learning Space: 25%, 35%, 43%, 36%

DFAR14 Data: from the 25 jury-recognized projects only

■ DFAR14   ▨ DFAR12
▨ DFAR13   ▨ DFAR11

Fitness / Wellness Amenity Spaces

Fountainview at Gonda Westside
Hillcrest Country Estates
The Summit at Rockwood South Hill
The Cottage at Cypress Cove
Rose Villa Pocket Neighborhoods & Main Street

Learning / Activity Amenity Spaces

Fountainview at Gonda Westside
Fountainview at Gonda Westside
Shenyang Senior Living
The Burnham Family Memory Care Residence at Avery Heights
The Cottage at Cypress Cove
Caleb Hitchcock Memory CareNeighborhood at Duncaster Retirement Community

Casual dining venues were once again more common than formal settings.

The popularity of outdoor amenities continues to grow, as seen in the most prevalent common theme, connection to nature, reported later in this chapter.

Dining Amenities

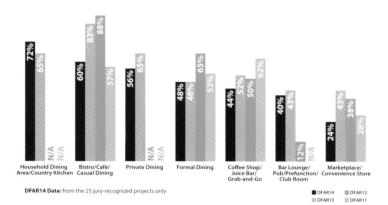

Household Dining Area/Country Kitchen: 72%, 65%, N/A, N/A
Bistro/Café/Casual Dining: 60%, 83%, 88%, 57%
Private Dining: 56%, 65%, N/A, N/A
Formal Dining: 48%, 48%, 65%, 53%
Coffee Shop/Juice Bar/Grab-and-Go: 44%, 52%, 50%, 62%
Bar Lounge/Pub/Prefunction/Club Room: 40%, 43%, 12%, N/A
Marketplace/Convenience Store: 24%, 43%, 38%, 28%

DFAR14 Data: from the 25 jury-recognized projects only

■ DFAR14 ■ DFAR12
■ DFAR13 ■ DFAR11

Outdoor Amenities

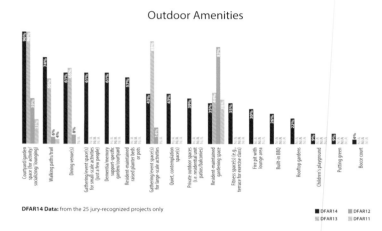

DFAR14 Data: from the 25 jury-recognized projects only

■ DFAR14 ■ DFAR12
■ DFAR13 ■ DFAR11

Dining Amenity Spaces

Abiitan Mill City

Edenwald Café

The Burnham Family Memory Care Residence at Avery Heights

The Summit at Rockwood South Hill

The Trousdale Assisted Living and Memory Care

Well-Spring Resident Activity Center + Expansion

Well-Spring Resident Activity Center + Expansion

The Woodlands at John Knox Village

Outdoor Amenity Spaces

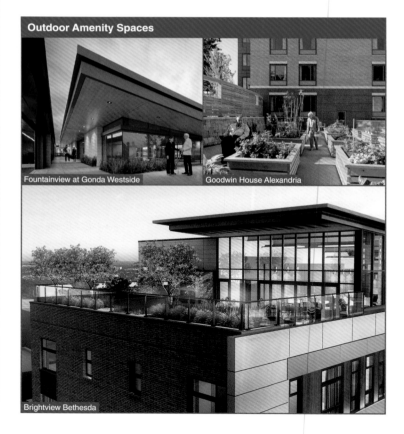

Fountainview at Gonda Westside

Goodwin House Alexandria

Brightview Bethesda

With regard to design challenges, just fewer than half of the 25 jury-recognized projects discussed site issues, such as addressing a small or tight site, stormwater management, grading or slope conditions, and / or parking (which was reported by projects located in urban areas), and 20% reported zoning or code issues. A handful of projects described challenges associated with space planning, particularly in terms of fitting their project's program into a limited building footprint. One quarter of the projects described challenges working within existing conditions or constraints, such as mitigating acoustic issues, phasing to relocate existing residents, or unifying varied aesthetic styles on a campus.

The jury-recognized projects also wrote about their innovative or unique features, with technology being a common thread. Such self-described innovations included: providing a setting for telemedicine (Elm Place); wireless resident monitoring, integrated nurse call systems, and silent fire alarms (Fountainview at Gonda Westside, Linden Park Apartments, Goodwin House Alexandria, North Ridge at Tacoma Lutheran); lighting systems that support circadian rhythms or direct people to bathrooms (The Cottage at Cypress Cove, Brightview Bethesda, The Burnham Family Memory Care Residence at Avery Heights, The Trousdale Assisted Living and Memory Care); a "digital dashboard" that acts as an events calendar, but can also be used to monitor building / systems performance (Elm Place); digital menus and ordering at dining facilities (Edenwald Café); hearing loops and wireless headphone systems in auditorium-type spaces (Brightview Bethesda, Well-Spring Resident Activity Center + Expansion); and robust and adaptive IT systems (The Seasons at Alexandria).

Other innovative and unique features the jury-recognized projects described included: the adoption of the Dutch *woonerf* concept to create a pedestrian-focused plan (Abiitan Mill City); a theater designed especially for an older population, with a quiet and draft-free HVAC system (Well-Spring Resident Activity Center + Expansion); floor plans that can easily adapt for different levels of care or that are staggered to let in more natural light (The Trousdale Assisted Living and Memory Care, Fountainview at Gonda Westside); or that advance memory support care and environments by doing such things as further deinstitutionalizing spaces, reducing distractions, and providing above-grade outdoor courtyards (Abiitan Mill City, Babcock Health Care Center, North Ridge at Tacoma Lutheran).

A large percentage of jury-recognized DFAR14 projects also described how they collaborated during the planning and / or design phases of their project in a manner that went beyond the expected teaming that is typical of the traditional design process. How teams collaborated, however, varied. Fifty-six percent of the jury-recognized projects gathered and incorporated

input from various stakeholders (e.g., administration, staff, residents, local neighborhood groups), five of which described using a charrette process. As Abiitan Mill City's submission explained, focus groups with the local senior community provided "invaluable [feedback that was] integral to the overall design of the development." Likewise, those involved with Cuthbertson Village Town Center Renovation noted, "This depth of experience and access [to stakeholders] was invaluable to the project."

Collaboration was not just with stakeholders; 36% of the jury-recognized DFAR14 projects described using a multidisciplinary approach in which the design team, consultants, and contractors collaborated and coordinated throughout the design of the project. Twenty percent discussed engaging an expert to consult on such topics as Small House design, wellness programming, active aging, feng shui, performance venue design, and Passive House design strategies. Two projects also described interesting partnerships with local artists, small businesses, hospitals, and / or institutions of higher learning.

Project Themes

Though the 25 DFAR14 projects recognized by the jury are quite diverse, several common and often interrelated project themes were identified based on the similarities among the submissions' narratives about project descriptions and goals. The following describes the jury-recognized DFAR14 projects' common themes, listed in order from most to least common.*

The common themes described by the jury-recognized DFAR14 projects include:

- Connection to nature (92%)
- Contemporary interior aesthetics (70%)
- Household model, culture change, and person-centered care (52%)
- Connecting to the greater community (52%)
- Promoting a sense of community (52%)
- Homelike environments (39%)
- Ecological sustainability (28%)
- Addressing the current market, repositioning to be competitive (28%)
- Designing for flexibility and aging in place (28%)
- Fitting the local context (24%)
- A focus on wellness, active living (20%)

*Note: For each of the themes listed in this section, the analysis only counted the projects that included narrative text related to the thematic concept. It is likely that additional jury-recognized DFAR14 projects also include elements similar to what is being reported, however, unless the project's application form content included text specifically related to the thematic concept at hand, that project is not part of the analysis presented herein.

Connection to Nature

Ninety-two percent of the jury-recognized DFAR14 projects described a connection to nature, increasing significantly from DFARs 11, 12, and 13 (at 67%, 65%, and 76% respectively), though comparable to DFAR10's 97%.

Connection to Nature Theme

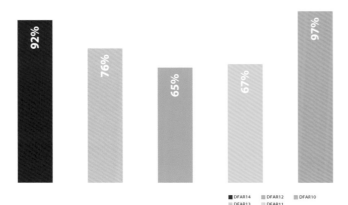

92%   76%   65%   67%   97%

■ DFAR14   ■ DFAR12   ■ DFAR10
■ DFAR13   ■ DFAR11

DFAR14 projects recognized by the jury that described their connection to nature include:

- Abiitan Mill City
- Babcock Health Care Center
- Brightview Bethesda
- Caleb Hitchcock Memory Care Neighborhood at Duncaster Retirement Community
- Cuthbertson Village Town Center Renovation
- Elm Place
- EmpathiCare Village
- Fountainview at Gonda Westside
- Frasier Meadows Retirement Community Independent Living Additions and Renovations
- Goodwin House Alexandria
- Hillcrest Country Estates
- Legacy Place Cottages
- Linden Park Apartments
- North Ridge at Tacoma Lutheran
- Rose Villa Pocket Neighborhoods & Main Street
- Shenyang Senior Living
- The Burnham Family Memory Care Residence at Avery Heights
- The Cottage at Cypress Cove
- The Plaza at Waikiki
- The Seasons at Alexandria
- The Summit at Rockwood South Hill
- The Trousdale Assisted Living and Memory Care
- The Woodlands at John Knox Village

Connection to Nature—Outdoor Spaces

Fountainview at Gonda Westside

Hillcrest Country Estates

Goodwin House Alexandria

EmpathiCare Village

Hillcrest Country Estates

North Ridge at Tacoma Lutheran

The Burnham Family Memory Care Residence at Avery Heights

The Plaza at Waikiki

The Trousdale Assisted Living and Memory Care

Connections to nature included:

- Access to outdoor spaces / indoor-outdoor connections (83% of the projects with a theme of connecting to nature), including secure courtyards, screened-in porches, raised planter beds, walking paths, arbors / pergolas with seating areas, fire pits, rain gardens, and other water features
- Extensive daylighting (70% of the projects), primarily via large windows
- Views to the outdoors (70% of the projects), which varied from city skyline vistas to woodlands to intimate garden scenes
- The incorporation of biophilic design principles (12% of the projects)

Connection to Nature—Daylighting

Babcock Health Care Center

Cuthbertson Village Town Center Renovation

Edenwald Café

Goodwin House Alexandria

Rose Villa Pocket Neighborhoods & Main Street

Shenyang Senior Living

Connection to Nature—Views

Frasier Meadows Retirement Community
Independent Living Additions and Renovations

Caleb Hitchcock Memory Care Neighborhood at Duncaster Retirement Community

The Summit at Rockwood South Hill

The Seasons at Alexandria

"The great rooms that provide the shared hub for each household have a strong visual connection to the exterior, large windows providing natural light, and access to secure courtyards on the ground floor… [there are] views to the exterior immediately upon entering, since views and natural light support feelings of well-being."

Shenyang Senior Living

"Within the building design, spaces have visual and physical connectivity to the outdoors. Patterns and materials found in nature are incorporated within the architecture and interior design. Biophilic design principles were introduced and embraced as a standard and directive for design and sustainability."

The Cottage at Cypress Cove

"Residents are encouraged to explore the outdoors within the tropical memory garden which has been designed to be a space that is pleasant, reflective, restorative, and an engaging experience. Relaxing elements include a rain chain waterfall, rain gardens, dancing water jets, and fountains. Ornate rain chains provide a unique visual connection to the outdoor courtyard and promote conversation without distracting, disruptive noises heard during a rainstorm. Residents can watch and listen to the soft-water sound of a waterfall while inside the household or from the adjacent covered porch areas."

Caleb Hitchcock Memory Care Neighborhood at Duncaster Retirement Community

"Connection to nature was a driving force in the design concept. This was emphasized by 'bringing the outside in' through an abundance of natural light in every space, corner windows that provide two-sided views in resident rooms, and a focused view of a majestic 100-year-old oak tree that is affectionately known on campus as the charter oak that became an organizing element in the design… [A goal was to provide] maximized daylighting and views to the outdoors, installing exceptionally even and higher artificial lighting levels and selecting highly efficient lighting with a color temperature upward of 3000 kelvins, closer to natural spectrum for visual clarity and a calming effect. Result: Owners are seeing a drop in resident sleep disorders as the bright and natural light is helping maintain the residents' circadian rhythm."

Elm Place

"The site design creates a variety of outdoor spaces for residents while grounding the building in the town's emerging urban landscape. The front lawn and covered drop-off provides a welcoming front door for residents and visitors. To the east, the building creates a small courtyard for outdoor picnics and gardening. The raised beds are at different heights— some work best for those in walkers while others work best for a resident using a scooter or wheelchair. The gardens are full and well used. The rear garden features a multitude of edibles along a small walking path. Aristolochia grows up a modern pergola—a contemporary take on a classic Vermont porch. This large-leafed vine creates a welcome dappled shade in the summer, but dies back in the winter to let the sun through. A new bocce court is centered inside the walking loop—a gentle activity for long summer days."

Rose Villa Pocket Neighborhoods & Main Street

"Each garden is themed and provided with various amenities like arbors, boulder seating walls, rose gardens, fire pits, and even pet drinking fountains. A multi-use pavilion structure bounding one of the gardens is available for social gatherings and events."

The Woodlands at John Knox Village

"Designed with a direct relationship to the outdoors, each home has large floor-to-ceiling windows that look out to a beautiful, landscaped courtyard and the site's natural asset—the woodland area. Adjacent to the open dining and hearth rooms is a well-positioned screened-in porch which provides the elder an opportunity to go out and experience the lovely sea breezes without having to leave the home. For those with the ability to leave the home, centralized elevators are positioned for ease and convenience, which connect the residents to the ground floor. From there, the building's featured landscaped courtyard and park-like woodland area are only a few steps away."

Contemporary Interior Aesthetics

Ever since DFAR10, when the Insights Study's comparison of projects with contemporary versus traditional aesthetics began, the rate of contemporary projects has increased. This culminated in DFAR13 with the highest percentage yet: 72% of the jury-recognized projects were classified as having a contemporary aesthetic (with 14% of projects having a traditional setting, and another 14% exhibiting a mixture of the two). The submissions to DFAR14 maintain this trend, with 70% exhibiting a contemporary aesthetic and the other 30% classified as having a mixture of contemporary and traditional interior aesthetics. None of the jury-recognized DFAR14 projects were described as having a fully traditional style.*

Contemporary Interior Aesthetics Theme

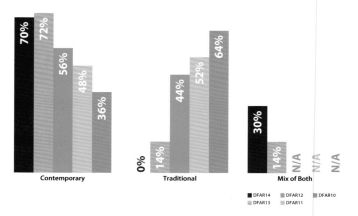

Such features as clean lines, geometric and orthogonal patterns, and minimal details help define a contemporary interior aesthetic. A traditional interior aesthetic, on the other hand, is more likely to include crown and base molding, rolled-arm furniture, pleated curtains, and details and patterns that are more ornate and / or curvilinear in nature.

*Note: The analysis of this theme did not include two jury-recognized DFAR14 projects, which did not submit photos or renderings of interior spaces that could be used for the categorization of aesthetic style.

DFAR14 projects recognized by the jury that were categorized as having a contemporary interior aesthetic include:

- Abiitan Mill City
- Babcock Health Care Center
- Brightview Bethesda
- Caleb Hitchcock Memory Care Neighborhood at Duncaster Retirement Community
- Elm Place
- EmpathiCare Village
- Fountainview at Gonda Westside
- Goodwin House Alexandria
- Linden Park Apartments
- North Ridge at Tacoma Lutheran
- Rose Villa Pocket Neighborhoods & Main Street
- Shenyang Senior Living
- The Burnham Family Memory Care Residence at Avery Heights
- The Plaza at Waikiki
- The Summit at Rockwood South Hill
- The Trousdale Assisted Living and Memory Care

Goodwin House Alexandria

Elm Place

Shenyang Senior Living

The Plaza at Waikiki

The Burnham Family Memory Care Residence at Avery Heights

The Summit at Rockwood South Hill

DFAR14 projects recognized by the jury that were categorized as having a mixture of contemporary and traditional interior aesthetics include:

- Cuthbertson Village Town Center Renovation
- Edenwald Café
- Hillcrest Country Estates
- Legacy Place Cottages
- The Cottage at Cypress Cove
- The Woodlands at John Knox Village
- Well-Spring Resident Activity Center + Expansion

Babcock Health Care Center

The Cottage at Cypress Cove

Edenwald Café

Household Model, Culture Change, and Person-Centered Care

Because operational and design decisions can affect building occupants' mental, social, emotional, and physical well-being—and, therefore, quality of life—it is important to provide person-centered care and physical environments that empower people.[3] "Household" is the term used herein to describe such sites, where small-scaled clustering of residents coupled with organizational policies support person-centered care. Households are typically defined as 10 to 12 private residential bedrooms organized around a shared living / dining / kitchen area. "Neighborhoods," on the other hand, are typically two to three groups of 10 to 12 private residential bedrooms (typically totaling 15 to 20+ residents) organized around one shared living / dining / kitchen area.

"Person-centered care promotes choice, purpose, and meaning in daily life. Person-centered care means that nursing home residents are supported in achieving the level of physical, mental, and psychosocial well-being that is individually practicable. This goal honors the importance of keeping the person at the center of the care planning and decision-making process."[4]

Goodwin House Alexandria

Legacy Place Cottages

North Ridge at Tacoma Lutheran

The Woodlands at John Knox Village

Fifty-six percent of the jury-recognized submissions that included a residential component reported that their project includes a Household (compared to DFAR13's 62%). However, after analyzing floor plans, we found only 52% actually provided layouts that were Households or Neighborhoods.

Of the jury-recognized projects that did indeed have a Household and / or Neighborhood plan, 54% of these submissions discussed Households, culture change, and / or person-centered care within their project description text, which is greater than past cycles (with DFAR13 at 38%, DFAR12 at 35%, DFAR11 at 29%, and DFAR10 at 35%). Of that 54%, based on floor plan analysis, 69% have a Household, 15% include a Neighborhood, and 15% offer both Households and Neighborhood layouts in their design (with layouts varying based on level of care, e.g., assisted living or rehabilitation neighborhoods versus memory care Households).

Household Model and Person-Centered Care Theme

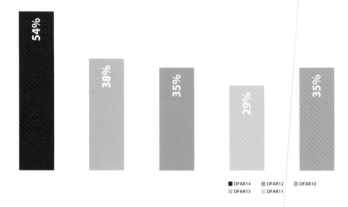

54% 38% 35% 29% 35%

■ DFAR14   ■ DFAR12   ■ DFAR10
■ DFAR13   ■ DFAR11

Facility types that incorporated a Household model varied: 15% of the projects that included a Household model were Assisted Living facilities; 85% Assisted Living Dementia / Memory Support; 38% Long-Term Skilled Nursing; 23% Skilled Nursing Dementia / Memory Support; 38% Short-Term Rehab; and 8% (one project) was a Hospice.

Floor plan

This floor plan, from Goodwin House Alexandria, shows two Household wings. A Household is typically defined as 10 to 12 private residential bedrooms organized around a shared living / dining / kitchen area.

Floor plan

This floor plan, from Legacy Place Cottages, shows a Neighborhood—in this case, two wings off a shared common area. A Neighborhood is typically defined as two to three groups of 10 to 12 private residential bedrooms (typically totaling 15 to 20+ residents) organized around one shared living / dining / kitchen area.

By facility type, the values are:

- Assisted Living Households*—the average size was 11,003 square feet (with a range of 9108 to 12,400 square feet) for an average of 13 residents (with a range of 10 to 17 residents). The average size was 866 square feet per resident, with a range of 729 to 958 square feet per resident.

- Assisted Living Dementia / Memory Support Households—the average size was 10,254 square feet (with a range of 6800 to 15,990 square feet) for an average of 14 residents (with a range of 11 to 20 residents). The average size was 673 square feet per resident, with a range of 500 to 958 square feet per resident.

- Long-Term Skilled Nursing Households*—the average size was 13,217 square feet (with a range of 10,950 to 15,484 square feet) for an average of 18 residents (with a range of 15 to 20 residents). The average size was 752 square feet per resident, with a range of 730 to 774 square feet per resident.

- Skilled Nursing Dementia / Memory Support Households*—the average size was 10,325 square feet (with a range of 9850 to 10,800 square feet) for an average of 14 residents (with a range of 11 to 16 residents). The average size was 799 square feet per resident, with a range of 616 to 982 square feet per resident.

- Short-Term Rehab Households*—the average size was 8,610 square feet (with a range of 5620 to 10,710 square feet) for an average of 17 residents (with a range of 11 to 20 residents). The average size was 516 square feet per resident, with a range of 500 to 536 square feet per resident.

- Hospice Households—[*insufficient data*]

*Calculations based on fewer than five projects.

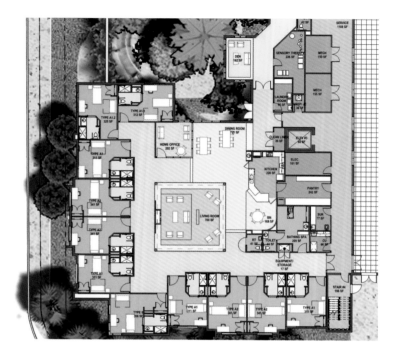

This floor plan, from EmpathiCare Village, shows a Household design where the common spaces are at the center of the plan. There is minimal separation between public and private zones of the house.

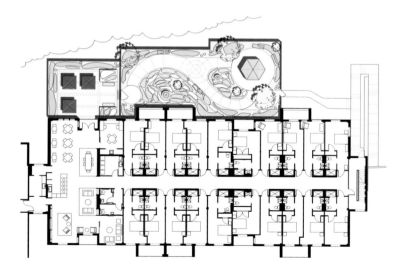

This floor plan, from The Burnham Family Memory Care Residence at Avery Heights, shows a Household design where the common spaces are pulled away from the bedrooms, allowing for greater separation between public and private zones of the house.

Connecting to the Greater Community

Fifty-two percent of the jury-recognized DFAR14 projects described a connection to the greater community surrounding their building or campus, from taking advantage of local amenities to opening up their common spaces and offering services to the public. This is comparable to DFAR13's 55%, which was significantly higher than previous DFAR submissions that came in at 29% for DFAR12 and 42% for DFAR11. The frequency of this theme, however, is comparable to the DFAR10 rate of 53% of jury-recognized submissions.

Connecting to the Greater Community Theme

52% | 55% | 29% | 42% | 53%

■ DFAR14   ■ DFAR12   ■ DFAR10
■ DFAR13   ■ DFAR11

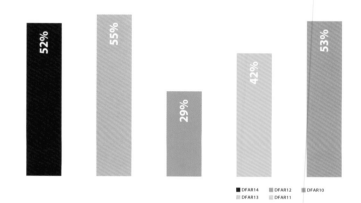

Brightview Bethesda
Rose Villa Pocket Neighborhoods & Main Street

Abiitan Mill City

Forty-six percent of the projects that connect to the greater community are located in urban settings and 54% are suburban. None are in a rural location. This is different from DFAR13, in which 59% were located in urban settings, 35% suburban, and 6% (one project) in a rural location.

Several projects described their urban connectivity (Abiitan Mill City, Brightview Bethesda, Fountainview at Gonda Westside, Rose Villa Pocket Neighborhoods & Main Street, Shenyang Senior Living, The Trousdale Assisted Living and Memory Care). These projects are located within a mixed-use development and / or are adjacent to or can easily access various service providers and public amenities. In fact, of the 25 jury-recognized DFAR14 projects, 68% have sites within 1000 feet of public transportation, such as a bus stop or rapid transit line (up from DFAR13 at 58%), and 44% are within 1000 feet of everyday shopping and / or medical services (also up from DFAR13 at 38%). However, if only those projects that described connecting to the greater community are considered then 77% are within 1000 feet of public transportation, and 62% are within 1000 feet of everyday shopping and / or medical services.

Others described providing public access to their amenities, such as dining venues and commercial retail spaces (Abiitan Mill City, Brightview Bethesda, Frasier Meadows Retirement Community Independent Living Additions and Renovations, Rose Villa Pocket Neighborhoods & Main Street, The Trousdale Assisted Living and Memory Care, Well-Spring Resident Activity Center + Expansion).

Multiple projects (The Cottage at Cypress Cove, Elm Place, Frasier Meadows Retirement Community Independent Living Additions and Renovations, Hillcrest Country Estates, EmpathiCare Village, The Plaza at Waikiki, Well-Spring Resident Activity Center + Expansion) described the outreach and services they provide to the greater community, including homecare for non-residents, educational sessions and counseling / support groups, therapy

and wellness services, PACE programs, and hosting regional events such as wellness fairs and fundraisers that support older adults.

Four projects (Abiitan Mill City, Brightview Bethesda, Elm Place, Fountainview at Gonda Westside) specifically noted they were designed to support aging in community.

IN THEIR OWN WORDS...

Abiitan Mill City

"Seniors will have the opportunity to age gracefully in an urban environment with easy access to the city's many attractions and amenities, plus multiple modes of public transit, which can reduce or eliminate the need to drive. Current Minneapolis residents will be able to remain within their own community, even as they age and their needs change."

Brightview Bethesda

"The project is strategically located in Bethesda's Woodmont Triangle, an area that is home to a number of exciting multi-family developments, both mid- and high-rise, as well as desirable retail, restaurants, and small businesses at the street level that create a dynamic mixed-use environment... Residents will be surrounded by restaurants, specialty shops, and retail service providers. Grocery stores, a movie theater, library, and more allow residents to continue an active life as part of their community instead of isolation... The street level features commercial retail uses accessible to both residents and the general public."

Fountainview at Gonda Westside

"It is designed to engage with the urban lifestyle Playa Vista offers with walking paths and easy access to restaurants, retail, and recreational opportunities. Inside the project, multiple communal program elements build upon the active and engaging Playa Vista culture."

Shenyang Senior Living

"The design connects the site to the city's adjacent park system providing residents from within the community and adjacent neighborhood the ability to connect... The housing is collaged into neighborhoods with varied amenities and programs providing unique destinations. Within close proximity to the Life Plan Community, retail, office, medical, and a school with daycare offer community resources. The school and daycare are adjacent to the Life Plan Community and physically linked encouraging connectivity."

Promoting a Sense of Community

Research has shown that social activities and productive engagement are as influential to elder survival as physical fitness activities.[5] Thus, it is important to encourage residents to leave their private homes to interact with others, encouraging relationships to form and promoting a sense of community.

Fifty-two percent of the jury-recognized DFAR14 submissions described ways in which their project promotes a sense of community—a significant increase from DFAR13's 31%, DFAR12's 26%, DFAR11's 33%, and DFAR10's 26%.

Promoting a Sense of Community Theme

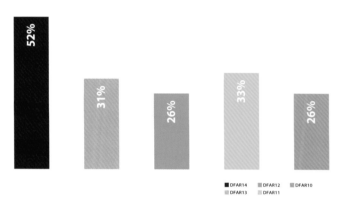

Among the jury-recognized DFAR14 submissions with this theme, sense of community is being promoted by common spaces that encourage socialization—both informal / spontaneous social interaction spaces (e.g., residents running into each other in laundry rooms, at sidewalks and shared yards, and by participating in Household activities), as well as formal / planned social interaction spaces (e.g., the interactions that occur in an activity room or theater).

> **DFAR14 projects recognized by the jury that promoted a sense of community include:**
>
> - Elm Place
> - EmpathiCare Village
> - Fountainview at Gonda Westside
> - Goodwin House Alexandria
> - Legacy Place Cottages
> - Linden Park Apartments
> - Rose Villa Pocket Neighborhoods & Main Street
> - Shenyang Senior Living
> - The Seasons at Alexandria
> - The Summit at Rockwood South Hill
> - The Trousdale Assisted Living and Memory Care
> - The Woodlands at John Knox Village
> - Well-Spring Resident Activity Center + Expansion

Elm Place

"We also paid particular [attention] to creating community within the building through the design of shared spaces. The building is an armature for individual expression as well as collective gathering."

Linden Park Apartments

"The architect added new sitting areas and laundry facilities on each floor versus previously having only one central laundry room. This allows for greater communal opportunities and interaction amongst residents, as well as providing greater convenience."

Rose Villa Pocket Neighborhoods & Main Street

"Each pocket neighborhood consists of seven cottage homes organized around an intimate garden setting that promotes a close-knit sense of community. Neighbors are naturally acquainted by the simple fact of shared space and small-scale living."

Shenyang Senior Living

"China is changing and developing quickly, and while new traditions are born, ties to traditional cultural activities and events remain important. The site design provides spaces for traditional outdoor markets, exercise and dance, tai chi, performances, holiday gatherings and parades, and socialization. Program spaces are purposefully located to promote passive and active interaction between people, culture, and nature."

Homelike Environments

Thirty-nine percent of the jury-recognized DFAR14 projects that had a residential component (from independent living through all levels of care) specifically described a residential approach or a desire to create homelike environments, a new theme for the DFAR Insights Study. From building layout to interior design decisions, operations, and programming, these projects strove to create environments that feel familiar, comfortable, and support each resident's personal dignity, unique interests, and daily rhythms.

Babcock Health Care Center

"Provide a true homelike environment. Key to this goal was providing fresh, cooked-to-order food as well as a resident-accessible kitchen where residents can sit and relax."

EmpathiCare Village

"The design approach creates a secured 'village' designed to provide neighborhood residential settings along with a variety of amenities for residents that emphasize the rhythms of daily living and familiar settings… This approach will provide residents with a full range of stimulating indoor and outdoor experiences and options that are much more similar to a residential or hospitality lifestyle versus a hospital-like environment."

North Ridge at Tacoma Lutheran

"The layout of North Ridge is intuitive—spaces are found as they would be in any home. The kitchen, dining room, and living room are all open to each other and to the short residential hallways. Residents may visit the living room for socializing with friends and family. A den is located adjacent to the living room to allow for quieter activity or visits with family. The dining room accommodates residents, staff, and family at meal times. In the kitchen, a lower seating area is built into the kitchen island so that residents can participate in meal preparation or baking activity—familiar and meaningful activities of family life."

The Cottage at Cypress Cove

"The project team envisioned a therapeutic environment and program that actually treats the symptoms of the disease while creating a familiar, comfortable home."

The Trousdale Assisted Living and Memory Care

"Located in a rapidly growing area with new housing development, the design team worked to create a modern and contemporary look that maintains a residential feel."

The Woodlands at John Knox Village

"Thoughtfully planned to protect elders' privacy, honor their personal choices, and assure their dignity, design of The Woodlands has eliminated the institutional feel of traditional nursing homes and created a home, which is the fundamental philosophy of The Green House® Project."

Ecological Sustainability

Ninety-six percent of the jury-recognized DFAR14 projects (and 91% of the 53 submissions) reported having ecologically sustainable features. However, only 28% of the jury-recognized DFAR14 projects actually discussed ecological sustainability within their project description text (less than DFAR13's 38%, and more than DFAR12's 24%).

Ecological Sustainability Theme

■ DFAR14   ■ DFAR12   ■ DFAR10
■ DFAR13   ■ DFAR11

Thirty-two percent of the jury-recognized DFAR14 projects (and 25% of all submissions), compared to DFAR13's 26% (and 29% of all submissions), are or are registered to be certified as ecologically sustainable by an independent organization, including LEED, Passive House, Enterprise Green Communities, WELL Building, and Energy Star. An additional 16% of the jury-recognized submissions were designed to meet green standards, but will not be going through a formal certification process.

Among the jury-recognized DFAR14 submissions, the green features with the greatest impact to the project include: energy efficiency, maximized daylighting, and conscientious choice of materials. The first two were also in the top three influencers for DFARs 11, 12, and 13, however, in this cycle, more applicants selected conscientious choice of materials as having an important impact.

Most Impactful Green Features

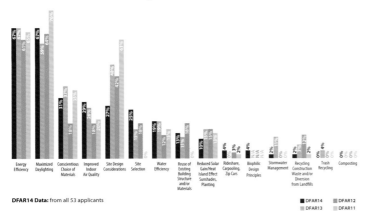

DFAR14 Data: from all 53 applicants

■ DFAR14 ■ DFAR12
■ DFAR13 ■ DFAR11

In addition, for the jury-recognized DFAR14 submissions, 40% are built on greenfield sites (no previous development other than agricultural or natural landscape); 16% are on greyfields (an underused real estate asset or land, such as an outdated / failing retail and commercial strip mall); and 4% are on brownfields (land previously used for industrial or commercial use, often requiring remediation of hazardous waste or pollution).

Projects' Site Classification

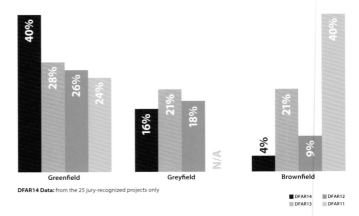

DFAR14 Data: from the 25 jury-recognized projects only

■ DFAR14 ■ DFAR12
■ DFAR13 ■ DFAR11

When asked about the primary motivation for including ecologically sustainable features, responses were similar to those from DFARs 11, 12, and 13. Supporting the mission / values of the client / provider was, again, the most popular response among all jury-recognized DFAR14 submissions. Like DFAR13 (at 67%), improving building occupants' health / well-being was also a major motivation at 50% (both up from 9% in DFAR12).

Primary Green Motivations

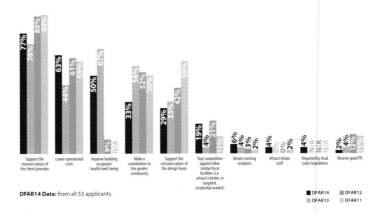

DFAR14 Data: from all 53 applicants

■ DFAR14 ■ DFAR12
■ DFAR13 ■ DFAR11

The DFAR14 submission form asked about the challenges the projects faced when the design team attempted to incorporate green features. These varied greatly, with no common challenges. Applicants discussed issues with site remediation of a greyfield, stormwater management, implementing a green roof, first-cost premiums, working with an uneducated client, and the cost and availability of products (due to that particular project's location and need to import from overseas).

Fountainview at Gonda Westside

"This project aims to set a new standard for senior living communities by delivering high-quality care for the elderly with a focus on the needs of the 'whole person.' It offers a place to live a physically and intellectually engaging lifestyle to enrich the quality of life for seniors. Strategically located in the heart of Playa Vista, Fountainview is not another isolated senior living community… It is designed to engage with the urban lifestyle Playa Vista offers with walking paths and easy access to restaurants, retail, and recreational opportunities. Inside the project, multiple communal program elements build upon the active and engaging Playa Vista culture."

The Summit at Rockwood South Hill

"Using biophilic design to illuminate and support the seven dimensions of wellness, the Summit (and Ridge) tower now offers the opportunity for a healthy, productive lifestyle in a LEED-Silver Certified building… [including] an expanded first-floor community space focused on wellness… wellness relates to everything they offer, including food services, activity programs, community connections, and creative endeavors."

DFAR14 Insights and Innovations Photography Credits

Page 185 *Fitness / Wellness Amenity Spaces* (clockwise from top left): Tricia Shay Photography / Admiral District; Gensler / Ryan Gobuty; Benjamin Benschneider Photography; Nathan Cox Photography; Thomas Watkins; *Learning / Activity Amenity Spaces* (clockwise from top left): Gensler / Ryan Gobuty; Robert Benson Photography; Robert Benson Photography; Alise O'Brien Photography; Perkins Eastman

Page 186 *Dining Amenity Spaces* (clockwise from top left): Troy Thies; Nathan Cox Photography; Benjamin Benschneider Photography; CJMW Architecture; C. J. Walker Photography, Inc.; CJMW Architecture; Alexis Denton; Robert Benson Photography; *Outdoor Amenity Spaces* (clockwise from top left): Gensler / Ryan Gobuty; Sarah Mechling; Hord Coplan Macht

Page 188 *Connection to Nature—Outdoor Spaces* (clockwise from top left): Gensler / Ryan Gobuty; Tricia Shay Photography; c.c. hodgson architectural group; Benjamin Benschneider Photography; David Franzen; Alexis Denton; Robert Benson Photography; Tricia Shay Photography; Sarah Mechling

Page 189 *Connection to Nature—Daylighting* (clockwise from top left): Atlantic Archives, Inc. / Richard Leo Johnson; RH Wilson Photography; Sarah Mechling; Perkins Eastman; Nathan Cox Photography; Alain Jaramillo Photography; *Connection to Nature—Views* (clockwise from top left): Robert Benson Photography; Hord Coplan Macht; Benjamin Benschneider Photography

Page 191 *Contemporary Interior Aesthetics* (clockwise from top left): Sarah Mechling; Carolyn Bates; David Franzen; Benjamin Benschneider Photography; Robert Benson Photography; Perkins Eastman; *A Mixture of Contemporary and Traditional Interior Aesthetics* (clockwise from top left): Atlantic Archives, Inc. / Richard Leo Johnson; Alise O'Brien Photography; Nathan Cox Photography

Page 192 *Household Model, Culture Change, and Person-Centered Care* (clockwise from top left): Sarah Mechling; Nathan Cox Photography; C. J. Walker Photography, Inc.; Jesse Young

Page 194 *Connecting to the Greater Community* (clockwise from top left): Hord Coplan Macht; Nathan Cox Photography; Troy Thies

Notes

1 Yeginsu, C. (January 17, 2018). U.K. Appoints a Minister for Loneliness. *The New York Times.* Retrieved May 15, 2018 from https://www.nytimes.com/2018/01/17/world/europe/uk-britain-loneliness.html.

2 Bentayeb, M., Simoni, M., Norback, D., Baldacci, S., Maio, S., Viegi, G., & Annesi-Maesano, I. (2013). Indoor air pollution and respiratory health in the elderly. *Journal of Environmental Science and Health, Part A, 48* (14), 1783–89.

3 Gabriel, Z., & Bowling, A. (2004). Quality of life from the perspective of older people. *Aging & Society, 24,* 675–91.

4 The Advancing Excellence in America's Nursing Homes Campaign. Retrieved March 17, 2014 from http://www.nhqualitycampaign.org/star_index.aspx?controls=personcenteredcareexploregoal.

5 Glass, T. A., Mendes de Leon, C., Marottoli, R. A., & Berkman, L. F. (1999). Population-based study of social and productive activities as predictors of survival among elderly Americans. *BMJ, 319,* 478–83.

Student Design Awards

Introduction

Emerald Expositions

The 2018 Environments for Aging (EFA) Expo & Conference held in Savannah, Georgia, brought a first to the event: a student design competition. The idea was born from a partnership between the EFA Expo and *Environments for Aging* magazine, AIA Design for Aging Knowledge Community, KaTO Architecture, and Savannah College of Art and Design (SCAD). The program tasked third-year SCAD students seeking Bachelor of Fine Arts degrees to consider and answer the challenges that come with rebuilding dwellings within communities affected by the natural disasters that devastated Puerto Rico in 2017.

Projects were required to consider very specific requirements, including supporting a variety of familial groups, providing adequate mobility for seniors, delivering modularity and the ability to make additions over time, and integrating passive design solutions such as photovoltaic panels and rainwater collection—all at a budget of $25,000 per unit. It posed a daunting task for any designer, but we were collectively blown away by what the students delivered, and honored to showcase their work at the EFA Expo. We also can't wait to see what ideas the finalists take with them to Puerto Rico as these concepts are brought to life.

We here at EFA Expo and *EFA* magazine are delighted to support this competition and be part of bringing true innovation and life-changing solutions to the people who need it most. We also consider this the first of many more design competitions to come that engage students and identify populations in need—particularly those that include seniors—and how to serve them through design. Thank you to AIA Design for Aging for coordinating this effort and all future ones, and congratulations to the competition winners.

Kevin Gaffney
Show Director
Emerald Expositions

Background

In the rural and mountainous community of Barrio San Salvador, Oscar and Lilian (husband and wife) were hard hit by Hurricane Maria. The strongest storm to strike Puerto Rico in 85 years arrived as a Category 4 hurricane on September 20, 2017, and ripped through the middle of the island of Puerto Rico.

This unprecedented disaster destroyed hundreds of thousands of buildings, leaving many of the 3.4 million residents without adequate shelter, working electricity, and clean water. Concrete and block structures lost roofs while buildings of wood construction were often completely destroyed. For Oscar and Lilian, only a wood platform on block stilts remains as evidence of their home.

For community residents, there were only two options. Move to another area where new housing is being constructed or accept an offer of $25,000 from FEMA to repair or rebuild their homes. Oscar and Lilian have title to their land, and although currently living with friends, want to return home to their community.

Back in the United States, Ingrid Fraley, past chair and member of the American Institute of Architects Design for Aging (DFA) Knowledge Community began a discussion with Angelica Santana, a Virginia-based lighting designer who was on her way to Puerto Rico to help her family and to provide additional assistance to other communities. At the same time, connections with like-minded individuals and companies were being formed with the goal of maximizing talent, identifying expertise, and coordinating opportunities that could help Puerto Ricans get back on their feet and rebuild their homes.

DFA engaged with Emerald Expositions, providers of the 2018 Environments for Aging Expo & Conference, to establish a unique collaboration with Savannah College of Art and Design. DFA agreed to format a design competition for third-year architecture and design students, but raised the bar by replacing a theoretical project with the design of a modular home to be constructed in Puerto Rico.

With students and faculty embracing the idea, DFA needed a champion to structure the competition. Kyle Murphy, founder and executive director of KaTO Architecture, accepted the challenge, visited the community of San Salvador, and introduced Oscar and Lilian to the students via the competition design brief. Design requirements included a modular design that could be expanded to accommodate families while providing supportive elements for older adults. Without losing sight of the FEMA budget and local material supply chains, student teams designed structures incorporating solar and rainwater collection devices, developed story boards, and constructed models. Five weeks later, 13 teams presented their solutions to a jury of design professionals at the EFA Expo & Conference.

All of the submissions were thoughtfully conceived and four teams were specifically acknowledged: a merit award winner (Team 11—Nueva+Vida) and three honorable mentions (Team 02—Bóveda, Team 01—Esperanza, Team 07—Lumina). KaTO and its engineering consultants generously volunteered their time and expertise to blend the best elements of these designs into one final design concept. SCAD students will have opportunities to stay involved as the project moves forward to final construction drawings and implementation.

The American Institute of Architects Design for Aging Knowledge Community sincerely thanks Emerald Expositions, sponsor of the Environments for Aging Expo & Conference, the faculty, staff, and students at Savannah College of Art and Design, KaTO Architecture, the jurors, and the donors (T.R. Martin & Associates, Inc. and Kellex Seating) who helped fund the winning team.

If you are interested in helping DFA and KaTO with this project, please contact Ingrid Fraley at ifraley@aol.com.

Top: Oscar and Lilian's house after being hit by Hurricane Maria in 2017
Photography: Kyle Murphy, KaTO Architecture

Competition Brief Description

Rebuilding communities in Puerto Rico: module by module

Rebuilding communities, young and old, affected by natural disasters is a team effort. EFA has partnered with KaTO and SCAD to deliver a student competition in architecture and interior design disciplines, which takes into account the challenges of rebuilding dwellings that both create and rebuild communities affected by the natural disasters that struck the island of Puerto Rico in 2017. The competition entry involves numerous national organizations such as the AIA, EFA, and stakeholders in professional and academic practice to put forth a proposal developed by third-year Bachelor of Fine Arts students at SCAD.

Dwelling units should be comprised of modular size, such that an addition or subtraction of the modular components of the proposal produces a defined "tranche." The dwellings must take into account a wide variety of familial groups of people, to include direct and indirect family members and provide an adequate environment for aging and mobility-limited family members. It is estimated that the dwellings should comprise an area anywhere between 400 square feet and 1200 square feet, depending on the proposed familial occupancy. Regardless of proposed dwelling size, the project must accommodate the ability for the dwelling to be subsequently enlarged over time.

The proposed solution should also provide the ability for residents of Puerto Rico to utilize the project modules to be adapted to existing dwellings where minor damage has occurred, in such a way that these modular pieces can also serve other community members whose dwellings were only partially damaged.

The proposed solution should also incorporate the use of passive climatic solutions for cooling and heating the interior spaces. The dwellings should incorporate the use of photovoltaic panels to provide electricity for these dwellings. Other applicable passive design solutions to include are rainwater collection and raising the internal floor plan above the ground in order to mitigate future flooding (e.g. concrete or CMU foundation pillars above grade). The dwellings should also be adaptable to a wide variety of terrains and provide for enough flexibility for these to be assembled in-situ regardless of topography.

The project should consider that the proposed "working" solution could be built with a very reduced budget of $25,000 per recipient of FEMA federal assistance funding. Regardless of federal funding for recipients, participants must bear in mind that the proposed solution must be cost-conscious and be built with "modularity" over time, if possible.

Opposite, above, left and following page: Dwellings in Barrio San Salvador, including Oscar and Lilian's house, after being hit by Hurricane Maria in 2017

Photography: Kyle Murphy, KaTO Architecture

Team 11
Nueva+Vida

Sophia Regan
Ralph Nickles
Isabella Rodriguez Durrego

"Nueva+Vida is a modular system for starting a new life. It is a panelized structure that can be replicated, reproduced, and repaired at the convenience of the owner. Utilizing dimensional lumber as interchangeable parts. This will keep construction and economical wastes lower. The idea is understandable allowing construction to be continued and carried out by the families who live in these homes."

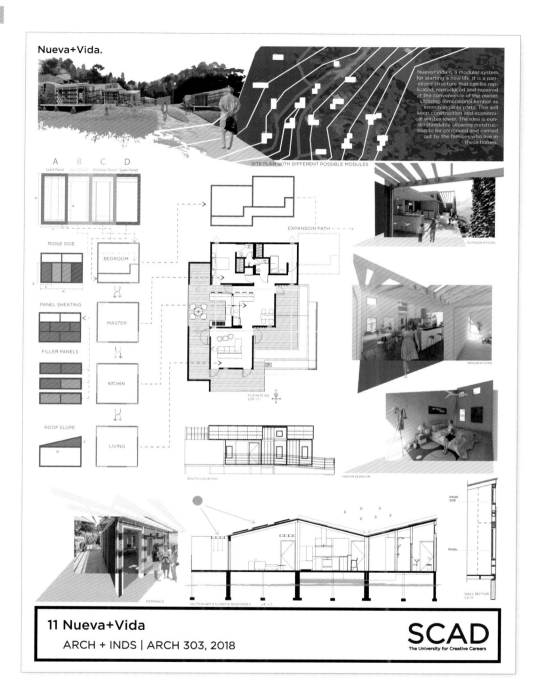

Nueva+Vida.

Nueva+Vida is a modular system for starting a new life. It is a panelized structure that can be replicated, reproduced and repaired at the convenience of the owner. Utilizing dimensional lumber as interchangeable parts. This will keep construction and economical wastes lower. The idea is understandable allowing construction to be continued and carried out by the families who live in these homes.

SITE PLAN WITH DIFFERENT POSSIBLE MODULES

EXPANSION PATH

OUTDOOR KITCHEN

INDOOR KITCHEN

MASTER BEDROOM

FLOOR PLAN

SOUTH ELEVATION

ENTRANCE

SECTION WITH CLIMATIC RESPONSES

WALL SECTION

11 Nueva+Vida
ARCH + INDS | ARCH 303, 2018

SCAD
The University for Creative Careers

Team 01
Esperanza

Tyler Wilson

Cameron Currie

Blake Albritton

Emily Havlicek

"Inspired by the hexagonal form, Esperanza aims to restore the lives of those in Puerto Rico with an intricate bamboo structure. For a community that lost so much, our design is meant to restore hope and allow users to feel a sense of security in their new home."

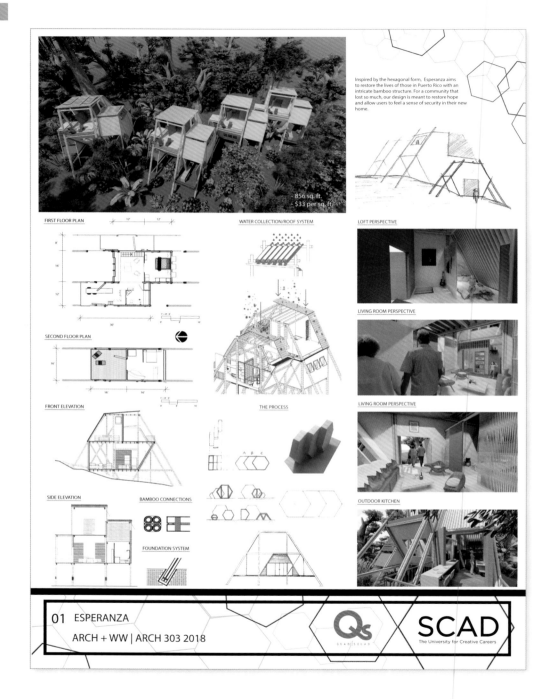

Inspired by the hexagonal form, Esperanza aims to restore the lives of those in Puerto Rico with an intricate bamboo structure. For a community that lost so much, our design is meant to restore hope and allow users to feel a sense of security in their new home.

- 856 sq. ft.
- $33 per sq. ft.

FIRST FLOOR PLAN

SECOND FLOOR PLAN

FRONT ELEVATION

SIDE ELEVATION

BAMBOO CONNECTIONS

FOUNDATION SYSTEM

WATER COLLECTION/ROOF SYSTEM

THE PROCESS

LOFT PERSPECTIVE

LIVING ROOM PERSPECTIVE

LIVING ROOM PERSPECTIVE

OUTDOOR KITCHEN

01 ESPERANZA

ARCH + WW | ARCH 303 2018

Qs

SCAD
The University for Creative Careers

Team 02
Bóveda

Will Kyle
Marco Mourao
Rachel Andert

"The Bóveda is a residence which keeps its most valuable assets protected, behind a fortified wall which acts as the spine and lifeline to the rest of this modular home. By keeping each component of the home connected to its lifeline, it can adapt and function efficiently while providing its owner a revitalized lease on life."

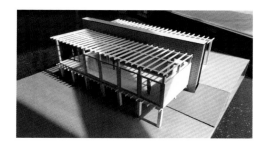

Team 07
Lumina

Mia Arenburg
Jacqueline Traudt
Ana Masuk

"Following the devastation of a hurricane, people seek comfort within the revival of their community. With its optimistic glow, Lumina will bring hope to the victims of Puerto Rico, and illuminate the island."

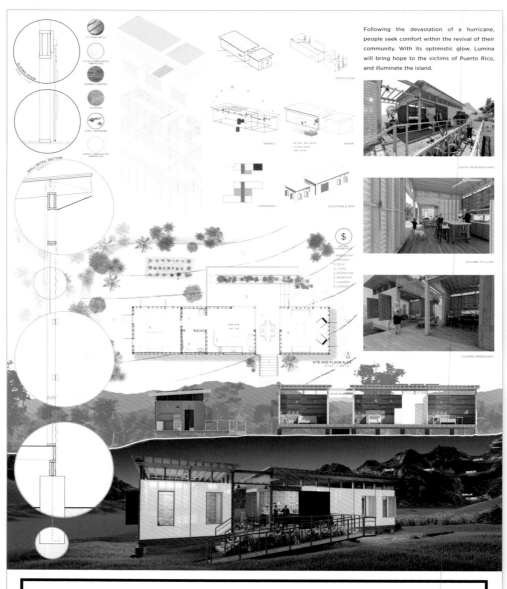

Following the devastation of a hurricane, people seek comfort within the revival of their community. With its optimistic glow, Lumina will bring hope to the victims of Puerto Rico, and illuminate the island.

07 LUMINA
ARCH + INDS | ARCH 303, 2018

SCAD
The University for Creative Careers

Team 03
Project Aevum

Kelsey Dempsey
Dillon Twigg
Meagan Flynn

"Project Aevum gives a wider range of adaptability to the permanent structure, allowing for residences to open up and remain semi-exposed when convenient, but to allow for the building to close up on itself as a protective unit in the event of a natural disaster. Steps have been taken to allow this unit to continually expand as time progresses, making it truly adaptable to any scenario. This residence addresses the act of growing alongside its occupants by allowing those at any stage in life to have easy access and use of the building. Project Aevum serves as a beacon of hope, rising up from the earth in the aftermath of disaster. Built to withstand that which may come, but designed to celebrate that which is already here; family, community, and life."

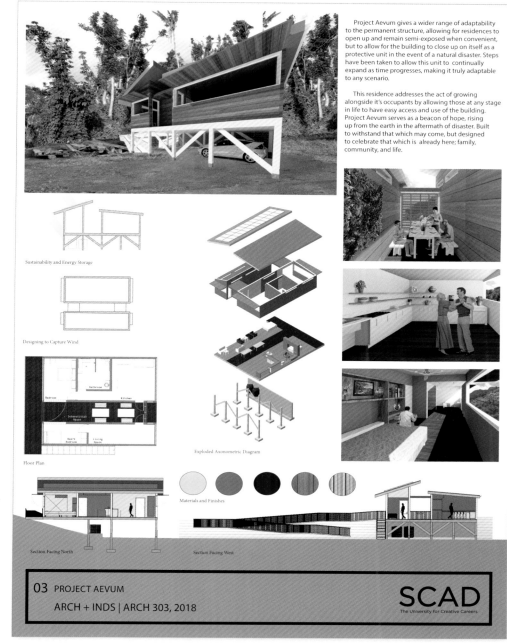

Project Aevum gives a wider range of adaptability to the permanent structure, allowing for residences to open up and remain semi-exposed when convenient, but to allow for the building to close up on itself as a protective unit in the event of a natural disaster. Steps have been taken to allow this unit to continually expand as time progresses, making it truly adaptable to any scenario.

This residence addresses the act of growing alongside it's occupants by allowing those at any stage in life to have easy access and use of the building. Project Aevum serves as a beacon of hope, rising up from the earth in the aftermath of disaster. Built to withstand that which may come, but designed to celebrate that which is already here; family, community, and life.

Sustainability and Energy Storage

Designing to Capture Wind

Floor Plan

Exploded Axonometric Diagram

Materials and Finishes

Section Facing North

Section Facing West

03 PROJECT AEVUM
ARCH + INDS | ARCH 303, 2018

SCAD
The University for Creative Careers

Team 04
Shift

Ajane Ramsey
Nick Hammond
Madison Cotterill

"This simple, self-sustaining design is intended to provide a secure home for Puerto Rican families recovering from the aftermath of Hurricane Maria. By combining the elements of a courtyard and a pathway, a new typology of community is created, reflecting the vernacular of the island. The modularity of the design allows for the opportunity to expand, which encourages multi-generational communities. The simplicity of the design enables families to participate in the construction of their new home, and aids in the return to normalcy."

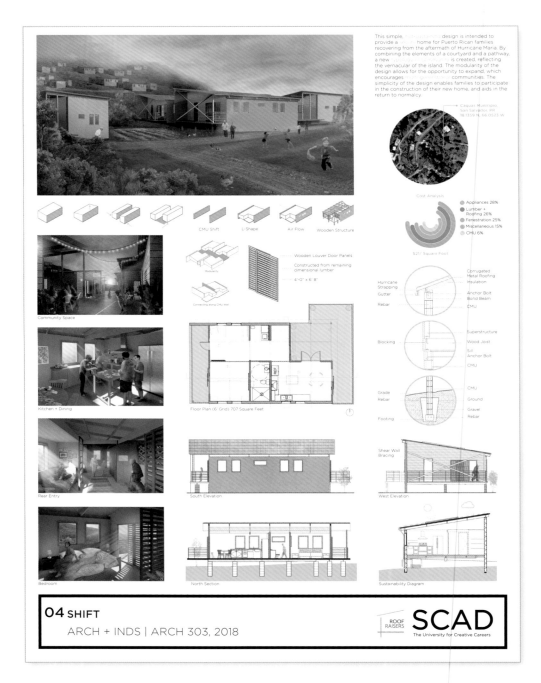

04 SHIFT

ARCH + INDS | ARCH 303, 2018

ROOF RAISERS

SCAD
The University for Creative Careers

Team 05
Vivir

Emma Davis

Will Cao

Julie Cheong

"To withstand a disaster such as Hurricane Irma, Vivir uses passive systems independent from losses of electricity or water, and thrifty but sturdy construction techniques. Vivir expands through a modular system from a systems-and-utilities core, providing the best fit to every family and making it easy to expand the home to fit every generation."

Team 06
Enlightenment

Natalie Tang
Daniel Ha
Wan-Yi Tan (Irene)

"The Enlightenment is a project for the celebration of life. It focuses to provide a universal, sustainable, simple, and unique living space for the community. This project focuses on embracing the community, culture, and nature. It also aims to reflect the core value of Puerto Rico and let the residents enjoy every moment within the house."

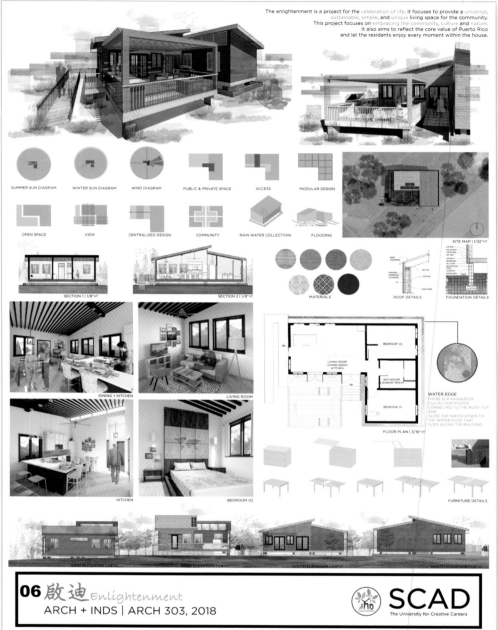

The enlightenment is a project for the *celebration of life*. It focuses to provide a *universal, sustainable, simple, and unique living space for the community*. This project focuses on embracing the community, culture and nature. It also aims to reflect the core value of Puerto Rico and let the residents enjoy every moment within the house.

SUMMER SUN DIAGRAM   WINTER SUN DIAGRAM   WIND DIAGRAM   PUBLIC & PRIVATE SPACE   ACCESS   MODULAR DESIGN

OPEN SPACE   VIEW   CENTRALIZED DESIGN   COMMUNITY   RAIN WATER COLLECTION   FLOODING

SITE MAP | 1/32"=1'

SECTION 1 | 1/8"=1'   SECTION 2 | 1/8"=1'

MATERIALS   ROOF DETAILS   FOUNDATION DETAILS

DINING + KITCHEN   LIVING ROOM

KITCHEN   BEDROOM 02

FLOOR PLAN | 3/16"=1'

WATER EDGE

FURNITURE DETAILS

EAST ELEVATION   WEST ELEVATION   SOUTH ELEVATION   NORTH ELEVATION

06 啟迪 Enlightenment
ARCH + INDS | ARCH 303, 2018

SCAD
The University for Creative Careers

Team 14
Hogar

Nicole Niava
Rodrigo Soria
Bernarda Barahona

"For our design, we chose the kitchen to be the heart of the residence; it is the most important space as it is the connection between the rooms and the outdoor spaces. The program is simple to give residents comfort and the flexibility to have their privacy as well as communal areas. The shape of the house was designed to accommodate the cultural traditions of Puerto Rico allowing the home to expand and create bigger communities. The design allows for passive heating and cooling strategies as well as rainwater collection and filtration system."

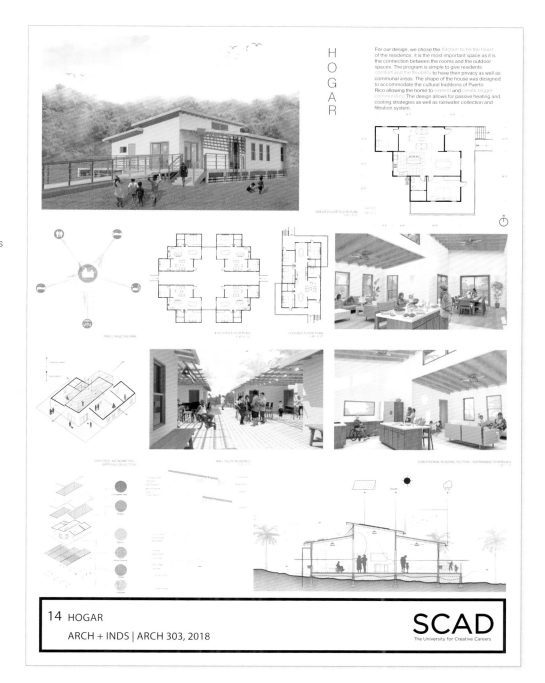

14 HOGAR

ARCH + INDS | ARCH 303, 2018

SCAD
The University for Creative Careers

Student Teams

01 Tyler Wilson, Cameron Currie, Blake Albritton, Emily Havlicek [Honorable Mention]

02 Will Kyle, Marco Mourao, Rachel Andert [Honorable Mention]

03 Kelsey Dempsey, Dillon Twigg, Meagan Flynn

04 Ajane Ramsey, Nick Hammond, Madison Cotterill

05 Emma Davis, Will Cao, Julie Cheong

06 Natalie Tang, Daniel Ha, Wan-Yi Tan (Irene)

07 Mia Arenburg, Jacqueline Traudt, Ana Masuk [Honorable Mention]

08 Hala Hamdi, Orianna Nardone, Mina Rhee

09 Riya Gupta, Sarah Black, Fabia Sainz

11 Sophia Regan, Ralph Nickles, Isabella Rodriguez Durrego [Merit]

12 Patrick Lucas, Hanna Milewski, Tiffany Tan

13 Mohammed Al Amoudi, Veronica Paulon, Camila Alban

14 Nicole Niava, Rodrigo Soria, Bernarda Barahona

Jurors

Greg Skinner, AIA, Hussey Gay Bell

Kyle Murphy, KaTO Architecture

Ann Smith, FAIA, NCARB, Lominack Kolman Smith Architects

Jerry Lominack, FAIA, NCARB, Lominack Kolman Smith Architects

David Banta, AIA Design for Aging Knowledge Community, Wiencek + Associates Architects + Planners

SCAD Faculty Associated with the Design Competition (studios)

Ivan S. Chow, AIA, NCARB, Dean, School of Building Arts

Joaquin E. Roesch, Architect (AZ, FL), RIBA, AIA, NCARB, Chair of Architecture and Urban Design

Elaine Gallagher Adams, AIA, LEED AP BD+C, Professor of Architecture and Urban Design

Huy Sinh Ngo, Professor of Architecture

Alice Guess, Professor of Architecture

Competition Partners

American Institute of Architects Design for Aging Knowledge Community

The mission of the American Institute of Architects Design for Aging (DFA) Knowledge Community is to foster design innovation and disseminate knowledge necessary to enhance the built environment and quality of life for an aging society. This includes relevant research in characteristics, planning, and costs associated with innovative design for aging. In addition, DFA provides outcome data on the value of these design solutions and environments.

Savannah College of Art and Design

Mission: SCAD exists to prepare talented students for professional careers, emphasizing learning through individual attention in a positively oriented university environment.

Vision: SCAD, an institution with distinctive yet complementary locations, will be recognized as the leader in defining art and design education. By employing innovation in all areas, SCAD will provide a superior education through talented and dedicated faculty and staff, leading-edge technology, advanced learning resources, and comprehensive support services.

Values: Being a student-centered institution; providing an exceptional education and life-changing experience for students; demonstrating quality and excellence in every aspect of operations; sustaining a respectful and honest university environment; growing while continually improving; being innovative and results-oriented; promoting a cooperative team spirit and a positive can-do attitude; going the extra mile.

Design for Aging
_____
an **AIA** Knowledge Community

AIA

SCAD
The University for Creative Careers

KaTO Architecture—Kyle Murphy, Executive Director

In conjunction with Syska Hennessy Group (MEP engineering) and Walter P Moore and Associates, Inc. (structural engineering).

KaTO Architecture focuses on social projects for education, health care, disaster relief, clean water solutions, and other critical needs in underprivileged communities internationally. KaTO currently has projects under construction and in development in the U.S., Mexico, Costa Rica, Peru, Dominican Republic, India, and Pakistan.

In the aftermath of any disaster, the greatest concern is that families will rebuild in ways that are not able to withstand future hurricanes and other natural disasters. KaTO has leveraged its extensive network of design and construction professionals to create a model house project in the community of San Salvador. The intent is for the project to make a significant impact in the rebuilding process, beyond the model house itself, by demonstrating to other homeowners the proper ways of rebuilding.

KaTO intends to work with local contractors and professionals to implement the first model house on a selected site, and make the drawings available to the rest of the community upon completion. The owners of the site to receive the first model house have agreed to allow others from the community to tour the house.

KaTO is a registered 501(c)(3) non-profit organization.

Competition Sponsors

T.R. Martin & Associates, Inc.—Cathy Martin, President

T.R. Martin & Associates, Inc. is an independent sales organization representing Fairfield Contract, Senior Living Division, Samuel Lawrence Health Care, Space Tables, and Dura Care Seating. T.R. Martin & Associates, Inc. represents these manufacturers in the states of Virginia, West Virginia, Maryland, North Carolina, South Carolina, and Washington, D.C.

Kellex Seating—Chris Rice, Doug Fawcett, and the Kellex family

When Kellex Seating was founded, more than 20 years ago, it made the commitment to put U.S. manufacturing first. It vowed to provide customers with the quality and service that are the benchmarks of "Made in America." The company had two goals: to become the best furniture manufacturing partner to its customers, and to provide employment opportunities to families and communities devastated by factory closings resulting from outsourcing to foreign countries. Kellex Seating developed a simple message to stay focused on that commitment: Make it happen, make it here.

Kellex Seating makes its products in the U.S. and supports the regional economy by partnering with local suppliers. In many cases, it owns and manages its most critical manufacturing components. From 15 acres of factory floor (the equivalent of 20 football fields) in North Carolina, Virginia, and Mississippi, orders go from the sawmill to frame operations, foam fabrication, finishing, upholstery, and out the door through shipping. Every piece of furniture is measurable in hours and those hours create jobs in the U.S.A.

Rob Mayer: A Look Back

Hulda B. & Maurice L. Rothschild Foundation
Signature Regulatory Reform in Long-Term Care
American Institute of Architects Design for Aging

In Memory of Dr. Robert Nathan Mayer

Introduction
Dr. Debra E. Weese-Mayer, President of the Hulda B. & Maurice L. Rothschild
  Foundation, and President of The Mayer-Rothschild Foundation

The FGI-Rothschild Foundation Task Force on Acoustics
David M. Sykes

Building Performance Guidelines
James E. Woods

Pioneer Network Projects
Cathy Lieblich, Penny Cook, Karen Schoeneman, Carmen Bowman,
  Bonnie Burman, Amy Carpenter, Linda Bump

**Guidelines for the Design & Development of Residential Health, Care, and
Support Facilities**
Doug Erickson

Low Vision Task Force with the National Institute of Building Sciences
Stephanie Stubbs

**Standards for Nursing Home and Assisted Living Residences in Toileting
and Bathing for Elders**
Jon A. Sanford

Closing Remarks—Personal Reflections
Bonnie Burman

Robert Nathan Mayer, Ph.D., Founder and President of the Hulda B. & Maurice L. Rothschild Foundation

On behalf of the Hulda B. & Maurice L. Rothschild Foundation, our family would like to express our deep appreciation to the American Institute of Architects and its biennial *Design for Aging* publication for recognizing the paradigm-shifting accomplishments of our beloved Dr. Robert Nathan Mayer in strategically working to improve the ways that older adults live in long-term care settings. In honoring Rob's unique contributions to improving the built environment and to developing best practices in person-centered care, *Design for Aging Review 14* celebrates Rob's legacy of vision-creating action where he deemed inactivity to be simply unacceptable. In joining Rob's colleagues here in saluting his life's accomplishments, we are humbled by the breadth of the list of his singular achievements in regulatory eldercare reform.

Rob was the Founder and President of the Hulda B. & Maurice L. Rothschild Foundation. For more than two decades under Rob's leadership, the Foundation was identified as a pioneer and lamplighter in eldercare reform both at the national policy level and local levels, to strengthen and broaden the person-centered care movement. Through a wide range of initiatives, including the eight national regulatory task forces highlighted in this publication, Rob and the Foundation sought to enhance the quality of life and the experience of residents, patients, and families alike in long-term care communities. This commitment was recognized in 2009 by the Council on Foundations with the Critical Impact Award, given for innovative leadership and bold vision to solve societal issues and enhance the common good. In 2012, Rob was named one of the eight most influential people in health care design by *Healthcare Design Magazine* for moving the health care industry to embrace new person-centered approaches. In 2016, after his untimely passing, Rob was named the second recipient of the Pioneer Award from the Facility Guidelines Institute for his vision and leadership as a driving force in the removal of barriers to achieving person-centered environments and effecting significant and meaningful regulatory changes for nursing homes and other long-term care settings. The 2018 edition of the *Guidelines for Design and Construction of Residential Health, Care, and Support Facilities* was dedicated to Rob for his success and vision.

As a family, we have redoubled our dedication to promoting Rob's vision of person-centered care by creating The Mayer-Rothschild Foundation in Chicago in Rob's honor. This new Foundation is dedicated to promoting person-centered care in assisted living facilities, Continuing Care Retirement Communities, and nursing homes across the nation. One of our key strategic initiatives continues Rob's keen sense of the need to promote person-centered values and practices broadly through consumer education, industry awareness, and a deep integration of contemporary marketing and communications to lift the bar across the field. This publication reaffirms those values in highlighting these Rob-specific accomplishments.

We salute the work of the American Institute of Architects and applaud the 26th anniversary of its Design for Aging initiative. Our children and I are delighted to join the resounding response from leaders in the discipline as we recognize these life accomplishments of our luminary and beloved Dr. Robert Nathan Mayer. Many organizations, agencies, and individuals were influenced by Rob during his life time and continue to support his ideas of person-centered care.

With sincere gratitude,

Debra E. Weese-Mayer, M.D.
President
Hulda B. & Maurice L. Rothschild Foundation
The Mayer-Rothschild Foundation

The FGI-Rothschild Foundation Task Force on Acoustics

The fifth dimension: designing "soundscapes" for health care

At age 65, 60 percent of Americans have hearing disorders. At 85 years of age and over, 80 percent of people suffer from hearing disorders that can be disabling and, for many, painful. Dr. Mayer wanted to address this long-overlooked problem by "changing the soundscape" of residential care communities in America.

One July day in 2014, my desk phone rang. I'm seldom at my desk—I usually work in a comfortable chair elsewhere—so, curious and seated there, I answered it. A polite, soft-spoken stranger identified himself as Dr. Robert Mayer from Hulda B. & Maurice L. Rothschild Foundation in Chicago. Understand, the president of a foundation doesn't just call up strangers. I run a non-profit, so for people like me, conversations with foundations usually begin with jumping through hoops and over hurdles, filling out applications, and enduring cool questions from bureaucrats who know lots of ways to say no. Clearly Rob Mayer was an unusual guy. He had a simple, forthright request: Would we be interested in forming an expert task force to address the abysmal noise problems in nursing homes? I was astonished.

Here's the thing Dr. Mayer understood: People can't see sound, and for architects and designers it doesn't show up in drawings or VR simulations— it's virtually invisible. But for the occupants who inhabit finished spaces— particularly elders who live in residential care communities—sound / noise is invisible but often disorienting and disturbing; it's a virtually inescapable fifth dimension. Their inability to hear clearly or to understand conversation amidst background noise leads to social isolation and depression, to growing problems with balance (your ears are your balance mechanism), and poor balance can lead to an increased incidence of falls. This is serious stuff. It's a ubiquitous life-safety problem.

For occupants, being in a room can be like living inside a drum or a guitar or a piano. They are captive to reverberant, inescapable, and sometimes cacophonous sounds—"noise." Specialists call this the "soundscape."

If you are a designer, you create the soundscape whether you mean to or not. There are lots of sounds none of us want to hear. In fact, that's how physicists and engineers define "noise;" it's unwanted sound. But, as the U.S. Centers for Disease Control and Prevention and other agencies point out, noise can also be harmful to health and well-being. It can be a life-safety problem, and, since a majority of people of 65 years of age suffer some form of hearing disorder or loss, it is a public health problem, albeit an under-recognized one. That's why sound and vibration are formally recognized as important parts of Indoor Environmental Quality (IEQ) in LEED and other building quality rating programs.

In fact, the U.S. Centers for Disease Control and Prevention and the World Health Organization both point to a growing epidemic of harmful environmental sound. So much noise is not normal or even tolerable. It's a postmodern problem. A century and a half of modernism in philosophy, art, architecture, and industry transformed society in both bountiful and destructive ways, but also made it cacophonous—and unhealthy.

Who does it affect most? Populations at risk: the elderly, the very young, the sickest, the poorest among us. So that has been our focus for the past decade and a half. Patients and health care workers in all kinds of health care environments—hospitals, elder residential care communities, outpatient clinics, offices—trying to be productive in environments where their effectiveness is compromised by unwanted sound.

Dr. Mayer knew we had been working on this problem—the soundscape of health care facilities, specifically hospitals—for a decade, and that we were action-oriented. Through partnership with the AIA and its partner, Facility Guidelines Institute, we had been hard at work since 2004 developing criteria for the design and construction of quieter health care facilities. We had won the battle in hospitals and were just getting started on outpatient facilities, but we hadn't yet gotten to Dr. Mayer's chief concern, residential care communities. He wanted us to hurry up. He wanted us to publish comprehensive, code-level criteria in the next edition of the *FGI Guidelines* due out in 2018. That was a tall order!

Grateful for his concern, his urgency, and action-orientation, we got to work. In January 2015, we kicked off the FGI-Rothschild Foundation Task Force on Acoustics for Elders in Residential Care, having recruited 35 experts from medicine, public health, government, scientific research, architecture, engineering, and design. Then we formed a subcommittee to conduct both primary and secondary research and identified a research site.

Next time you start to work on the design of a residential care community, remember to thank Dr. Robert Mayer for his passionate commitment to making these places better for the people who inhabit them.

David M. Sykes, Chair
The Quiet Coalition
The Rothschild Task Force on Acoustics for Elders in Residential Care
The FGI Acoustics Working Group
ANSI S12 Work Group 44

Opposite: Well-designed soundscapes create comfort, safety, and enhance communication, even in open public areas such as this community space in a 12,000-square-foot adult day care center designed by JSR Associates. Designers followed the *FGI Guidelines* acoustical criteria and used sound-absorbing treatments on the ceiling, floors, walls, windows, and furnishings.

Lead architect: Jane Rohde. Interior designer: Shernise Richardson.
Photography: Nicole Lowder

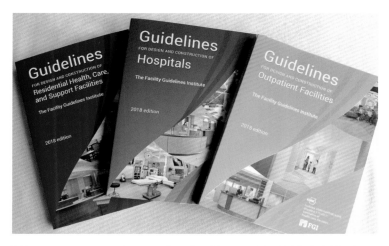

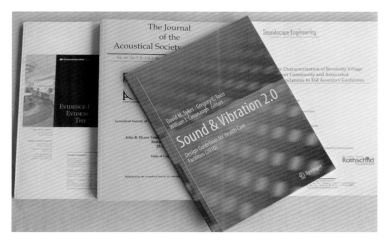

With encouragement and support from Rob Mayer and the Hulda B. & Maurice L. Rothschild Foundation, Facility Guidelines Institute developed comprehensive, code-level acoustical and noise-control criteria for residential care facilities, and to harmonize those criteria across the three-volume *FGI Guidelines 2018*. This set the standard for all types of health care design and construction, effectively establishing, for the first time, national standards that are also adopted by the U.S. Green Building Council (USGBC)-LEED Healthcare and for the International Code Council (ICC).

Photography: John Baptiste

Rob Mayer strongly supported the third-party research program ensuring the acoustical criteria developed for FGI, USGBC-LEED, and ICC was evidence-based. He also supported the professional outreach and educational program thereby accelerating adoption by regulatory agencies as well as professionals in design and construction.

Photography: John Baptiste

Building Performance Guidelines

Development of "Guidelines for Performance Evaluations of Occupied Elder Care Facilities"

During the formation of the Low Vision Design Committee by the National Institute of Building Sciences (NIBS) in 2011, I was first introduced as chair to Rob by Eunice Noell-Waggoner. From that introduction, until the publication of *Design Guidelines for the Visual Environment* on May 11, 2015, Rob provided his knowledge, insight, and support, especially with regard to needs of the elder population. During that time, Facility Guidelines Institute (FGI), which Rob also supported through the Hulda B. & Maurice L. Rothschild Foundation, published its 2014 edition of its *Guidelines* in two volumes: *Guidelines for Design and Construction of Hospitals and Outpatient Facilities*, and *Guidelines for Design and Construction of Residential Health, Care, and Support Facilities*. Neither volume provided guidelines for periodic or episodic evaluations of facility performance during occupancy (i.e., after construction). This omission led me and Rob into discussions in the summer of 2015 regarding the need for similar guidance in the operations and maintenance of occupied facilities. Rob suggested that we include Douglas Erickson, Executive Director of FGI, for subsequent discussions, which culminated in an agreement to develop a white paper that would explore this need with a focus on the elder population. The outline for the white paper was submitted to Rob on August 24, 2015.

To our sorrow, Rob passed away on December 3, 2015, just before the first draft of the white paper was completed. To honor his amazing contributions to the long-term care field, his family created The Mayer-Rothschild Foundation and invited Dr. Margaret (Maggie) Calkins to become Executive Director and carry on Rob's vision and work. The first draft of the white paper was completed on December 22, 2015, entitled "Are Guidelines Needed for Performance Evaluations of Occupied Elder Care Facilities?" The final draft of November 14, 2016 included responses to two rounds of peer-review by a diverse group of reviewers, who were selected by Maggie and Doug Erickson. The reviewers provided a wide range of opinions and supported the development of the concept by a substantial majority. Several issues were identified and prioritized in the white paper. These focused on

four fundamental attributes that encourage fiduciary relationships among stakeholders: credibility; accountability; affordability; and enforceability. On March 31, 2017, the Foundation approved and provided initial support for the development of a draft document entitled, "Guidelines for Performance Evaluations of Occupied Elder Care Facilities." The current draft 1.5 was presented to the Foundation on June 7, 2017. Further development of these performance guidelines is waiting funding.

The white paper and the developing performance guidelines have been dedicated to the memory of the visionary Rob Mayer. The purpose of these performance guidelines is to provide a set of evaluation procedures that include "continuous accountability" processes for all existing and occupied eldercare facilities. These draft guidelines focus on a contiguous methodology (i.e., standardized protocol) by which a site-specific facility can be credibly evaluated, throughout its occupancy period, in terms that relate outcomes, exposures, and system performance. They are intended to:

- Complement the 2014 (and subsequent) *FGI Residential Design Guidelines*, which focus on design and construction;
- Be consistent with measurable criteria and with other referenced material cited in the *Residential Design Guidelines*; and
- Focus on the quality of indoor environmental control.

The draft document consists of two parts:

1) An introduction, overview, and a set of nine guiding principles to be used as a basis for developing a standardized protocol and, subsequently, for an educational and training program

2) Guidance on developing and implementing a site-specific protocol for: defining evaluation criteria that are measurable; selecting and calibrating instruments; acquiring and interpreting data; evaluating results; and reporting findings, conclusions, and recommendations to accountable stakeholders in both oral and written forms

James E. Woods, Ph.D., P.E.
Indoor Environments Consultant

Pioneer Network Projects

Pioneer Network Projects funded by the Hulda B. & Maurice L. Rothschild Foundation for which Rob Mayer was not only a funder but a partner in the planning and implementation of all of the projects.

2008: Creating Home in the Nursing Home: A National Symposium on Culture Change and the Physical Environment Requirements

- Convened and sponsored by Pioneer Network and the Centers for Medicare & Medicaid Services (CMS). The Commonwealth Fund, American Health Care Association, and American Association of Homes and Services for the Aging (now LeadingAge) were co-sponsors and Rob was an active participant in the planning and implementation of the symposium and invitational workshop that followed the next day.

- National Fire Protection Association (NFPA) was also one of the presenters, which served as an opportunity to learn about the culture change movement.

- Second-day workshop: Invited participants developed recommendations for action, one of which was to advocate for changes in the Life Safety Code and the International Code Council (ICC) to support "Creating Home in the Nursing Home."

2008–2010: National Long-term Care Life Safety Code Task Force: Funded by the Hulda B. & Maurice L. Rothschild Foundation

- A National Long-term Care Life Safety Code Task Force was formed to review the pertinent sections of the current (at the time) NFPA 101 Life Safety Code and determine proposals for changes to be submitted to NFPA for the 2012 Life Safety Code that support the "creation of home in the nursing home."

- Ultimately, NFPA approved four proposals to create home in the nursing home, which became part of the 2012 Life Safety Code. The successful proposals included changes to the Code related to Cooking and Kitchens, Seating in the Corridor, Decorations, and Gas or Electric Fireplaces.

2010: Creating Home in the Nursing Home II: A National Symposium on Culture Change and the Food and Dining Requirements

- Pioneer Network and the Centers for Medicare & Medicaid Services (CMS) co-sponsored this symposium, which was funded by the Hulda B. & Maurice L. Rothschild Foundation. It ended up being a "virtual" symposium as there was a snowstorm in Washington, D.C. on the day it was scheduled, so Pioneer Network produced and hosted webinars. An in-person invitational workshop was convened in May 2010 to develop recommendations for next steps. One of those recommendations was to develop standards of practice supporting individualized care and self-directed living to improve the food and dining experience of nursing home residents.

2011: Food and Dining Clinical Standards Task Force: Funded by the Hulda B. & Maurice L. Rothschild Foundation

- A Food and Dining Clinical Standards Task Force was formed to develop standards of practice supporting individualized care and self-directed living to improve the food and dining experience of nursing home residents.

- The Standards seek to help long-term care providers protect individual safety and honor individual rights to make choices, to refuse treatment, and to make their own informed choices.

- Twelve national clinical standard-setting organizations agreed to the new Dining Standards and they were published by Pioneer Network. CMS publicly recognized them in a survey and certification letter to state survey agencies on March 1, 2013, also referring to a video CMS released in support of them.

2011–2013: International Code Council (ICC) Person-Centered Care Task Force: Funded by the Hulda B. & Maurice L. Rothschild Foundation

- An ICC Person-Centered Care Task Force was formed to develop proposals to revise the I-codes (including the International Fire Code and International Building Code) to support person-centered care environments, similar to what was done with the Life Safety Code in the areas of Fixed Seating in the Corridors, Open Kitchens, and Decorations. This Task Force was also a result of the National Symposium on Culture Change and the Physical Environment Requirements as well as the work of the National Long-term Care Life Safety Code Task Force.

- The Task Force members partnered with the ICC Code Technical Committee on Care Facilities to provide guidance and help enact additional changes. The resulting changes that were adopted as part of the 2015 edition of the I-codes included the following:

  o division of Occupancy Group I-2 to separate requirements for nursing homes and hospitals

  o separated Occupancy Group I-1 (Assisted Living) into Condition 1 and Condition 2, with added requirements for Condition 2, to allow for better clarification of memory support occupancy and those needing limited assistance in evacuation

  o expansion / clarification of what spaces can be open to corridors

  o allowing open kitchens

  o allowing for fixed furniture / seating in an 8-foot-wide corridor

  o providing allowances for combustible decorative materials, such as grandchildren's artwork, on walls

  o added language stating that corridors in Group I-2 are not required to be 8 feet wide when community does not move residents in beds

2012–2013: New Dining Practice Standards Toolkit Task Force: Funded by the Hulda B. & Maurice L. Rothschild Foundation

- A Task Force was formed to work with Carmen Bowman, Kim Clayton, and Pioneer Network staff to develop a New Dining Standards Toolkit to help long-term care communities implement the New Dining Standards.

- The Toolkit was published by Pioneer Network in 2014 and includes frequent references to the Dining Standards and to CMS regulations and interpretive guidance. The Toolkit includes the following resources to help nursing homes implement the standards: Model Policy and Procedures, Tip Sheets and Forms, Brochures for Residents and Families, and Additional Resources.

2012–2013: National Long-term Care Life Safety Code Task Force: Funded by the Hulda B. & Maurice L. Rothschild Foundation

- A Task Force, consisting of the members of the 2012 Life Safety Code Task Force, selected members of the ICC Person-Centered Care Task Force, and of FGI's Health Guidelines Revisions Committee, was formed to identify language in the 2012 edition of the Life Safety Code that may still be a barrier to person-centered care environments and to submit proposals to the NFPA for changes and additions to include in the 2015 Life Safety Code.

- Proposals that were approved by NFPA and became part of the 2015 Life Safety Code included disguising doors with murals, reducing required corridor widths to 6 feet in small household settings, and a clarification of limited cooking that allows the use of butter, oil, or cooking spray.

2014–2016: International Code Council (ICC) Person-Centered Care Task Force: Funded by the Hulda B. and Maurice L. Rothschild Foundation, later the Mayer-Rothschild Foundation

- Selected members of the previous Life Safety Code and International Code Task Forces were convened to further propose revisions to the I-codes (including the International Fire Code and International Building Code) to support person-centered care.

- The Task Force members also partnered with the ICC Code Technical Committee on Care Facilities to provide guidance and help enact additional changes.

- The resulting changes that were adopted as part of the 2018 edition of the I-codes included the following:

  o clarified and expanded spaces in Occupancy Group I-1 that could be open to the corridor

- o carried over the Open Kitchen requirements from Occupancy Group I-2 to Occupancy Group I-1
- o added language that clarified that artificial decorative vegetation, such as seasonal wreaths on doors, is permitted in Group I-1 and Group I-2 occupancies

2017: International Code Council (ICC) Person-Centered Care Task Force: Funded by The Mayer-Rothschild Foundation

- Selected members of the previous Life Safety Code and International Code Task Forces were convened to further propose revisions to the I-codes (including the International Fire Code and the International Building Code) to support person-centered care.
- The Task Force members also participated in the ICC Committee on Health Care, helping to provide the nursing home industry perspective and shape code change proposals.
- Proposals that were submitted for changes to the 2021 edition of the I-Codes included the following:
  - o scope changes to Chapter 11 (accessibility) of the International Building Code to allow equivalency percentages for assisted toileting and assisted bathing
  - o remove erroneous requirement that UL 300A hoods must only vent to the outdoors
- Hearings for the 2021 edition of the I-Codes begin in April 2018. This work will be carried on by Dr. Margaret Calkins and Amy Carpenter.

Cathy Lieblich, Pioneer Network
Penny Cook, Pioneer Network
Karen Schoeneman, CMS
Carmen Bowman, Edu-catering
Bonnie Burman, CMS
Amy Carpenter, SFCS Architects
Linda Bump, Actionpact

Guidelines for Design and Construction of Residential Health, Care, and Support Facilities

The 2018 edition of *Guidelines for Design and Construction of Residential Health, Care, and Support Facilities* is dedicated to Robert Nathan Mayer, Ph.D, a visionary exemplar whose passion for respecting the personhood of every individual infused his work as President of the Hulda B. & Maurice L. Rothschild Foundation for more than 35 years. Rob initiated and successfully implemented some of the most significant and meaningful regulatory changes in nursing homes ever proposed. His concern for understanding and supporting the well-being of elders who live in shared residential care communities was a contributing factor for separating residential care settings from acute and outpatient centers in 2014, and provided critical insights for the further refinements incorporated into this 2018 edition. Rob's inspirational ideals, everything-is-achievable attitude, and visualization of fully embraced person-centered approaches live on through the many organizations, agencies and individuals he has profoundly influenced in his lifetime and beyond.

Doug Erickson
Facility Guidelines Institute

The Pioneer Award
of the
Facility Guidelines Institute
In Honor of Robert N. Mayer, PhD, President, Hulda B. & Maurice L. Rothschild Foundation

PROCLAMATION:

Only a few individuals or organizations in our midst are compelled by the vision of a new path to embody the pioneering spirit and perseverance to pursue that path. The dedication and passion of these few compel others to new levels of performance; they are the pioneers and adventurers who lead us to a preferred future.

The Pioneer Award of the Facility Guidelines Institute (FGI) honors select individuals or organizations of outstanding character who influence or create the future of health and residential care facility design and construction through their participation and support of the mission and vision of the Facility Guidelines Institute.

One such individual is *Robert N. Mayer, PhD.*

Dr. Mayer always believed that one should not sit back and let the past dictate the future but to break traditional models and inspire new thinking to benefit all.

Dr. Mayer was passionate about transforming elder services, based on person-centered values and practices. He understood the significant implications design and construction of residential communities have on the creation of person-centered cultures and the need to create built environments where both elders and their caregivers are able to express choice, and practice self-determination in meaningful ways at every level of daily life.

Therefore, be it proclaimed by the Board of Directors of the Facility Guidelines Institute that *Robert N. Mayer, PhD,* shall be the second recipient of the FGI Pioneer Award.

Kurt A. Rockstroh, FAIA, FACHA
President, Facility Guidelines Institute

Douglas S. Erickson, FASHE, CHFM
Chief Executive Officer, Facility Guidelines Institute

Joseph G. Sprague, FAIA, FAHCA, FHFI
Immediate Past President, Facility Guidelines Institute

Presented this day, February 27, 2016

FGI

Low Vision Task Force with the National Institute of Building Sciences

The National Institute of Building Sciences, Low Vision Design Committee honors the late Robert N. Mayer

The Low Vision Design Committee (LVDC) of the National Institute of Building Sciences was founded in late 2011 on a wing and a prayer and seed money provided by the Hulda B. & Maurice L. Rothschild Foundation, at the recommendation of its Founder and President Robert N. Mayer. Since that time, this small group of architects, medical professionals, engineers, interior designers, lighting designers, federal agency representatives, and community activists, several of whom have low vision themselves, have dedicated their time to amalgamating the knowledge of their separate vocations into tools that can be used cross-profession to create supportive environments for an ever-growing population with low vision. Rob Mayer was an advocate and active contributor to the LVDC until his passing in late 2015.

The LVDC has devoted the lion's share of its efforts to creation of the *Design Guidelines for the Visual Environment* and subsequent work toward morphing the *Guidelines* into a national standard. "Not only did Rob provide critically needed funding from the outset, he enthusiastically participated in our meetings, where he shared his wisdom," said past LVDC chair James E. Woods. "His passion for eldercare gave strong direction to the development of our *Guidelines*. I hope we can continue his vision."

Rob supported the committee, financially and technically, through the arduous and sometimes contentious rounds of corrections and changes that shaped the *Guidelines* throughout the four years of its development. It was a labor of love, and Rob was right in the thick of it with all of us. He carved the time out of his impossibly busy schedule to attend LVDC meetings and absorbed sometimes esoteric architectural details, processing them in a way that could coax consensus from opposing corners. After six revisions and two public reviews, when the *Guidelines* was published in May 2015, Rob, as was his wont, gave the credit to others and expressed his appreciation of the group. "We owe a great debt of thanks to all of those who took the considerable time and reflection to carefully review a tremendous amount of detail in order to help strengthen the document," he wrote to the committee.

Rob further used his communications and networking savvy to connect the *Design Guidelines for the Visual Environment* as a reference to the *FGI Guidelines 2018*. "Since the Committee was first convened in 2011 with Foundation support, we have stayed true to our initial objective of providing design guidance to the various organizations tasked," he said. In this light, the Rothschild Foundation and Rob also offered the financial support to enable the LVDC to meet in person, and to spread the word about low vision design at industry conferences. In 2015, he worked with the committee at our first national Environments for Aging Conference, held in Baltimore, to facilitate reach to a broader audience.

In 2015, shortly before his passing, Rob, through the Rothschild Foundation, awarded a grant to the Institute to expand its reach to create a listening panel to bring together health care facility stakeholders to examine how varying design, construction, and operations requirements impact delivery of person-centered care. The Institute currently is developing a report based on the outcome of that panel.

The Institute honored Rob posthumously at its annual banquet on January 14, 2016. "We have lost not only a generous contributor, but also a caring, actively involved committee member," said President Henry L. Green, Hon. AIA, himself a founding member of the LVDC. "Rob worked with us on the front lines of our four-year effort to create design guidelines for supportive environments for people with low vision, and, more recently, to turn those guidelines into a building standard. We will all miss him and his thoughtful guidance a great deal."

The Low Vision Design Committee continues its work today, inspired always by the generous and caring spirt of Rob Mayer, who gave us our first chance and believed deeply in our mission to create better built environments for seniors and for all people.

Stephanie Stubbs
National Institute of Building Sciences

Standards for Nursing Home and Assisted Living Residences in Toileting and Bathing for Elders
(Supplement to the Americans with Disabilities Act)

Beyond ADA: designing toilet rooms to meet the needs of frail seniors and their caregivers

Research and best practices have repeatedly demonstrated that the Americans with Disabilities Act (ADA) Accessibility Standards for toilet grab bar configurations, which are based on the capabilities of young people who transfer independently and generally have good upper-body strength, do not adequately meet the needs of older adults or their care providers. Nonetheless, neither prior studies nor anecdotal evidence from practice provided sufficient data about spatial and dimensional requirements of grab bar configurations to justify specific changes to the current technical requirements in the ADA Accessibility Standards. With funding from The Mayer-Rothschild Foundation and in collaboration with the U.S. Access Board, which promulgates the ADA Accessibility Guidelines, the goal of this project was to provide sufficient information to make definitive recommendations for "supplementary senior accessibility guidelines" that would support the transfer needs of frail seniors living in residential facilities covered by the ADA. To do so, the specific aims were to identify the optimal spatial and dimensional requirements of grab bars that effectively supported both independent and one- and two-person assisted toilet transfers by older adults.

A two-phased study with older adults and care providers in residential facilities was conducted to determine the optimal requirements for grab bars. In phase one, transfers were evaluated for three grab bar configurations to identify optimal characteristics for safety, ease of use, comfort, and helpfulness. These characteristics were then validated for independent and one- and two-person assisted transfers in phase two. An aluminum framing system was used to fabricate a reconfigurable 5-foot by 7-foot portable toilet test rig for simulation testing.

The optimal configuration derived in phase one included fold-down grab bars on both sides of the toilet (14 inches from centerline of toilet, 32 inches above the floor, and extending a minimum of 6 inches in front of the toilet) with one side open and a side wall 24 inches from centerline of toilet on

the other. Phase two feedback was significantly positive for independent and one-person transfers, and somewhat lower, albeit still positive, for two-person transfers.

Findings from this study supported prior work to provide substantial evidence that bilateral grab bars are significantly more effective than those that comply with current ADA Accessibility Standards. In addition, unlike like previous studies, this study also provided evidence to specify the technical requirements for grab bar configurations that would be most effective in senior facilities.

Findings and recommendations from this study were received with great interest and enthusiasm for change when presented to the Access Board in the fall of 2018. Unfortunately, while there is now sufficient data and attention to develop a senior standard, given the current political climate in Washington, D.C., such a conclusion is unlikely to occur at the current time without an extensive lobbying effort.

Jon A. Sanford
Director, Center for Assistive Tech and Environmental Access (CATEA)
Professor
College of Design
Georgia Tech

Closing Remarks—Personal Reflections

I wanted to add a few personal reflections on why Rob was so successful at making the right things happen in the right way for all the right reasons. Thank you for this opportunity.

Rob understood better than anyone I know that real change could never ever happen if we all continued to surround ourselves with what he called the "us'ns"—that is, the usual cast of characters. The folks that were in "our orb." The folks who spoke the "same language" and had the same concerns. We would look at each other and exclaim, "Well, what about the 'them'ns'? Shouldn't they be at the table too?" And the question Rob always asked was, "Who else should we include? Who else needs to sit at the table?" (Literally and figuratively.) After all, shouldn't all voices be heard?

And thus, Rob ensured that each one of the efforts and projects he participated in was all inclusive; that all the right people were in the room even if—or especially if—they had a different perspective. I venture to say this had not happened in our field before. Each of the efforts Rob championed included new partners with very different points of view. For example, I can still remember the first time Robert Solomon came to one of our initial gatherings. He later told me that he really couldn't understand why he was there. We all figured it out quickly, especially Robert. And the rest, as they say, is history.

And once Rob ensured that there no longer were "us'ns" and "them'ns," Rob's leadership style made the rest of the difference. Five key elements of Rob-ness stand out in my mind.

First, Rob was the listener extraordinaire. And he didn't just listen, he heard. Everyone. It was his uncanny ability to recognize that everyone mattered that made the end products so exquisite. When in Rob's presence, people who rarely spoke up could be heard stating, "I was thinking…" He brought out the best in everyone.

Second, if Rob could have made himself invisible, he would have. Rob wanted no attention. He wanted no glory. He wanted no thanks. He just wanted to make life better for the elders he held so dear. Being selfless made him the strong self he was. How ironic.

I don't have magic powers, but I just know that if we could see Rob from the inside out we would note that there is no space between his head and his heart. It is rare to see such reasoned passion in action. He never just thought. He never just felt. He thought and felt at all times. It was magical. And it is that magical power that is the third key element of Rob-ness.

While Rob knew how much our elders needed us now!—he certainly had an extraordinary sense of urgency—somehow, he had a degree of patience that was superhuman. Element four, of course. I remember our first Life Safety Code meeting in Cleveland. It was super cold out; folks in the lobby were dressed in layers galore to go to a Browns football game. I'm not sure how the Browns did that day, but I can tell you, we didn't do so well. As we presented drafts of our proposed changes the questions doubled. And then they multiplied. We were speaking different languages. I remember leaving that first meeting thoroughly dejected—until I saw Rob come bounding (literally) out of the room.

His pep talk went something like this: "Good start;" "We have to be patient;" "Slow and steady." Were we in the same meeting? But he was right. After just a few more sessions and more revisions than I would like to count, we got to "yes" and the changes to the Life Safety Code that would enhance the lives of our elders while keeping them safe were passed.

The fifth and final element of Rob-ness is impossible to put into words. Rob was just Rob. And that was more than enough. I miss him daily. He deserves to be remembered and honored always.

Here's to Rob.

With admiration and total awe,

Bonnie Burman
CMS and Pioneer Network

In memory of Rob Mayer, 1949–2015

Appendix

PROJECT DATA // INDEX OF ARCHITECTS

Project Data

Abiitan Mill City

Client / Owner / Provider: Ecumen; Shoreview, Minnesota
Architect: BKV Group
General Contractor: Frana Companies
Landscape Architect: BKV Group
Structural Engineer: BKV Group
Mechanical Engineer: BKV Group
Civil Engineer: Pierce Pini + Associates, Inc.
Electrical Engineer: Kirby Electric
Energy Design Assistance Consultant: The Weidt Group
Hydrology Consultant: Wenck Associates
Historical Consultant: Hess Roise and Company
Public Funding Consultant: Landon Group

Building Data

Independent living: Total GSF: 115,400
Independent living: Total NSF of residential spaces: 110,500
Independent living: Total NSF of common spaces: 4900
Assisted living—dementia / memory support: Total GSF: 29,700
Assisted living—dementia / memory support: Total NSF of residential spaces: 19,200
Assisted living—dementia / memory support: Total NSF of common spaces: 10,500

Independent Living			
Unit type	Number of units	Size range (NSF)	Typical size (NSF)
Studio	3	540–573	540
One-bedroom	60	694–752	700
One-bedroom plus den	1	890	890
Two-bedroom	16	979–1431	1150
Two-bedroom plus den	4	1498–1671	1500
Three bedroom	4	1892–2204	2200
Total (all units)	88		

Adaptable independent living units (%): 5
Other independent living units (%): 95

Assisted Living—Dementia / Memory Support			
Unit type	Number of units	Size range (NSF)	Typical size (NSF)
Private room*	48	365–668	365
Total (all units)	48		

*single occupant

Project Costs (actual or estimated if the project is yet to be built; not including FF&E, site, or soft costs)

Independent living: Total cost for new construction ($): 23 million
Assisted living—dementia / memory support: Total cost for new construction ($): 5 million

Gender Breakdown of the Residents

Women (%): 55
Men (%): 45

Status of the Residents

Single (living alone) (%): 60
Living with a spouse / domestic partner (%): 40

Source of Resident Payments

Private payment (%): 100